ALGER HISS

WHY HE CHOSE TREASON

CHRISTINA SHELTON

An Introduction by Richard Pipes

THRESHOLD EDITIONS

New York London Toronto Sydney New Delhi

Threshold Editions
A Division of Simon & Schuster, Inc.
1230 Avenue of the Americas
New York, NY 10020

First Threshold Editions hardcover edition April 2012

THRESHOLD EDITIONS and colophon are trademarks of Simon & Schuster, Inc.

For information about special discounts for bulk purchases, please contact Simon & Schuster Special Sales at 1-866-506-1949 or business@simonandschuster.com.

The Simon & Schuster Speakers Bureau can bring authors to your live event. For more information or to book an event, contact the Simon & Schuster Speakers Bureau at 1-866-248-3049 or visit our website at www.simonspeakers.com.

Designed by Renata Di Biase

Manufactured in the United States of America

10 9 8 7 6 5 4 3 2 1

Library of Congress Cataloging-in-Publication Data
  Shelton, Christina.
    Alger Hiss : why he chose treason / Christina Shelton.—1st Threshold Editions hardcover ed.
      p.   cm.
    Includes bibliographical references and index.
    1. Hiss, Alger.   2. Spies—United States—Biography.   3. Communism—United States—History—20th century.   4. Espionage, Soviet—United States—History—20th century.   5. United States. Dept. of State—Officials and employees—Biography.   6. United States. Congress. House. Committee on Un-American Activities.   7. Hiss, Alger—Trials, litigation, etc.   I. Title.

  E743.5.H55S54 2012
  327.12092—dc23
  [B]
                                                                2011038985

ISBN 978-1-4516-5542-1
ISBN 978-1-4516-5545-2 (ebook)

For my daughters—
Taryn and Valerie

Forsan et haec olim meminisse iuvabit
—Virgil, *Aeneid,* 1.203

And my grandchildren—
Alexander, Matthew,
Hannah, Talia, and Emma

ACKNOWLEDGMENTS

My special thanks to those who have so generously shared their thoughts and ideas with me on this subject. I am particularly appreciative to the following scholars, senior intelligence officers, and government officials for the insights they have brought to the project: Kenneth deGraffenreid, former deputy undersecretary of defense for policy support; John Dziak, former senior official at the Office of Secretary of Defense; M. Stanton Evans, author and journalist; Carl Linden, professor emeritus of political science and international affairs, George Washington University; Hayden Peake, former Army and CIA intelligence officer; Paul Redmond, former chief of counterintelligence, CIA; David Thomas, Defense Intelligence Agency (DIA) senior intelligence officer; and Graham Turbiville, associate fellow, U.S. Special Operations Command/ Joint Special Operations University and senior consultant for the Department of Defense and intelligence community. And my particular thanks to Herbert Romerstein, former head of the United States Information Agency's Office to Counter Soviet Disinformation and former professional staff member for intelligence committees of the U.S. House of Representatives, who was always available to answer questions and who encouraged me in this project. My deepest gratitude to these individuals for the hours they spent to assist me. They have inspired my work and provided invaluable guidance; but for all assessments and judgments in the book I take full responsibility, as well as for any errors.

My appreciation also goes to those mentors, colleagues, and

friends who supported me over the years and encouraged me to persevere and whose integrity and honesty were unwavering: Harriet Fast Scott, author of books on the Soviet armed forces; David Sisson, former Counterintelligence Division Chief, DIA; John Sloan, former director of policy support, DIA; Alice Jourdain von Hildebrand, Roman Catholic philosopher and theologian and former professor at Hunter College; and to the memory of Charles F. Elliott, professor, George Washington University, Sino-Soviet Institute; Ercell McGuire Kullberg, executive administrator at Trinity Parish's Chapel of the Intercession Episcopal Church and at Earl Hall, Columbia University; James T. Reitz (colonel, ret., U.S. Army), Soviet military affairs intelligence specialist; and the ultimate renaissance man, Uncle Jerry.

CONTENTS

INTRODUCTION
BY RICHARD PIPES

Although the "Hiss affair" is more than half a century old, there are still people who disregard the incontrovertible evidence that Alger Hiss was a Soviet spy, proclaiming him a victim of anti-Red hysteria. It is indeed difficult to understand how a member of the American elite could maintain a double existence. Christina Shelton has collected all the available evidence about this controversial figure and in the process illuminated the motives behind his treachery. Hiss belonged to the class of Americans who, persuaded by the Depression that the country's political and economic regime was doomed, looked to the Soviet regime for salvation. They betrayed their country convinced that in so doing they were serving it. Hiss, she concludes, "closed his mind, blind to the inhumanity of Communism, and adopted Lenin's notion that the choice of revolution is ultimate and irrevocable, an act of passion as well as intellect. Hiss worked hard to appear urbane and sophisticated, and behind this persona was his single-minded devotion to Communism, leading to a lifetime of defiance and denying any wrongdoing." This judgment is supported by a wealth of evidence that illuminates the complex story of Soviet espionage in the United States. The main characters involved in this story are convincingly portrayed and their motives explained. This account should put to rest any lingering doubts about Alger Hiss's treachery.

Richard Pipes
Cambridge, Mass.
October 2011

FOREWORD

During the late 1940s, a high-level State Department official, Alger Hiss, was accused of spying for the Soviet Union by a senior editor of *Time* magazine, Whittaker Chambers, who previously had been a Soviet agent and Hiss's "handler." For two years, the political drama of the congressional hearings and Hiss trials made headline news throughout the country. The case was particularly contentious, given Hiss's prominence, the political climate of an incipient anti-Communism movement during the Truman administration, and, most importantly, because of the ideological rupture that unfolded. Battle lines were drawn between the right and the left that remain to this day. Hiss eventually was convicted of perjury related to espionage. The evidence that was crucial to the government's case included stolen State Department classified documents, microfilms with classified material, and handwritten notes—all of which came to be known collectively as the "Pumpkin Papers"—that Hiss had turned over to Chambers for passage to Soviet military intelligence. Chambers had secreted them prior to his defection for his own future protection and then presented them shortly before the perjury trials began.

For scholars and intelligence professionals versed in Soviet espionage, this book covers familiar ground, such as the biographical material on Whittaker Chambers and Alger Hiss, as well as details of the case. However, for most readers today, the Hiss story is unfamiliar territory. It is history—and little-known history at that, in an age when biogenetics and nanotechnology studies take precedence over branches of learning in history. If they know anything about the Hiss saga, even some older current-day readers have only a vague, distant memory of a spy story, pumpkin papers, and a typewriter. This book makes the Hiss story accessible to the modern reader and draws attention to its relevance today.

The book describes and assesses many aspects of Hiss's complicated life and looks at the importance of the Hiss story from a variety of perspectives. Foremost among them, and unlike most other books that have been written on the subject, this account views the Hiss story as much more than a spy case; it goes beyond the case itself, beyond the "Pumpkin Papers," taking it to another dimension. The first and most important perspective of this narrative is the ideological one. This assessment focuses on placing Hiss in the strategic context of American political philosophy and Communist ideology. An ideological perspective is essential to the Hiss story since it is what drove his political thinking and his behavior. The philosophical political struggle within the United States for more than two centuries, and so evident today, has been between individuals like Hiss, who believed in statism—concentrating extensive power in the federal government—and those who advocate individual liberty and limited, decentralized government. A further aspect of the ideological struggle in Hiss's day played out on the international stage. Particular attention is paid in the book to the nature of Communism and Fascism, the Nazi-Soviet Pact, Stalin's role at Yalta, and the reasons for Chambers's break with the party and Marxism-Leninism, which revealed the true nature of the Soviet system. These events and issues were an intimate part of Hiss's life; how he reacted to these developments is closely examined.

The book also draws attention to the ongoing intellectual perversity of American academia in its mistaken assessment of the historical realities of the crimes of the Soviet system. This intellectual willfulness has been exposed—in all the unlikely places and by all people—in a May 2010 interview with *Izvestiya* by Russian president Dmitri Medvedev. In the most damning public assessment of the Soviet Union to date by a Russian leader, Medvedev accused the Soviet state of being "totalitarian in nature . . . a regime that suppressed basic rights and freedoms" and he acknowledged the crimes against humanity by both Stalin and the Soviet system. By contrast, during the past half century in the United States, if one described the Soviet Union as a totalitarian state one was considered a troglodyte by most in American academia. The primary themes of ideology, Communism, and the Soviet system are interwoven throughout this book because they are intrinsic to the Hiss story and what motivated him. In addition to viewing Hiss in terms of ideology, I address the actual case against the backdrop of Communist infiltration of the U.S. government and the politics of the 1930s and 1940s, specifically the New Deal administration. New Deal politics were fundamental to Hiss's beliefs and career; and Hiss was devoted to its policies.

A second perspective concerns the personalities of the main players. I examine the backgrounds of those individuals who had a great influence on Hiss and were important to understanding Hiss's life, including his wife, Priscilla, and Whittaker Chambers, Hiss's close friend, Soviet "handler," and ultimately his accuser. Hiss's experience at Harvard Law School and his relationship with his mentor, Felix Frankfurter, also provide insights into his political thinking. Some of Hiss's associates in the International Juridical Association and his professional colleagues in the Ware Group, an underground Soviet intelligence cell based in Washington, D.C., contributed to his political development and they are discussed at length. A few of them were forceful influences and prime movers in Hiss's radicalization. In sketching the biographies of some of these men, it becomes clear how they fit the template used by Soviet intelligence for recruitment at that time: highly intellectual, educated, credentialed, and well-placed persons who could be moved into government positions that provided access to state secrets.

I also explore the significance of Soviet influence operations. Hiss's various roles at the State Department are relevant here, including the position he held when he was responsible for wartime China policy and especially his roles at the Yalta and UN conferences. Hiss's story is about not just espionage, but also how he was in a position from his post at the State Department to influence U.S. foreign policy to accommodate Soviet objectives. In this sense Hiss was a key figure in the history of the twentieth century.

Hiss's character and the different dimensions of his personality form another important aspect to this story. I draw attention to the human side of Hiss and his affection toward his wife, Priscilla, and especially his son, Tony. Material consisting of hundreds of Hiss's family papers and personal correspondence, recently made available at New York University's Tamiment Library archives, reflects a warm, caring, and sensitive person. Moreover, a striking aspect of his personality was his drive to develop the "persona" of a well-bred, sophisticated intellectual, which he spent the first half of his life accomplishing; the second half of his life was devoted to a remarkable, unceasing drive to achieve vindication. True to Leninist morality, Hiss never broke.

Finally, the book underscores the many missed opportunities and cases of poor judgment in terms of identifying Hiss's ties to Soviet military intelligence. In fact, the Hiss story represents a huge American counterintelligence failure. Part of this resulted from scotomas, or blind spots, about Hiss and about the nature of the Soviet system. This theme, of scotomas blocking objective assessments about Hiss, runs throughout this book. At the time, government officials such as former U.S. secretary of state Dean Acheson were unable "to see" the evidence even after the FBI briefed them on Hiss as a security risk. Over the years, blind spots continued to prevent Hiss's defenders from processing the cumulative evidence against him.

The book ends with an amassing of the evidence available to date on the case. Much of it is known. Some relatively recent and very important information, such as data from the KGB archives, is covered in *Spies: The Rise and Fall of the KGB in America*, an outstanding, comprehensive book by John Earl Haynes, Harvey Klehr, and Alexander Vassiliev on the overall threat of Soviet espionage in the United States during the 1930s and 1940s. But for the first time, all the available evidence involving Alger Hiss, including data from the Hungarian archives, is presented in a book specifically on Hiss.

To this day, the Hiss case remains controversial, although his band of supporters has diminished, especially as KGB archival evidence has been uncovered that clearly points to Hiss as a Soviet military intelligence agent. Nonetheless, Hiss remains a symbol, an iconic figure for those who are more concerned about what he stood for (a collectivist worldview) than about what he did (betray his country).

Christina Shelton
New York City
September 2011

PROLOGUE

I CAN HEAR the critics now: another Hiss book—not again—it never ends. Well, true, it doesn't ever go away; and for good reason. The unending Hiss saga is more than just a famous spy case of the 1930s and 1940s involving Alger Hiss, a high-level government official indicted for perjury, and his nemesis, Whittaker Chambers, a former Soviet military intelligence agent who accused Hiss of espionage against the United States. The players in the Hiss drama are long gone, as are the specific politics of the time that affected the story (the New Deal; President Roosevelt's wartime accommodation of Stalin's diplomatic and political objectives; President Truman's reelection concerns; the start of the Cold War; and "McCarthyism"). At various levels, the Hiss story is of historical importance: on the individual level (the Hiss-Chambers clash); on the national political level (the impact the Hiss case had on the politics of the 1950s); and on the international and strategic level (the effects of Yalta and the founding of the United Nations).

On the ideological level, however, the Hiss narrative is consequential and as current as today's news stories. The story doesn't go away, because it has become a symbol of the ongoing struggle for control over the philosophical and political direction of the United States. It is a battle between collectivism and individualism; between centralized planning and local/state authority, and between rule by administrative fiat and free markets. It prompts the question of where does one stand on the relationship of power between the state and the individual, and where does one draw the line in that relationship in order to have stable, rational constitutionalism governing society and to prevent concentration and centralization of power in the state, which always comes at a cost to individual liberty and freedom. Socialist precepts acknowledge this cost by claiming that the collective *should* take precedence over the individual.

The Hiss case embodies and reflects this ongoing struggle for power. The particular battle playing out during the Hiss-Chambers story in the 1930s and 1940s was between the collectivism and tyranny of Communism and Fascism on the one hand and constitutional democracy on the other. A benign, nonideological contest over the limits of government power existed even between two of the Founding Fathers, Jefferson and Hamilton; this cleavage, however, took place within the context of constitutional limits to power. Jefferson believed limited government offered the best chance of preserving liberty. He argued that to the extent a central government was necessary a strong Congress with a weak executive would be a critical counterbalance. Hamilton, by contrast, wanted a strong central government and executive, at the expense of the legislature. Jefferson saw state sovereignty as a way to check federal encroachment of power, while Hamilton wanted to subordinate local government to centralized power.[1]

For more than two hundred years, the political course of the United States has reflected an effort to maintain a measured balance between these two positions, to allow individuals the opportunity and freedom to pursue their goals within a contractual framework with the state. During the Hiss era, the New Deal administration, in the name of addressing the economic crisis of the Depression, was upsetting that balance and swinging far over to comprehensive, centralized government control. The issue of overreach and upsetting that balance is back again today. The battle over these two worldviews continues.

In a variation of the dichotomy between individual liberty and tyranny of government, George F. Will, journalist and author, points out, "James Madison asserted that politics should take its bearings from human nature and from the natural rights with which we are endowed, and which pre-exist government. Woodrow Wilson . . . argued that human nature is as malleable and changeable as history itself, and that it's the job of the state to regulate and guide the evolution of human nature and the changeable nature of the rights we are owed by the government that—in his view—dispenses rights [a view shared by Marxists], . . . Madison said rights pre-exist government. Wilson said government exists to dispense whatever agenda of rights suits its fancy, and to annihilate, regulate, attenuate, or dilute others."[2] Wilson's statist views, which won wide support among "progressives," were subsequently adopted by Hiss during the New Deal. Hiss firmly believed in a collectivist political ideology; he believed government was the ultimate instrument of power for solving problems and that the U.S. Constitution should be bent or bypassed to support this view. Hiss put his political belief into practice in his support for Communism and loyalty to the USSR, a state where government authority and power were not limited by the rule of law—in fact it would brook no limit.

Another significant aspect of the Hiss case is how the battle lines were drawn between both sides—the defenders of Hiss and those of Chambers. Which player one supported generally identified a person on the political spectrum, evidence of guilt or innocence notwithstanding. This clear "divide" was particularly true at the time of the Hiss case. Two opposing camps developed, with little middle ground. To put a name to the more obvious members of each camp: Victor Navasky, former publisher of the *Nation*, was among the most public pro-Hiss supporters; William F. Buckley Jr., founder of the *National Review*, was representative of those who were pro-Chambers. During the 1950s some of the liberal/left intelligentsia deserted Hiss, including Arthur Schlesinger, Murray Kempton, Lionel Trilling, Leslie Fiedler, I. F. Stone, and Sidney Hook. Over the years, as more and more evidence was disclosed that implicated Hiss as a Soviet asset, other prominent persons who were not on the "right" began to disavow Hiss, such as John Kenneth Galbraith and Senator Daniel Patrick Moynihan.[3]

Down through the decades, as individuals other than Whittaker Chambers surfaced to identify Hiss as a Communist, and as documentary and archival material has been uncovered in Eastern Europe and the former Soviet Union pointing to Hiss as a Soviet military intelligence asset, the evidence of Hiss's guilt has become overwhelmingly compelling, cumulative, and convincing.

Yet some Hiss defenders have "dug in" with their strategy of not addressing the conclusive evidence but rather continuing their ad hominem attacks, particularly against Chambers and Richard Nixon, the junior congressman who investigated Hiss during the 1940s hearings of the House Committee on Un-American Activities, and even against Senator Joseph McCarthy, who did not pontificate on the issue of espionage in the United States until *after* the two Hiss trials were over. This pro-Hiss defense was superbly summed up years later by Anglo-American author and journalist Christopher Hitchens: "If Hiss was wrong, then Nixon and McCarthy were right. And that could not be."[4] Some Hiss defenders even go so far as to cast doubt on the validity of Soviet archival material.

The Hiss defense is understandable when coming from Tony Hiss, Alger Hiss's son. But other defenders have vested professional reputations in their positions and do not want to suffer what they likely see as the embarrassment of retraction. Some supporters believe that if Hiss were guilty, it would cast a dark shadow over the New Deal, the Yalta Conference, and the United Nations. To them, those stakes would be too high and retraction not worth the price.

Another group of Hiss defenders represents something more troubling. These individuals have a blind spot, or scotoma, from the Greek word for blindness. This phenomenon helps to explain why the Hiss defense continues to this day and keeps the story alive. A scotoma indicates that an individual fails to see or is blind to alternatives; as a result of a sensory locking out of information from the environment, one observes only limited possibilities.

People develop scotomas to the truth about the world because of preconceived ideas and beliefs, other people's preconceived ideas (flat worlds or cultural trances), and past conditioning.[5] Scotomas prevent a change in views because people gather information selectively to verify what they already believe. Their minds see what they want to believe; they want to hold on to their version of reality. At times, however, what seem like blind spots may actually be purposeful deceptions.

Now, just who was Alger Hiss as a person? Tony Hiss characterized his father as a complicated and complex person. In his book *The View from Alger's Window*, Tony described the "three faces of Alger." The first was the face he was closest to—the private, personal Alger who was effervescent, playful, gentle, considerate.[6] This was how he saw his father. Indeed, the hundreds of letters written by Hiss to his wife during the 1930s and to his wife and son while he was in prison reflect these very qualities.[7] It is impossible to read this personal correspondence without seeing the very warm side of Hiss—affectionate and concerned for his wife and especially for his son. Interestingly, Whittaker Chambers also saw this face of Alger; he described Hiss as "a man of great simplicity and a great gentleness and sweetness of character."[8] Tony wrote that the second face was turned outward—Hiss's public persona, which was somewhat stilted, cautious, not showing any part of his inner self, polished, sophisticated, lawyerly, and aloof. The third face, which Tony did not acknowledge but described as the "Chambers-defined face," was the dark side: the spy for the Soviet Union.[9] An analysis of Hiss's life reveals that he thoroughly perfected the ability to compartmentalize these different aspects of his persona.

In addition to Tony Hiss's view, there is a consensus in the body of Hiss literature that Alger was charming—and disarmingly so. I can confirm that to be the case. I had the opportunity to see some aspects of face one and face two of Hiss. I met Alger Hiss at his seventy-fifth birthday party in November 1979 and witnessed the charming side of Alger, as well as his other side: guarded and detached. I had received a phone call from a friend of a friend of a friend who said that Hiss's annual birthday celebration was coming up but that Alger was somewhat annoyed because the same group of people (in other words, sycophants) was always invited to this event each year, and Hiss wanted some diversity. The person who called me asked if I was interested and of course I jumped at the chance to see this historical figure up close. I also had a professional curiosity, given my background in Soviet affairs. A few days later I caught the shuttle from Washington, D.C., to New York and went to the apartment where the event was taking place.

When I arrived I was the first guest, and the host escorted me into the living room. A few minutes later Alger Hiss walked into the room. He was rather tall, quite thin, and distinguished looking. As I remember, he wore a turtleneck sweater and sport jacket and seemed very relaxed. He clearly had a presence. I introduced myself and had a chance to spend the next fifteen or twenty minutes with him before the others arrived. At one point I had asked some question about Chambers's book, *Witness,* and Hiss said he had never read it. Astonished, I loudly and somewhat brashly exclaimed: "What? How is that possible?" I then proceeded to enumerate all the reasons why he should have read it, despite the fact that it was written by his accuser. Hiss mostly listened and said little. Then as the guests arrived, I got up and started to leave the room; Hiss also stood up and asked me to stay. I was standing next to him as each of his many guests came up to him to wish him a happy birthday; some of them really fawned over him. What was strange was that Hiss introduced me to each and every one: "I'd like you to meet Mrs. Shelton." That was all he said because that was all he knew about me. Each guest looked at me with an expression of intense bewilderment. Evidently they were all part of a small, closed circle of New York's "left" intelligentsia and thus able to spot an outsider immediately. I am sure they wondered who the hell I was and what I was doing at a birthday party for Alger Hiss.

For the duration of the party, Hiss seemed somewhat indifferent.

He glanced across the room, watching whom I was chatting with at different times. The only guest I recall from that evening was a former Communist who had too much to drink and was lamenting to me over lost opportunities. Just to annoy him (he wasn't sober enough for serious discussion), I reminded him that Stalin had millions of innocent people murdered; he said, with tears in his eyes, "You don't understand, we were building a new world." I remember thinking how that Marxist-Leninist "call to action" had such power over man's ego (a chance to change the planet is, after all, an ego grabber) that it enabled him to dismiss mass murder offhandedly.

When I started to leave to catch the last shuttle back to Washington, Hiss approached me and said he wanted me to meet his son, Tony. We made our way through the crush of people, by now about fifty or more, to the kitchen, where Tony was entertaining guests. After a quick introduction, Hiss helped me with my coat and walked me to the front door. The feedback I received the next day was that I made a big hit with Hiss. To this day I cannot imagine why, after my adversarial fifteen-minute lecture on why he should have read *Witness*. But I suppose that I was the diversity that he had requested.

In 2009, thirty years after that birthday celebration, I read Tony Hiss's book on Alger's prison stay, *The View from Alger's Window*. In it, Tony indicated that Alger had read *Witness* in prison in 1952, when it was serialized in ten consecutive installments in the *Saturday Evening Post*.[10]

PART ONE

The Early Years

I.

GROWING UP IN BALTIMORE

The Escape from Shabby Gentility

D
URING THE HISS-CHAMBERS congressional hearings in 1948 and the two Hiss perjury trials (May 31, 1949–July 8, 1949, and November 17, 1949–January 21, 1950), Alger Hiss supporters consistently used certain adjectives to describe his "persona" in an attempt to prove his innocence through a character defense: this highly credentialed person, this handsome, well-connected, sophisticated patrician from a socially prestigious family who became a senior State Department official, could not possibly be a Communist spy; the liar certainly must be his accuser, Whittaker Chambers, the stumpy, fat, sloppy, poorly dressed, brooding ex-Commie with particularly bad teeth. Never mind that Chambers was an intellect of a higher order than Hiss, and a senior editor for *Time* magazine; the narrative in the press of the comparative physical and character descriptions of the two men continued for the duration of the trials, and for that matter, for decades more as well. One of the reasons for Hiss's lifelong crusade to prove his innocence—in addition to his adherence to Leninist morality, serving the cause as a symbol of American injustice, and protecting the legacy of the New Deal, Yalta, and the UN—was his determination to preserve the "persona" he so assiduously had developed.

The journalist Murray Kempton once famously suggested that Alger Hiss was a product of "shabby gentility."[1] That is not quite on the mark. The Hiss family may have come from gentility but it was certainly not shabby. Growing up, all five children had music and art lessons, as well as German language lessons for Alger. They attended private colleges or universities and vacationed on Maryland's Eastern Shore. During college, the three boys spent summers in Europe. Not too shabby. Alger Hiss himself, in an obvious reference to Kempton's description, portrayed the economic circumstances of his early years as "modest" but "not particularly shabby."[2] While the Hisses did represent the gentility of an old Baltimore family, whose first ancestor arrived from Germany in the mideighteenth century, they were not blue-blooded, distinguished, or upper class, as even Kempton noted. Mrs. Hiss may have thought of the family as socially prominent, but a more accurate designation would have been "middle class."

So while Hiss was not a person born into the upper class, he always displayed great self-control and composure, typical characteristics of that class. By virtue of his intelligence and highly successful academic career at Johns Hopkins University and Harvard Law School, as well as his distinctive charming manner, grace, good looks, and sophistication, he turned himself into an exemplar of the eastern upper-class liberal establishment. From the 1920s to 1940s, Hiss gave the impression of good breeding and wealth, when he really used his talents to successfully develop this "persona" while networking with prominent upper-class people he came in contact with during his years at Hopkins and Harvard Law, then his Supreme Court clerkship. Thus did he gain a foothold in their class. In short, he became "the fair-haired boy" of the elite establishment even though his origins did not put him in their class. Moreover, this was an upper-class establishment noted for loyalty among its members. Mrs. Hiss had urged her children to strive for professional and social prominence, and none succeeded more than Alger.

Alger Hiss was born in Baltimore on November 11, 1904, to

Charles Alger Hiss (1864–1907) and Mary Lavinia Hughes Hiss (1867–1958). Charles was of German ancestry; his great-great-great-grandfather had changed his name from Hesse to Hiss. His middle name, "Alger," was given for his grandfather's old friend, Russell Alexander Alger, who became secretary of war under President McKinley.[3] Charles, the last of six children, was educated in Baltimore public schools. After high school, he became a salesman for the Troxell Carriage and Harness Company. He then worked in a cotton textile mill and after that as a salesman and executive for a major Baltimore wholesale dry goods store, Daniel Miller and Company.[4] Charles also was an officer of the Fifth Regiment in Baltimore's National Guard unit. In 1888 he married Mary Hughes, known as "Minnie," the daughter of a middle-class Baltimore family of English ancestry; according to her, she was directly descended from the Earl of Leicester. Minnie was educated at the Maryland State Teachers College.[5]

Minnie was by most accounts a devoted mother but she also maintained a busy schedule of club meetings. She was a member of many of Baltimore's civic and women's groups, serving as president of the Arundel Club and on the boards of the Women's Civic League of Women Voters and District Federation of Women's Clubs.[6] Minnie pushed her children to succeed professionally, financially, and socially. According to Whittaker Chambers, Hiss did not speak much of his early years but Chambers's impression was that "his relations with his mother were affectionate but not too happy. She was perhaps domineering."[7] William Marbury, one of Hiss's closest friends, also considered Minnie domineering.[8]

Charles and Minnie had five children: Anna (1893–1972), Mary Ann (1895–1929), Bosley (1900–26), Alger (1904–96), and Donald (1906–89). In 1895, one of Charles's older brothers, John, died at the age of thirty-three from a heart attack and left a widow and six children. According to one of Hiss's biographers, John Chabot Smith, Charles became the "financial and emotional care taker of his brother's family."[9] Thus Charles and Minnie's five children grew up in a rather large extended family, with their six cousins who lived a few blocks away. The eleven children played together (board games, charades, spelling bee contests), had family meals together, and went to church and Sunday school at the neighborhood Episcopal church every Sunday. Religious training and Bible reading played a central role in the Hiss household. Minnie later transferred to the Presbyterian Church and after that to the Unitarian Church.[10] Alger remained an Episcopalian but stopped going to church when he left home.[11]

The Hiss family lived near Lanvale Street in Baltimore, a middle-class neighborhood, in a three-story, semidetached brick house. Charles prospered in his business and eventually became part owner of the Daniel Miller Company. He helped his wife's brother, Albert Hughes, get a job at his company as treasurer. Unfortunately for Charles, Albert seemed to have become involved in some unsuccessful investments of company funds,[12] which Charles felt obliged to repay by selling his own company stock. In the process, Charles lost his job. He was forty-two years old, the mainstay of eleven children, in poor health, and he was unable to find another job. An older brother, George, offered to take him in as a partner to help run his successful cotton mill in North Carolina. Charles would have accepted, but Minnie refused to leave Baltimore; she valued her place in Baltimore's "genteel" society as a respected woman who attended concerts and art galleries and belonged to the proper clubs.[13] Charles's depression grew deeper and on April 7, 1907, he committed suicide by slitting his throat with a razor blade.[14] Alger was about two and a half years old.

The suicide of Alger's father was kept a close family secret. The Hiss children were so protected from it that the tragedy was treated as a nonevent in their family. Alger revealed in his memoir that he and his brother Donald did not learn of it until they were about ten and eight, respectively, when they overheard neighbors refer to them as "the children of the suicide."[15] Alger related this comment to his older brother, Bosley, who apparently also had been unaware of the family tragedy. Bosley confirmed the suicide from an obituary in the *Baltimore Sun*. This is how the three sons learned of their father's death about eight years earlier. Alger revealed that hearing the comment by the neighbors was one of the most painful episodes in his early years. Yet he claimed he did not feel resentment at not being told, and that when he did learn of the secret, he "joined in the family policy of silence."[16]

Charles left Minnie with their five children to raise, and his deceased brother John's widow and six children to care for as well. Minnie did receive a $100,000 insurance policy, in addition to having the family home, and each of her five children inherited a $10,000 trust (equivalent today to about $200,000).[17] Given their financial position, it is curious that during Alger's early life he always indicated that he lacked money. He said, "As our family financial resources were moderate, I applied for and received scholarships each year at Hopkins and Harvard."[18] He also claimed, according to one of his biographers, Meyer Zeligs, that "for financial reasons" he needed to go to college in Baltimore in order to live at home.[19] At the end of his sophomore year at Hopkins, Hiss was able to afford a trip to Europe only because of the newly innovated Student Third Class, which made European travel affordable for "students of modest means like myself," Hiss said. Traveling in Europe, he was on a budget of four dollars a day and he lamented that he could afford only an "occasional bottle of decent wine."[20] Not exactly the profile of a patrician.

Given the rather substantial trust he inherited, it is unclear why Alger did feel so strapped for money during these years and thought it necessary to depend on school loans and family money. Perhaps, in relative terms, he *felt* poor because he had surrounded himself with so many people of wealth and privilege. When he was at Johns Hopkins, he recalled that he was moved by the book *What Price Glory,* which, according to John Chabot Smith, "confirmed his antiwar views and his distrust for militarism." Yet he was in ROTC, which he said provided him with a modest stipend and a uniform to wear once a week, which saved him money on his other clothes! So he stayed in ROTC for the monetary benefits.[21] Even later in life, when he was earning a good salary at a prestigious law firm at the beginning of the Depression, his letters to his wife, Priscilla, reflected this same preoccupation with insufficient money. For example, in one letter Hiss enumerated the Christmas gifts he bought for his family in Baltimore; one was for an aunt—a pair of skating socks for eighty-five cents—and he was going to split the cost with his brother Donald and give it to her as a joint gift. In fact, he wrote that he bought eight Christmas gifts and Donald's share for them was $4.60.[22] As an attorney for a prestigious law firm in Boston, Hiss wrote in a letter to his wife in March 1932 that "I found a restaurant that has a great lunch for fifteen cents."[23] Years later, in 1947, after he moved to New York as president of the Carnegie Endowment, with a sizable salary, Alger rented a small third-floor walk-up apartment in Greenwich Village. Chambers observed that Hiss did not seem to be interested in "things"—his home furnishings, cars, and taste in food were all rather simple. Nonetheless, there was always enough money for a maid or a cook for his wife, Priscilla; private schools for his son, Tony; and season tickets to concerts and the theater.

The first of Minnie's children was Anna. She played a minor role in the Hiss family over the years and is rarely mentioned in the Hiss literature. She attended Hollins College in Virginia for a year, then graduated from Sargent College (now Boston University) in 1917. After teaching for a year in Baltimore, she moved to Austin to become a physical education instructor at the University of Texas. She spent the next four decades establishing a separate and independent life, attaining a very successful career and making many contributions and innovations to the development of programs and facilities for women's athletics. Anna became head of the university's athletic department while also doing graduate work at a variety of universities in the United States and overseas. She retired after spending thirty-six years organizing an advanced women's athletic program, then moved back to Baltimore in the late 1960s. Anna, who never married, had limited relations with the Hiss family by virtue of living in Texas for so many years.[24]

Minnie's second child and second daughter, Mary Ann, attended Bryn Mawr School in Baltimore, then went to Smith College. In 1920 she married Elliot Emerson, an upper-class, well-to-do Boston stockbroker who was seventeen years her senior. In the mid-1920s, Emerson suffered serious financial setbacks and had to borrow money from the Hiss family to avoid bankruptcy. His financial situation remained problematic for the next several years. Mary Ann and her husband had fierce quarrels and separations. She began having emotional problems and was hospitalized two times, once briefly in a sanitarium.[25] The Hiss family, again in their secretive way, did not tell Alger, who was in college at the time. Hiss was close to his sister Mary Ann, having had contact with her outside of their Baltimore home, when he was at school from 1921 to 1922 at a private academy in Massachusetts, and when he went to Harvard Law School in 1926. In May 1929, the month before Hiss graduated from Harvard Law, Minnie told Alger that Mary Ann had swallowed a bottle of Lysol, killing herself. She was thirty-four years old. Since Alger was unaware of the emotional and financial stresses in her life, the suicide seemed "sudden and irrational." He was shocked when he heard the news of her death.[26]

Bosley (or "Bos" as he was often called) Hiss was Minnie's third child, and first son. After Charles's death, Bosley was treated as "the man of the house" even though he was only seven years old at the time. Alger looked up to his older brother and was very fond of him. Bosley turned out to be something of a teenage rebel, running away from home several times. According to Alger, Bosley was handsome, charming, a nonconformist adventurer who drank a lot and partied and womanized.[27] Bosley attended Johns Hopkins on scholarship and after he graduated he went to work as a reporter for the *Baltimore Sun*. He became very ill at a young age and spent time convalescing at Minnie's house. This arrangement was not successful and led to an estrangement between mother and son.

By the spring of 1924 Bosley was an invalid with malignant Bright's disease (chronic nephritis). He left home and went to Rye, New York, to live with Margaret Owen, a woman in her forties with whom he had had a relationship before he became ill. Margaret nursed him and, although he was dying, married him.[28] Because Margaret, a professional interior decorator, had to be in New York City every day, Alger moved to Margaret's place in Rye, north of the city, in Westchester County, to help take care of Bosley. It was the summer of 1926 and Alger had just graduated from Hopkins. He drove his brother to the hospital for treatments and read to him and shopped for him. He regarded it as a family duty; Alger considered himself as "the family's deputed representative."[29] Two months after Alger started law school, Bosley died in November, at age twenty-six. Unlike Mary Ann's death, this one was expected; Bosley had been seriously ill for almost four years. The deaths of Alger's siblings were like bookends, one occurring when he started Harvard, the other when he finished.

Despite the family tragedy of his father's suicide, Alger, the second son and fourth of five children, viewed his life as happy and active. In his memoir he said that on the whole, "my childhood memories are of a lively and cheerful household" and a "warm family spirit."[30] Alger was surrounded mostly by women—mother, aunts, and sisters. He was fond of one aunt in particular. After his father's death, Aunt Lila, his father's unmarried oldest sister, moved into the Hiss house at 1427 Linden Avenue to help Minnie take care of the children. Minnie also had a maid to do the cooking and housework. Uncle George in North Carolina, well-to-do from his cotton mill business, supplied regular financial help. Another aunt, Aunt Lucy, moved in with John's widow and six children to help care for that family. The Hiss clan really seemed to come together to provide support for one another in the face of crises.

Later in life Alger said that his mother and his aunt Lila were the two adults he remembered best from his childhood.[31] He revealed that he was in many ways closer to his aunt Lila, who was warm and affectionate and the more sympathetic confidante. His mother was too busy running the family and attending club meetings. Alger felt that his mother's emphasis on materialism and her ambitions for her children's success were balanced by Aunt Lila's commitment to spiritual matters. Aunt Lila shared with the Hiss kids her love for literature and learning and morality. Alger had a fond memory of Aunt Lila reading aloud to them and teaching them how to read aloud as well, as with "modulation of tone, and rhythm and pitch and volume."[32]

A cousin Elizabeth recalled that Alger had "a most normal upbringing. He was never unhappy. He cooperated with his dominating mother." Alger remembered "spending much time in the streets, backyards, and parks roller-skating and playing baseball and football."[33] In addition, Alger delivered spring water to families in the Lanvale neighborhood, who would pay fifteen cents a quart or $2.50 for a five-gallon demijohn of fresh, cold springwater that came out of a spigot in Druid Hill Park. Alger and a school friend walked their wagonful of empty bottles up the hill, filled the bottles, then came back down, selling the water along the way.[34]

Hiss said his happiest memories were the summers he spent at Aunt Tege's farm near St. Michaels, on the Eastern Shore of Maryland. He picked tomatoes, helped milk the cows, sheared sheep, and harvested wheat.[35] When he was thirteen years old, Minnie thought Alger had outgrown the summer farm life. In 1918 and 1919 she sent him to Camp Wildwood in Maine, where he met boys from elite New England prep schools, such as his lifelong friend, Henry Hill Collins III, and counselors from Ivy League schools. He did well, winning a medal at the end-of-season track meet. He learned bird-watching, which became a lifetime hobby.[36]

Alger attended high school at Baltimore City College. After graduation, Minnie thought he was too young at sixteen years old to go to college, so she sent him to Powder Point Academy in

Duxbury, Massachusetts. To save money, he lived with his sister
Mary Ann, who had a place in Duxbury.[37] He entered Johns Hopkins, class of 1926. After he graduated from Harvard Law School
in 1929, he married Priscilla Fansler on December 11, 1929. They
had one son, Tony, born in 1941.

Donald was Minnie's third son and youngest child. Two years
older than Donald, Alger was closest to this sibling and apparently
had a great deal of influence over him. Donald Hiss followed a career track that closely paralleled Alger's: Johns Hopkins and Alpha
Delta Phi, Harvard Law School, legal secretary to Oliver Wendell
Holmes, government service in the New Deal, membership in the
Ware Group, and a State Department position. However, Donald did not make law review at Harvard, as Alger had, and this
"brooded on his mind all his life."[38] Donald worked as an attorney
at the Department of the Interior, then the Department of Labor.
In 1938 he went to work in the State Department until the end
of World War II, during which time he was an assistant to Dean
Acheson. In 1945, Donald resigned from the State Department for
health reasons, he said. He joined the prestigious law firm of Covington, Burling, Rublee, Acheson, & Shorb in Washington, D.C.,
until his retirement in 1976. He also was a part-time professor of
international law at the Johns Hopkins School of Advanced International Studies in Washington, D.C. Donald married the former
Catherine Jones and they had three children, Bosley, Cynthia, and
Joanna.

II

HOPKINS AND HARVARD LAW

Hiss Cultivates an Upper-Class,
Eastern Establishment Persona

I N HIS MEMOIR, *Recollections of a Life,* Alger Hiss devoted
only nine pages to his entire early childhood and wrote almost
nothing about his college years at Johns Hopkins. In fact,
the book skips from the chapter on his childhood in Baltimore to
the chapter on his Harvard Law School experience. He wrote at
length about a trip with his brother Donald to Giverny, France,
in the summer of 1929. But he made only a few references to his
college days. He mentioned that at Hopkins he majored in history
and romance languages.[1] Another reference was during his discussion of becoming a New Dealer: he said that in his college days he
"scorned" politics and thought of it as a "dirty business." Apparently
in retrospect (Hiss wrote his memoir in 1988) his life at Hopkins
more than six decades earlier left little impression on him; but he
did fault Hopkins for its neglect in covering some of the great political issues of the time. Hiss wrote that "political apathy was the
mood of the university."[2] He recalled that there had been "few if
any references in Johns Hopkins classes to the Soviet revolution
or to the Sacco-Vanzetti case," one of the most famous trials of the
twentieth century.[3] Despite this criticism from a 1988 perspective,

while attending Hopkins in the 1920s Hiss did not seem to have these intellectual concerns or misgivings about political and social justice. He himself claimed that while in college he was enjoying a cultural, cosmopolitan life.

Hiss's college record showed that he was highly successful. He participated fully in student activities. He was the editor of the college newspaper, president of the drama club, and president of the student council. He was in ROTC all four years, in his senior year the cadet commander, and ended up with a second lieutenant's reserve commission. Alger was elected a member of Phi Beta Kappa in his junior year and also to the prestigious Tudor and Stuart Club. He was a member of Alpha Delta Phi, a fraternity that pledged only the wealthiest and most socially acceptable men. He was a member of the Cane Club, a Prohibition-era drinking society whose members carried canes and wore white carnations on special occasions. Hiss was well liked and successful both academically and in extracurricular activities. He was ambitious and driven, but not in a noticeable way, according to Murray Kempton.[4] Alger was already developing the persona of a very engaging man. He was voted the "most popular" and the "best all around" and the "best hand-shaker."[5] The yearbook editor's description of him was "the epitome of success" and most cultured and learned. The editor ended with "Alger is a nice chappie, in spite of his attainments."[6]

Alger loved the theater; he and his fraternity brother Charles Ford Reese attended regularly. Charles, who had season tickets, was from the Ford family that owned the Ford Theatre in Baltimore and in earlier generations the famous Ford Theatre in Washington, D.C., site of Lincoln's assassination. They saw every play that came to Baltimore, sitting in the Ford family's box. During Christmas recess, Alger would go to New York to see Theater Guild productions of such playwrights as George Bernard Shaw, Luigi Pirandello, and Eugene O'Neill. He stayed at the fraternity club house on Forty-Fourth Street with another fraternity brother.[7]

Hiss considered himself a Democrat, which was his family's

political affiliation. One of his favorite teachers was Broadus Mitchell, an economics professor who was a socialist. However, Hiss commented years later that "we were so thoroughly inoculated by prevailing social and economic views against his mildly Socialistic opinions that they made no impression on us."[8] Mitchell was liked by most students because he was affable and a lenient grader.[9] Hiss said Mitchell's views may have tended to fortify the distaste that some students had developed for business as a career, but they did not lead them to consider the possibility of structural defects in industrial society.

Hiss was picking up strong antibusiness ideas, being a fan of H. L. Mencken and Shaw. He did not study Marx and Lenin, because these subjects were not taught at Hopkins at the time. Hiss observed, again, decades later, that there was no school of thought that advocated forthright government intervention in the economic life of the nation to redress the lot of those who failed to share in the benefits of the economy. His biographer, John Chabot Smith, said that Hiss's interests in intellectual matters were not very strong during his college days.[10] In fact, Hiss said that of the books he read in college he was most moved and influenced by Somerset Maugham's *Of Human Bondage*.[11] The book, probably Maugham's best, is an absorbing novel but no great intellectual challenge.

Whittaker Chambers found Hiss's intellectual interests lacking. Chambers maintained that his friendship with Hiss was "one of character—not of mind." Despite his strong legal abilities, "Hiss was not a highly mental man," compared to the minds Chambers was exposed to at Columbia University (such as Clifton Fadiman, Meyer Schapiro, or Mark Van Doren). Chambers observed that ideas did not interest Hiss, except for Marxist-Leninist doctrine, but even that was only as it applied to current politics, not theory or history. Chambers said Hiss never drew his attention to important books; moreover, Hiss didn't like Shakespeare, calling the Bard's works "platitudes in blank verse."[12] The comment was later denied by some Hiss supporters.[13]

In an unpublished paper by Hiss, cited in Ivan Chen's 2008 on-line account of Hiss at Harvard, Hiss wrote about the foundations of his liberalism and claimed that he was already politically and socially progressive when he went to college.[14] There doesn't seem to be evidence to support this position; most of the Hiss literature actually portrays him as politically neutral while at Hopkins and more involved in developing his persona and in enjoying a cultured social life. The one exception was his acknowledged dislike for big business, which he voiced from time to time. Hiss also noted in the same unpublished paper that his idealism drew him to the subordination of private gain to the welfare of others.[15] Again, this view of redistribution appears to be a position Hiss may have held in theory only while in college. In practice, Hiss seemed thoroughly to enjoy the benefits of wealthy and prestigious friends. Hiss wrote that Harvard was where his "early liberal outlook had been strengthened and given focus." Much of this added "focus" resulted from the liberalism of Frankfurter himself, Hiss wrote.[16] The available information about his thinking at Harvard supports this particular claim.

Initially, Hiss had wanted to pursue a career in the Foreign Service; a family friend and professor of international law, Manley Hudson, suggested law school as an avenue to prepare for entry into international diplomacy. Hiss enrolled at Harvard Law School in 1926. Going to Harvard Law was a defining experience, a formative and influential time in Hiss's life. A review of the literature on Hiss contains very few details about his years at Harvard, where he excelled academically, and where he developed his liberal leanings as well as close friends and important contacts. However, a recent research paper by Ivan Chen provides an impressive, detailed account and fuller appreciation of the three years Hiss spent at law school.[17] During Hiss's first year, Abbott Lawrence Lowell was the president of Harvard University and Roscoe Pound was dean of the law school. Pound was instrumental in turning the law school into a center of American legal and political leadership, according to Chen.[18]

The admissions process to get into Harvard Law was quite different in 1926 than it is now. No standardized tests were required (including LSATs); recommendations were not part of the application process, either. Admission was solely on the basis of one's undergraduate record, according to Chen. However, in 1926–27 about a third of the incoming class of students had graduated from Harvard, Princeton, and Yale. (Johns Hopkins was represented by only nine students, including Hiss.) Thus, contrary to Chen's comment that only undergraduate grades were used for admission, the large percentage of incoming students from Harvard, Princeton, and Yale would suggest that other unofficial criteria for admission were likely considered: family alumni status, financial contributions, attendance at Harvard College or other Ivies.

Although admission was easier then, it was more difficult to stay enrolled. Today, Chen claimed, nearly every student matriculating at Harvard Law graduates. In Hiss's time, about one-third of each entering class flunked out at the end of the first year, even though the required curriculum remained the same from 1926 until the 2007–2008 school year.[19] Hiss was one of 674 men who started law school in 1926. Early in his first year he applied for and won the Herbert Parker scholarship for $250, awarded to an outstanding student each December to cover the cost of that year. Letters of reference were acceptable for loan applications.

Hiss once told his son, Tony, that he had studied hard his first year, on nights and weekends. Yet he remained close to his family and visited home regularly.[20] The year-end exams for the five first-year courses (Civil Procedure, Contracts, Criminal Law, Property, and Torts) were open book; students had four hours to answer ten essay questions. Hiss did remarkably well; his A- average for first year placed him in the top 1.5 percent of the class. It also earned him an invitation to join the editorial board of the *Harvard Law Review,* along with the other thirteen highest-ranking students, several of whom became close friends with Alger.[21]

Only 426 of the original class of 674 returned for the second year. Alger continued to be a high achiever and got a B+ average at the end of his second year, one in which his editorial commitments to the law review took up a good deal of time. In addition to editing, Hiss also published a student note, titled "The 'Yellow Dog' Device as a Bar to the Union Organizer," in the review.[22] As was the custom, a colleague on the law review editorial board (in this case, Lee Pressman) had given Hiss this assignment. As a result, Hiss developed a strong interest in labor law and government affairs.

Yellow dog contracts, agreements between employers and employees that nonunion workers only would be utilized, were controversial in the late 1920s. Felix Frankfurter advocated their abolishment. In *Hitchman Coal & Coke Co. v. Mitchell,* the U.S. Supreme Court ruled that employers could go to a court and obtain an injunction—a court order—barring union leaders from even trying to unionize workers who had signed yellow dog contracts. In his law review note, Hiss criticized the Court for affording employers, and only employers, this special remedy. In all other labor disagreements, a party could go to court and sue only after a contract had been breached. Hiss believed that yellow dog contracts should not have been treated any differently. He believed that by ruling as it did in *Hitchman,* the Court unfairly granted employers a powerful tool—the right to enjoin or prevent a union from acting, even before it had done anything improper—that was not available to any other party to any other kind of labor contract.[23]

Some of Hiss's peers wanted to elect him president of the law review. However, Hiss threw his support to Herman Austern, who was the highest-ranking student in the Class of 1929. Hiss believed his own name was put forward only to prevent Austern—a Jew—from winning. In the end, Austern was elected.[24] Hiss later wrote that he felt he had shed what he perceived to be the anti-Semitic snobbishness and racist outlook of his mother's background.[25]

A number of Hiss's colleagues on the law review became his close friends, and some supported him during his perjury trials.

Among them were Erwin Griswold (a future dean of Harvard Law), who formed a strong friendship with Hiss, saying during the time of the trials that he had no reason to doubt his loyalty; Richard Field (a future Harvard Law School professor), a close friend of Alger and who chose him as his best man when he married; Edward McLean, who helped prepare Hiss's defense at both trials; Harold Rosenwald, a very close friend who was on Hiss's defense team during the second trial; and Lee Pressman, an admitted Communist and a member of the Ware Group—an underground Communist cell—from 1934 to 1935, who also worked with Hiss on the International Juridical Association (IJA) in 1932 and in the Agricultural Adjustment Administration from 1933 to 1935. Jesse Slingluff, although not on the law review, was perhaps Hiss's best friend before they were classmates at Hopkins and Harvard. Hiss's law review contemporaries continued to be among his close circle of friends long after they left Harvard.[26]

With regard to the faculty, Hiss developed a close relationship with Felix Frankfurter, the nationally prominent law professor. Hiss came to Harvard with a letter of introduction to Frankfurter from William Marbury, a Baltimore lawyer who was a mutual friend. Because of this, Hiss felt, he was one of the lucky few invited to the famous Sunday teas at Frankfurter's home on Brattle Street in Cambridge—along with his "august friends" carrying on "intellectual discourse." Frankfurter was the "idol" of the students who were favored and fortunate enough to be invited.[27] He had "a tendency to have close relationships with and to promote the careers of only those students who had conspicuously good grades."[28]

In his memoir Hiss recalled that Frankfurter was not popular with most students and faculty members, because he was "cocky and abrasive" and the leader of the liberal wing of the law faculty, which at the time was mainly politically conservative. For example, Frankfurter championed the innocence of Sacco and Vanzetti and felt their execution in 1927 represented a miscarriage of justice. This won him acclaim among liberals as a defender of civil liberties

but not so at Harvard. The president of Harvard, Abbott Lowell, served on the Massachusetts commission that recommended
against leniency for Sacco and Vanzetti.[29]

Hiss wrote that at Harvard Law School "the spirit of reform
was symbolized by Professor Felix Frankfurter."[30] Hiss believed his
relationship with Frankfurter helped shape his liberal views.[31] This
was especially true with regard to Frankfurter's efforts in labor laws,
where Hiss believed in the injustice of labor laws and the bias of
courts against labor. It was at this time that Hiss became convinced
of the need to reform and redress these social injustices.[32] Hiss was
also influenced by James M. Landis, later dean of Harvard Law
School, who brought Harvard its first course in labor law in 1928.[33]

Following graduation, Hiss kept up his friendship with Frankfurter, seeing him often when he was practicing law in a Boston
firm from 1930 to 1931. After Franklin Roosevelt's election,
Frankfurter in 1933 contacted a select number of his students,
including Hiss, urging them to go to Washington and into public
service, including the federal government's New Deal program.
During the Hiss trials in the late 1940s, Hiss's legal defense called
on Frankfurter to testify to Hiss's good character, which the justice did. Later Hiss kept in touch with him indirectly through his
brother Donald, who had a very close relationship with Frankfurter
as well, and in fact was the executor of his estate.[34]

After Roosevelt selected Frankfurter to become a Supreme
Court justice in 1939, Hiss perceived a "seeming paradox in the
contrast between Frankfurter's increasingly conservative judicial
opinions and his earlier liberal attitudes." The activism of the Warren Court did not follow the doctrine of judicial restraint and thus
Frankfurter, who advocated that doctrine, often found himself at
odds with the liberal faction of the Warren Court.[35]

Only 379 students of the original 674 returned to Cambridge for
the third year. During his last year at Harvard Law School, Hiss
not only attended Frankfurter's weekly teas but also took two of
his seminars. They consisted of about a dozen students, and in the

case of Federal Courts, Frankfurter handpicked the class from a group of outstanding students. Alger finished the third year with an A- average. According to Chen, Alger had straight A's except for a D in Conflict of Laws. His successful three-year performance earned him cum laude honors at graduation.[36] In addition, Frankfurter recommended Hiss for the distinction of a clerkship with Supreme Court justice Oliver Wendell Holmes.[37] In 1946, three years prior to the first perjury case, Frankfurter was asked about his view on Hiss. He replied that "Alger was a very nice person but . . . somehow he had not quite come up to the promise of his youth." Apparently Frankfurter came to believe that somewhere along the way Hiss had lost his focus, although the jurist later testified in Hiss's behalf.[38]

III

PRISCILLA HISS

Priscilla: It's Never a Nice Day
for the Sharecroppers in Oklahoma

A LGER HISS'S WIFE of thirty years, Priscilla Harriet Fansler, was born in Evanston, Illinois, on October 30, 1903, to Thomas L. Fansler and Willia Spruill Fansler. Her father, whose descendants were Dutch, was born in the 1850s in a log cabin his father built in Alton, Illinois. He became a general agent of the Northwestern Mutual Life Insurance Company and a trustee of Illinois College. On her mother's side, her Spruill and deRespass ancestors had been in the United States as long as or longer than the Hisses. Thomas and Willia had eight children; two died young.[1] Priscilla was the youngest of the remaining six children. Her oldest brother, Dean, eighteen years her senior, was a professor of English literature at Columbia University and later dean at the Philippine University in Manila. During World War II, he was interned by the Japanese for four years and died after his release in 1945. Another brother, Ralph, was a bank examiner in Detroit. Henry was a top advertising man on the *New York Herald Tribune*. Thomas Jr. was an English teacher. Her only sister, Daisy, was a music librarian at the Philadelphia Public Library.[2]

Priscilla spent her early years in Frazer, Pennsylvania, a Main

Line suburb of Philadelphia, graduating from Phoebe Ann Thomas High School. She received a bachelor's degree from Bryn Mawr College in 1924. Out of 119 graduates from Bryn Mawr, Priscilla was one of eleven cum laudes. She was listed as president of the Liberal Club.[3] She attended Yale University Graduate School, taking advanced English.

In the summer of 1924, following his sophomore year, Alger took a trip to Europe on a cheap student tour with Jesse Slingluff, his closest college friend. Alger met Priscilla on the ocean liner *The New Amsterdam*. He was very impressed by "her beauty and brains."[4] He detoured from his own itinerary to accompany her to London and stayed until the arrival of her friends. She was not impressed with him, and years later said she thought of him as brotherly at the time. After her return from Europe, Priscilla went to Baltimore to visit friends and happened to meet Alger again. She was now a graduate student at Yale and announced that she was engaged to Thayer Hobson, a divorced man. Hiss remembered hearing the news as a "cruel blow" but Priscilla claimed she did not remember the incident at all.[5] Alger moved on, however, and at Johns Hopkins started to date an attractive female graduate student from New Orleans. He said she was the only girl he ever wrote a poem about. They were engaged for a while but after he started law school, Hiss broke it off; he said he was not ready for marriage.[6] In 1925, Priscilla married Hobson, a fellow graduate student at Yale, and who later became a publisher in New York. They had one son, Timothy, born in 1926.

Priscilla worked at a new magazine, *Time,* as the office manager for its editors, Henry Luce and Briton Hadden. Luce was a friend of Hobson. She then enrolled at Columbia University graduate school and received a master's degree in literature. After less than four years, divorce proceedings were instituted by mutual consent; Hobson was the petitioner. The grounds for divorce: incompatibility. Hobson got a Mexican divorce in January 1929. He then married Laura Zametkin, who later became famous as Laura Z.

Hobson, author of *Gentleman's Agreement*.[7] Priscilla was given custody of their son. Twenty years later, during the Hiss trials, the FBI interviewed Hobson, then president of the William Morrow Company in New York. During the interview, he characterized his former wife, Priscilla, as a rather "fuzzy-minded idealist."[8]

Alger Hiss resumed his pursuit of Priscilla, following her divorce from Hobson; however, she became involved with a married man, William Brown Meloney, a New York newspaperman. At the end of the summer 1929, when Alger returned from Europe, he discovered, according to one version of the story, that Priscilla was about to enter a hospital for "surgery" (meaning an abortion); Meloney had refused to divorce his wife and marry Priscilla.[9] Alger traveled up to New York each weekend to see her. The Hiss literature includes contradictory accounts about the abortion: Priscilla said she told Alger about it when they first married; he claimed he did not find out until ten years later. However, when he discussed the incident with Allen Weinstein, author of *Perjury*, the comprehensive, monumental, and definitive account of the Hiss-Chambers espionage case, Hiss indicated that he knew in 1929, before they married, when he visited her in the hospital.[10]

After refusing Alger twice for other men, Priscilla, a single mother, now may have seen some merit in marrying Alger. For his part, Hiss thought of Priscilla as a "female intellectual"; they had shared interests in the theater and music and in the belief that "the problems of the world could be solved."[11] Priscilla married Hiss on December 11, 1929, and according to almost all accounts of their relationship, she proceeded to play a dominant and influential role in his life.

Alger's mother, Minnie, disapproved of Priscilla; she did not attend the wedding, which took place in Washington, D.C., in a friend's apartment, where they were married by a Presbyterian minister. Instead Minnie sent a telegram to Alger on their wedding day that read, "Do not take this fatal step." The reason for her rejection of Priscilla is unclear, but Priscilla never forgave her mother-in-law and stayed angry at Alger over the episode for years. Aside from his mother, one of Alger's closest friends, William Marbury, as well as Alger's brother Donald both felt uncomfortable around Priscilla. Donald apparently did not like her; she was too highbrow. According to a 1949 statement by his lawyer, Donald had little use for Priscilla, objecting to her "on personality rather than political grounds."[12] In addition, some of Alger's friends thought Priscilla was too radical and too intellectual. She, in turn, did not like Alger's Baltimore friends; she regarded them as part of his "undergraduate experience."[13]

Alger and Priscilla were married three months after he had started to clerk for Holmes. Justice Holmes had a rigid policy that his law clerks had to be single, which meant that Hiss was not to marry during his one-year term of office. It is not clear whether Hiss was aware of this policy when he married Priscilla; there are conflicting stories on this point in the Hiss literature. In any event, he apologized and Holmes accepted the apology. Priscilla found an apartment for them to live in from December 1929 to October 1930.[14] She became an assistant librarian for the Wickersham Commission, which was studying proposals for judicial reform, among other things, and had criticized the way the Sacco and Vanzetti case was handled. After Hiss finished his year clerking for Holmes, he had to change his earlier plan to practice law in Baltimore, where he had taken the Maryland bar. Priscilla was opposed to his taking a job in Baltimore. If Alger had any thought of moving back to Baltimore to practice law, Priscilla made sure that was not going to happen.[15] She would not end up the unwanted daughter-in-law in Minnie's world of "shabby gentility."

Armed with a recommendation from Marbury, Alger went to Boston to work for the prestigious law firm of Choate, Hall, & Stewart.[16] The Hisses took a place at 21 Chauncey Street in Cambridge. However, Priscilla "loathed" living in Cambridge,[17] apparently because Alger dominated that world as a result of his years at Harvard Law and the contacts he had developed. Thus, when

Priscilla received a grant from Carnegie Corporation to collaborate with her sister-in-law, Roberta Fansler, an art historian, on a book titled *Research in Fine Arts in American Colleges and Universities*, she left Cambridge and moved to New York in October 1931. She rented an apartment where her brother and sister-in-law lived, near Columbia University.[18] Alger went down on weekends to visit. About a year later, Priscilla influenced him to seek a job in New York, which he did.[19]

During the years 1929–32 Alger corresponded regularly with Priscilla. A review of the Hiss Family Papers archived at the Tamiment Library, New York University, including many hundreds of letters, reveals that Alger was an inveterate letter writer his whole life. During his forty-four months in prison, he wrote no less than 445 letters.[20] His letters provide insight into Hiss as an attentive and affectionate husband. Alger and Priscilla referred to each other as Hill and Pros or Prossy, and Priscilla adopted the Quaker use of *thee* and *thy* for those close to her. (Priscilla was Presbyterian, but she came from a Quaker family.)[21] There were affectionate Valentine and birthday cards, which Hiss would sometimes sign, "Thy husband Hill." (Tony Hiss said that he was not aware of the origins of his father's nickname "Hill.") The letters contained many terms of endearment.

Hiss's letters were very chatty: he talked about books and plays and art. He mentioned he liked T. S. Eliot and was reading Hemingway and Shaw; he was going to see *Journey's End*. He saw *Don Giovanni*; went to art exhibits at the Phillips Gallery; spent a day at the Laurel, Maryland, racetrack; played squash. In one letter he mentioned how he missed Pros and was lonely, and he indicated some annoyance because he thought her letters were not informative enough and he felt "shut out of thy life." He also was displeased when Priscilla did not respond to his letters promptly. The letters were at times pedestrian. They mentioned not only social activities (for example, going to museums, civic orchestra performances, Harvard glee clubs, parties) but also mundane financial concerns involving rents, leases, bills, and household issues such as plumbing leaks and heating problems.[22]

References to political issues in the correspondence were rather rare. In one letter to Hiss, Priscilla wrote about taking classes in 1931–32 through the Columbia University Extension Program in "The Worker in American History." Hiss's reply on October 16, 1932: "Thy story about 'The Norton Story of Jackety Lot' Eliot preparing his students for a proletarian revolution is certainly news. I had thought that the ideas now current, about which we talked last week, were peculiar—so far as capitalistic democratic America is concerned—to the present moment. It's discouraging to think that perhaps the panic of 1877 gave as vivid a lesson of capitalism as has today's Depression and that such a warning was ignored." The letter continues on about an article on pacifism, his work schedule, and paying bills.[23]

In New York, Priscilla Hiss had gravitated steadily to the political left and, along with her brother, Tom Fansler, joined the Morningside Heights Branch of the Socialist Party, according to the party's records.[24] She attended meetings during the time Alger worked in Boston. Her letters to Alger talked about dockworkers' strikes and unemployed sailors. The signs of the Depression were beginning to surface in the city: soup kitchens, bread lines, men selling apples, people living in shacks and tents. Priscilla was living in a walk-up cold-water flat at 180 Claremont Avenue, off upper Broadway near Columbia University. In a March 18, 1932, letter to Alger she discussed her attempts to organize a cooperative store "in connection with the unemployed relief that our branch of the Socialist Party is trying to start."[25] When Priscilla worked in the "feeding station" and voted in 1932 she identified herself as a Socialist. However, years later, in her testimony during the Hiss trials, she denied that she ever joined the Socialist Party.

In addition to her own words in the March 18, 1932, letter to Alger, FBI files have evidence of her falsifying her testimony at the Hiss trials. Under questioning from Hiss's defense attorney, Claude

B. Cross, on December 29, 1949, at the second trial, Priscilla Hiss said she never was a Communist Party member and never was a "fellow traveler." She said that she voted for Al Smith in 1928, Norman Thomas in 1932, and Harry Truman in 1948. When asked about any association with the Socialist Party, Priscilla acknowledged that she made contributions to a feeding station with the uptown branch of the Socialist Party near her home, and that she made sandwiches and coffee and dispensed them in the winter of 1931–32. The only time she attended any Socialist Party meetings, she claimed, was when she was working at the food station. She said she was never a member of the Socialist Party.[26]

At the second trial, August Claessens, executive secretary of the Social Democratic Federation, was called to the stand and examined by the government's attorney, Thomas F. Murphy. Claessens was a member of the Socialist Party and as a city organizer he had a file card from an application for party membership by Priscilla Hiss. A Blue Card bore Priscilla's name and her address at 180 Claremont Avenue, and stated that she was admitted on March 23, 1930, to the Morningside Heights Branch (government exhibit 63)—less than three months after she married Alger Hiss. Government exhibit 64 was a photostat of the two pages of the Board of Election book for the year 1932. Priscilla included for the question: "Party of enrolled voter, Soc." All of which impeached her testimony.[27]

In *Perjury*, Allen Weinstein claimed that Priscilla's Socialist Party commitment went beyond soup kitchens. She helped found an organization of left-wing dissidents called the American Labor Associates (ALA). In 1932 the ALA held meetings to gain supporters and raise funds for a magazine; the Advisory Board's letterhead included Priscilla's name, along with Communists, socialists, and nonaffiliated radicals. At one meeting attended by Priscilla, the group discussed a planning document that concluded that the task for radicals was to build an "organized purposive revolutionary movement."[28] Priscilla obviously was committed to radical social change while living in New York in the Depression years of 1932–33.

After Hiss left Choate, Hall in the spring of 1932 to work for about a year at Cotton, Franklin, Wright, & Gordon, a large Wall Street law firm, he and Priscilla upgraded to a nicer apartment at 378 Central Park West. It was October 1932. Priscilla ended her attendance at Socialist Party meetings at the Morningside Heights Branch. However, both Priscilla and Alger studied sporadically for a short time at the Socialist Party's Rand School, near Union Square.[29] There is no evidence that Hiss ever joined the Socialist Party, but his antibusiness and pro-union positions began to expand and harden during this period. He was convinced that "longstanding industrial and financial practices" could not solve the problems of the Depression.[30]

Hiss began to study the history of labor and social reform and "discovered Karl Marx, Robert Owen, and Sidney Webb."[31] He also had an opportunity to reestablish an old friendship with Lee Pressman, one of his classmates at Harvard Law School. Pressman was then with the law firm of Chadbourne, Stanchfield, & Levy. Hiss and Pressman both worked, pro bono, at night and on weekends for the IJA. Hiss described the IJA as an "editorial group specializing in putting out notes on labor causes." Pressman didn't stay long in New York. He moved to Washington and Hiss soon followed him there in March 1933. Years later, in 1951, in congressional testimony, Pressman confessed he had been a Communist Party member and a member of the Ware Group[32] in the early 1930s. But Pressman insisted that the Ware Group was a Marxist "study group," not an espionage cell.[33]

Biographical data on the Hisses indicates that while Priscilla seemed always to be politically on the left, Alger quickly caught up to her and they became "radicalized" in tandem. He probably was influenced by her, though certainly as much, if not more so, by colleagues such as Lee Pressman at the IJA. Chambers said that Priscilla Hiss also was a member of the Communist Party and influenced her husband in his Communist activities. There is no evidence to suggest that Priscilla recruited Alger into the Communist

Party; it appears he found his way there on his own at about the time he joined the Ware Group in 1933 in Washington, D.C.

Whittaker Chambers maintained that when he first met Alger, in the summer of 1934, Hiss was already a committed Communist. Chambers believed that Alger Hiss refused to break with the Communist Party, as he ended up doing in 1938, because of Priscilla's fanatical loyalty to the party.[34] Allen Weinstein and Sam Tanenhaus (author of the comprehensive bestselling biography on Whittaker Chambers) both pictured Priscilla as "short tempered, upper crust, politically obsessed." According to Weinstein, when a friend remarked to the effect, "What a nice day it is," Priscilla snapped back with something like "It's never a nice day for the sharecroppers in Oklahoma!"[35]

After practicing law for about a year at Cotton, Franklin, Alger moved to Washington, D.C., at the strong urging of Frankfurter. He and Priscilla rented a house in June 1933 in Georgetown at 3411 O Street NW.[36] Alger started his career as the consummate New Dealer, and Priscilla became involved in the Bryn Mawr Alumnae Association in Washington, of which she was the president from 1936 to 1937. Priscilla also taught English part-time at the Potomac School in Washington. In 1940–41 she worked for the Library of Congress on the staff of Julian Leavitt, then head of the Catalogue Division. She had been his assistant before, in 1930, when Leavitt was librarian of the Wickersham Commission. Hiss's biographer, Smith, said that when Leavitt was out of work during the Depression, living in a tiny shack in Norwalk, Connecticut, the Hisses visited him from New York. They would bring him crates of canned food and lend him money, which he repaid after his appointment to the Library of Congress.[37]

In May 1934, the Hisses moved again, to 2831 Twenty-Eighth Street NW. They left this apartment several weeks before the lease was up in July 1935 and moved to a house at 2905 P Street NW from April 1935 to June 1936. It was at the Twenty-Eighth Street home that, Chambers testified, he stayed with his family until the lease ran out, courtesy of Alger Hiss. The Hisses stayed at P Street for about a year and then moved to 1245 Thirtieth Street NW until about January 1938, when they moved to Volta Place in George-town.[38] The Hisses' last residence in Washington, D.C., before moving to New York City, was at 3210 P Street NW, from about 1943 to 1947.[39]

According to FBI files, the membership roster of the Washington Committee for Democratic Action contained Priscilla Hiss's name and address at 3415 Volta Place NW, where the Hisses lived from January 1938 to 1943. The FBI memo stated that the Washington Committee for Democratic Action was an affiliate of the National Committee for Democratic Action, a subversive organization within the purview of Executive Order 9835.[40] (This order established an employee loyalty program in the executive branch of the government and was the main impetus for the creation of the attorney general's List of Subversive Organizations.) The FBI's investigation regarding Priscilla Hiss developed information that she had knowledge of and aided her husband in his work for the Soviets. No evidence was developed that she specifically had been a Communist Party member but there were indications of strong sympathy for the Communist movement on her part. In a signed statement to the FBI, and later in trial testimony, Priscilla denied knowledge that her husband was engaged in espionage, or that she aided him by typing stolen State Department documents.[41] And FBI files state that after Alger was released from prison, when his son, Tony, was accepted as a student at the Putney School in Vermont, Priscilla and the family were driven to Vermont by an individual who was a former employee of the USSR's news agency, TASS, which was outspoken in the Alger Hiss defense.[42]

In the midst of their involvement with professional and political activities, the Hisses still had family obligations. According to John Chabot Smith, Alger tried to be a devoted father to Timothy, Priscilla's son from her first marriage to Thayer Hobson.[43] Tim called his mother and stepfather "Pros and Alger" as a child. He attended private schools; under the terms of the divorce settlement, his father, Hobson, paid for Tim's education. "Every effort seems to have been made to avoid open displays of emotion" on the part of Tim or his parents. For example, when Alger and Pros had a dispute, with Alger usually offering a compromise and Pros not accepting it, in the end it was done her way. Alger would go out for a walk to get rid of his anger; he had a temper but never allowed himself to show it.[44] Hiss's extraordinary self-control and reserve were visible throughout his life, especially in his nearly half-century-long crusade to prove his innocence.

When he was a teenager, Tim went to George School, a Quaker boarding school near Doylestown, Pennsylvania. Priscilla remembered that Tim's visits to his father were stressful for him; by contrast, Tim remembered enjoying them very much, especially when Hobson married a fourth time; Tim said he grew to love Thayer's fourth wife. Timothy Hobson was a young man at the time of the Hiss trials. Hiss made it a point not to have Timothy, who later was a medical intern at Mount Zion Hospital in San Francisco, called to testify. Hiss was concerned that rumors of his homosexuality would surface and become public. Timothy had an "undesirable" discharge from the navy in 1945 after a medical evaluation.[45] Such was Hiss's sensitivity toward his stepson (and Tim's mother, Priscilla) that he did not want him called to testify. However, the most Timothy could have done was to support Hiss's position that during the 1930s (when he, Tim, was only a boy of eleven years old) Chambers had not been a regular visitor to the Hiss house. On the other hand, Chambers claimed there was a "lack of warmth" in Hiss's relationship with his stepson.[46]

In the summers Tim went to camp on the Eastern Shore, near Chestertown, where for some years the Hisses rented an apartment in the summer in order to be near Tim.[47] In an interview with Weinstein in 1974, Tim said he had felt in the 1930s that Alger and Pros were not comfortable with each other in private, that they led no close personal life, and they filled their time with parties, dinners, shop talk over drinks, etc. He was very lonely and the household remained something of a blur to him.[48]

Tony Hiss was born on August 5, 1941; Priscilla was thirty-seven years old, Alger thirty-six, and Timothy almost fifteen. In his book *Laughing Last,* Tony claimed that Alger didn't offer too much of a hand in bringing him up. Others, he said, thought that he was spoiled and that "Alger would get mad at the way Pros indulged me." Tony remembered that his mother, Prossy, as he called her, played the piano, worked in the Library of Congress, was a civil defense warden in World War II, and taught in grade school. Tony wrote that people remember her as "slim, pretty, with long hair, talkative, opinioned; men rather liked her, women often found her a little scary."[49]

From what has been written by and about the Hisses, including their correspondence with one another, it seems that Timothy was close to capturing the nature of the relationship between Priscilla and Alger: it was socially and professionally busy, with each involved with his or her own separate career—especially Alger—yet there was a warmth there. Still, they seemingly had no close personal life. Their letters reveal a mutual affection and concern for each other and a social partnership, but only a small level of intimacy. What seemed to be lacking in their marriage was passion. Presumably that was reserved for ideological pursuits.

IV.

SUPREME COURT CLERK
AND ATTORNEY-AT-LAW

From Holmes's Surrogate Son to Radicalized Lawyer

FOLLOWING HIS GRADUATION from law school, Hiss earned a clerkship with Supreme Court justice Oliver Wendell Holmes. He was chosen on the recommendation of Felix Frankfurter, who selected Holmes's clerks each year.[1] William Howard Taft was the chief justice of the Supreme Court at the time. Holmes had been appointed by President Theodore Roosevelt to the Court in 1902, as an associate justice. He served for thirty years and had a new private "secretary" (today the term is "law clerk") every year. Since Holmes and his wife had no children, Hiss felt that his secretaries played a special role in his life, in some ways serving as "surrogate sons." This was probably especially true at the time of Hiss's appointment—Holmes was eighty-eight years old and a recent widower. Alger described his relationship with the justice as the "most profound" he ever had.[2] "No other honor or piece of good fortune has been such a source of delight for me as was that enchanted year I spent with Holmes beginning in 1929. And no other relationship has had a deeper or more lasting influence."[3]

Holmes told Hiss that when he was a boy, his grandmother told him of the British entering Boston. His family home on Beacon

Hill had been Lord Howe's headquarters for a time during the Revolutionary War. Holmes had a Queen Anne mirror from that house that Alger admired greatly and Holmes left it to him when he died. It became a treasured possession. Holmes was descended from privileged elite, yet he often said to Alger that the Civil War had taught him true democracy. Over and over again, Holmes told how "he had witnessed bravery and leadership on the part of poor, simple men" who lacked advantages of education or background.[4] Holmes had fought in the Civil War, receiving a commission as first lieutenant in the Twentieth Regiment of the Massachusetts Volunteer Infantry. He saw much action, from the Peninsula Campaign to the Wilderness, suffering wounds at the Battle of Ball's Bluff, Antietam, and Fredericksburg.[5]

In 1929, Holmes was living in a brownstone house at 1720 I Street NW in Washington, D.C. The legal secretary job was not demanding. Holmes wrote his own opinions and needed little help from his secretaries. Hiss's formal duties were primarily giving Holmes oral reports on petitions for review. For oral arguments Holmes did not ask Hiss to write memoranda summarizing briefs, nor did he require Hiss to attend arguments. For the cases that the Court took for full review and in which Holmes wrote an opinion, he seldom called on Hiss for discussion or research. His opinions were uniformly brief. They simply set forth the legal principles he thought to be applicable and the precedents he wished to rely upon.[6] In short, Holmes rarely used Hiss, or for that matter any of his other secretaries, for research or discussion of legal cases.

However, informal tasks increased and led to a close relationship with Alger. Holmes's wife of fifty-seven years died in April 1929. Thus Alger's year, starting in October, was somewhat of a transition, where the secretary's role took on some functions previously performed by the late Fanny Holmes. For example, Hiss responded to Holmes's correspondence for him and he wrote checks to pay household bills.[7] There was something new, however. At Hiss's suggestion (and Holmes's strong resistance at first), Hiss would read aloud to Holmes every day. For Alger this was the highlight of his year. He wrote, "I was the first one permitted to read aloud to Holmes." This offered an opportunity for a closer personal relationship with the justice than the position called for.[8] Hiss had lunch and tea with Holmes every day. He became very excited when he had access to the "Black Book"—a book with Holmes's diary-like notes and a list of the books he had read, which reflected a variety of his interests.[9] When Holmes retired in 1932, secretaries continued to serve him, Hiss's brother Donald among them. When Donald Hiss graduated from Harvard Law School, Felix Frankfurter selected him to clerk for Holmes.

During his year with Holmes, Alger Hiss claimed, he learned from the justice "lessons of character and of culture and, less important, of the law itself."[10] Hiss indicated that he wished to "emulate him in conduct and character." Holmes was "the most profound influence in my life," and "for me a paragon of virtue and charm."[11] Alger talked Holmes into letting him spend the summer of 1930—technically Hiss's term was over—at the justice's summer house in Beverly Farms, Massachusetts, on Massachusetts's north shore, the first secretary to have done that. Hiss said that he wanted to keep Holmes from getting lonely and, according to son Tony, he also wanted "just to hang around some more."[12] Hiss's then new wife, Priscilla, and stepson, Tim, who were living in Washington, D.C., during this time, went with Hiss. They rented a summer place of their own in the nearby Montserrat section of Beverly.[13]

Hiss's biographer, John Chabot Smith, wrote that Hiss remembered Holmes as a skeptic of the first order. Hiss did not entirely accept Holmes's skeptical views, attributing them to disillusionment with the abolitionists in Civil War days; they had been the idealistic movement of Holmes's generation. But when Hiss knew Holmes, the justice regarded the group as "a silly bunch of propagandists, and argued it was idle to try to solve the problems of the world through movements of any kind." One just had to deal with them as they came along; you do the best you can, you have a "humanistic outlook, but you don't think it's going to be the answer." Hiss thought this was "too skeptical—defeatist, cynical."[14] Hiss may have been very fond of Holmes, as he said, but based on these comments Holmes was not likely to have had a major influence on Hiss's activist political thinking. In this regard, Hiss may have been influenced more by Justice Louis Brandeis, a powerful patron of the New Deal, a liberal, and a supporter of labor unions.

After a year of clerking for Holmes, Alger and Priscilla moved in October 1930 to Boston, where Alger entered private law practice at Choate, Hall, & Stewart. Little information is available on his eighteen months at Choate, Hall; it may have been a quiet time. Hiss had little to say on the subject in his memoir and in his letters to Pros, who had moved to New York during that time. While at Choate, Hall, Hiss spent much time working on cases involving the Gillette Safety Razor Company and the Raytheon Company.

Hiss went to work for the New York law firm of Cotton, Franklin, Wright, & Gordon in the spring of 1932. This position also was an uneventful time, except for his second job, pro bono work, along with Lee Pressman and Nathan Witt, for the IJA. In his memoir Hiss indicated this was the start of his political commitment. His acceptance to work for Roosevelt and the New Deal he saw as the final step in the progression of his political attitudes.[15] Hiss was becoming radicalized. His political development was more than youthful idealism.

The IJA published a bulletin that dealt with the legal problems of "the union organizer, the striking worker, the unemployed, the hunger marcher, the disposed farmer, and the rioters who turned back the sheriff when he came to foreclose the mortgage." The labor union stories went to Lee Pressman and farm cases to Hiss.[16] The IJA, according to Murray Kempton, had since been described as under Communist control.[17] G. Edward White (whose father-in-law, John F. Davis, provided legal assistance to Hiss from 1948 to 1950) said in his book on Hiss that the IJA followed the Communist Party line; it was "an example of a 1930s 'Popular Front' organization where liberals and collectivists could secure political reforms" to meet the political and social crises of the Depression.[18]

Communists were active in the labor movement at that time and Pressman acknowledged he would accept their support whenever it was useful to him.[19] Nathan Witt, who graduated from Harvard Law School, also worked on the IJA and subsequently was hired by the New Deal's Agricultural Adjustment Administration (AAA), along with Hiss and Pressman. Hiss said he found his IJA work "much more exciting than the anti-trust cases that paid his salary"; it made him feel part of "The Movement."[20] He wrote that "without realizing it, I was already in touch with the grass roots of the New Deal."[21]

In *Perjury*, Weinstein noted that a member of the IJA group, Jerome R. Hellerstein, claimed some of the IJA members were Communists, such as Joseph Brodsky, who was then attorney for the Communist Party. But Hellerstein maintained that Lee Pressman and Nat Witt were not Communists at that time. Another member was Carol King. In congressional testimony years later, King said she thought that Hiss, whose name appeared on the letterhead of the IJA's National Committee, made a mistake in denying membership in this Communist-front organization. Weinstein concluded that Hiss had moved leftward during his IJA days, influenced both by his wife Priscilla's socialism and by the more radical views of Pressman and King, but stated it is doubtful that Hiss was a Communist during this period (1931–32).[22] Without any evidence to the contrary, that assessment may be accurate.

According to Hiss, a year later, in March 1933, Frankfurter sent him a telegram urging him to come to Washington, D.C., to work in the New Deal administration. Hiss maintained that he actually wanted to teach law for several years after private practice. But he left corporate law and went to Washington for a position with the Legal Division of the AAA, headed by Jerome Frank. Weinstein suggested in his book that Lee Pressman, despite Hiss's denials, did play a role in convincing Hiss to move to Washington and join the AAA. Weinstein stated that an exchange of letters between Jerome Frank, the AAA's general counsel from 1933 to 1935, and Pressman in April 1933 indicated that Pressman participated in Hiss's decision.[23] Hiss made the point of insisting that his move to the AAA was a result of urgings by Frankfurter and Frank and that Pressman had nothing to do with it. Yet Weinstein claimed that letters between Frank and Pressman suggested Hiss discussed accepting the AAA post with Pressman.[24] It is curious that there were different versions on such a seemingly innocuous issue as to who was responsible for Hiss moving to Washington. Why was that part of the narrative so important? When he arrived in Washington, Hiss associated with predominantly radical lawyers, some of whom were acknowledged Communists. After arriving to work for the AAA, Hiss joined the Ware Group (sometime between mid-1933 and mid-1934), a covert group of agents within the U.S. government who supported Soviet intelligence.[25]

Precisely how, when, and where was Alger Hiss "spotted" for potential recruitment? When was he recruited, and by whom? Did he join the Communist Party and then was he recruited into the Ware Group for underground operations? Or did Hiss join the Ware Group and the Communist Party simultaneously? If so, he would have been recruited directly by Soviet intelligence for underground work rather than becoming a member of the Communist Party first. In fact, Chambers indicated just that—that Hiss, like almost all the Washington Communists, belonged to a new breed of intellectuals who had gone directly underground without passing through the open party.[26] For their part, Whittaker Chambers and Noel Field, a former State Department official, were open party members before they moved into intelligence operations.

The American Communist Party (CPUSA) typically served as a recruiting ground for both the GRU (Soviet military intelligence) and the KGB.[27] According to a former Communist Party official, Louis Budenz, the CPUSA was a recruiting ground for espionage against the United States.[28] Information gaps exist on how exactly

Alger Hiss was recruited directly into a clandestine Soviet cell. How did a member of a law firm in New York become a member of an underground Soviet cell, the Ware Group, in Washington, D.C.? Chambers identified eight individuals, all of whom were Communists, who were leading members of the Ware Group in 1934, when he assumed control of the group: Nathan Witt, Lee Pressman, John Abt, Charles Kramer, Henry Collins, Victor Perlo, Donald Hiss, and Alger Hiss. Alger Hiss, Pressman, and Witt worked on the IJA after graduating from Harvard Law School and left New York for Washington, D.C., to work in the New Deal administration. Were the three of them already targeted for recruitment prior to going to Washington? Or did Harold Ware, who headed the Communist cell in Washington, recruit them after they arrived? Was Pressman already a member of the party by 1933? According to Weinstein, "in the early part of 1934 Pressman had been recruited to Communism by Harold Ware."[29] Did Pressman then recruit Alger? These questions have yet to be fully answered.

During the 1930s, Theodore Mally and Arnold Deutsch, KGB "illegals,"[30] were responsible for recruiting Soviet spies at Cambridge University. The so-called Cambridge 5—five individuals of the British Establishment who were also Soviet agents (Harold "Kim" Philby, Guy Burgess, Donald Maclean, Anthony Blunt, and John Cairncross)[31]—was one of the most successful operations in the history of Soviet intelligence. According to Oleg Gordievsky, a former KGB officer who defected to the West, "the KGB still considers the five leading Cambridge moles the ablest group of foreign agents it has ever recruited."[32] Recent archival material has revealed that Arthur Wynn, a prominent British civil servant and Communist Party member, similarly recruited Soviet agents from among Oxford University graduates.[33]

In England during this period of the 1930s, Moscow utilized a methodology of seeking out future operatives in universities in order to attract the best and brightest to support Soviet intelligence. Targeting a pool of students from the upper-class British

Establishment would result in the recruitment of individuals who could eventually attain high-level positions in the British government. From these posts, their value would be in having access to state secrets and being in place to influence foreign policy. If placed in British security or intelligence services (MI5 or MI6), they would be invaluable for counterintelligence purposes as well. For example, Kim Philby, a senior British intelligence officer, was British liaison to U.S. intelligence in 1949. He thus had access to the Venona project—a highly restricted program whereby U.S. code-breakers were able to read some Soviet intelligence cables between New York and Moscow intercepted during World War II. Philby alerted the KGB about the existence of Venona. Moreover, Philby was able to warn fellow Cambridge 5 members Maclean and Burgess that they were going to be exposed, thus enabling them to flee to the Soviet Union.[34]

It was equally important for Moscow to penetrate American intelligence and security services besides the British ones. General William Donovan's Office of Strategic Services (OSS), the forerunner of the CIA, was thoroughly penetrated. Donovan's personal assistant, Duncan Chaplin Lee, was referenced in the Venona decrypts and was identified as a Soviet spy by Elizabeth Bentley, a courier for a KGB network and who subsequently defected. Decoded Venona messages indicated that Lee provided Soviet intelligence, by way of Bentley, with British and U.S. diplomatic strategy for negotiating with Moscow over postwar Poland, as well as OSS operations in China and France. For her part, Bentley asserted that Lee turned over to the Soviets an OSS security list containing names the OSS had identified as Soviet sources, Communists, and Soviet sympathizers. Bentley's information on this subject was confirmed by Venona cables.[35] Lee also fit the Soviet intelligence mold for recruitment: a well-bred intellectual. He was descended from the Lees of Virginia; graduated from prestigious St. Albans School in Washington, D.C.; from Yale University in 1935, first in his class; attended Oxford as a Rhodes scholar; and returned to attend

Yale Law School. Like Hiss, Lee was a WASP intellectual whose elitist background led the press at the time to find the charge of his being a Soviet agent "ridiculous."[36]

More recent times provide further examples of the significance of penetrating an intelligence and security service. Soviet intelligence had two valuable spies inside U.S. services: FBI (Robert Hanssen) and CIA (Aldrich Ames). In 1979 Hanssen "gave up" General Major Dmitri Polyakov, a GRU officer who had been passing valuable information to the United States for twenty-five years. Polyakov was considered "the crown jewel" of sources.[37] Polyakov was merely sidelined after Hanssen identified him to Moscow, probably because of his status as a GRU officer on the General Staff. However, after Ames also identified Polyakov as a U.S. agent in 1985, Polyakov was executed.[38] Former CIA officer Ames, who had access to the names of U.S. sources in the Soviet Union, was responsible for compromising many Soviet agents who were providing the United States with intelligence.[39] When sources are exposed, not only is there a loss of intelligence but also a loss of these assets who are possibly providing names of American spies working for the USSR.

Did Moscow use this recruitment model (targeting university students) in the United States? One interesting aspect of this question reflects a fundamental flaw in the Hiss character/reputation defense. When Hiss was accused by Chambers of being a spy, the Hiss defenders, focusing on character issues, charged that it was not possible, given his credentials, intelligence, academic achievement, prestigious positions in government, and impeccable background. Yet these were the very same credentials that made each of the Cambridge 5 such attractive targets. William Harvey, the FBI/CIA official who was one of the first to suspect Philby, said "good breeding was not a bar to treason—and in fact was a positive incentive."[40] This was exactly the profile Soviet intelligence was utilizing for "spotting" and recruitment. And Alger Hiss, indeed, fit the template.

PART TWO

A Committed Communist

V.

THE NEW DEALER

*Hiss: Increase the Number of Supreme Court Justices
to Ensure a Majority with Liberal Views*

A LGER HISS REFERRED to himself as a "New Dealer to
the core."[1] By all accounts, he really was the consummate
New Dealer. In a 1986 interview with David Remnick
for the *Washington Post*, Hiss spoke of becoming radicalized by the
Depression and recalled Franklin Delano Roosevelt's greeting to
New Dealers: "Good morning, fellow socialists."[2] If this greeting
was an attempt at political humor, it was also accurate; many New
Dealers believed in socialism. Nonetheless, among those on the
"left" a decided reluctance to use the term *socialism* prevailed. This
New Deal mind-set is evident today. Socialists dressed as "progressives" are more palatable to the American people.

In fact, the New Deal administration was experimenting with
socialism as a form of government to address the economic ca-
tastrophe of the Depression. Yet New Dealers in general avoided
identifying themselves publicly as socialists as well as New Deal
legislation as socialist, probably because a majority of Americans
were (and are) devoted to individual freedom and are opposed
to socialism and its accompanying government controls, dictates,
and mandates. And for good reason: history, as well as current

events in Europe, show that socialist solutions are economically unsustainable.

However, the circumstances of the Great Depression temporarily anesthetized the basic innate impulse for privacy, individualism, and liberty on the part of many Americans. It was precisely because of the broad economic collapse, with its widespread bank failures and massive unemployment, that radical policies, socialism, and Communism assumed a certain amount of acceptability in the United States of the 1930s. Moscow's stand against the rise of Fascism also gave the left "cover." Moreover, the CPUSA made headway with many liberals because they sought common cause with them on race relations, civil rights, and unions. As John Ehrman, a former CIA official, writes, some "progressives such as former Vice President Henry A. Wallace (1941–1944) viewed Moscow's intentions as benign and were willing to work with American Communists on domestic issues."[3] The United States formally recognized the USSR in 1933; the Soviet Union had joined the community of nations in anti-Fascism and proclaimed a unity of interest between the United States and itself.

New Dealers were young (all but one in the Ware Group were under thirty years old), energetic, educationally advanced, and ready to fundamentally transform the structure of the United States to meet the economic crisis of the country; to substitute free markets for bureaucratic fiats. They had the levers of power in their hands. As Hiss saw it, those affected by the New Deal were the "unemployed, labor, small home owners, small farmers, the negroes, and other minority groups"—groups where there was "popular support" for "a changed relation between government and the public."[4] Among New Dealers, there was camaraderie and excitement at the thought of making a difference. Some were liberals, some socialists, and others Communists. A national emergency existed and the New Dealers were the "Young Turks" ready to seize the opportunity to meet it. They were going to make America over. Hiss boasted that "we were a band of brothers—members of a citizens' militia in mufti, mustered to fight the ills of the Depression."[5] Hiss described how he felt about being a New Dealer: "It was a homogeneous group, imbued with an esprit de corps; solidarity; comradeship; a sense of community; a common set of values; we were inseparable."[6] New Dealers were small bands of roommates; associates in the same governmental agencies. In his memoir, Hiss focused on who the New Dealers were, not as much on what the New Deal actually accomplished.

Many New Dealers were lawyers. Hiss felt he and his colleagues were part of an elite group that manned many legal jobs of the New Deal for good reason—because the Supreme Court was viewed by New Dealers as a roadblock to innovative legislation. Hiss wrote, "Each new program had to be drafted with a wary eye to the Court's obstructionist views. This special need resulted in the prominence given to the lawyers."[7] And New Deal lawyers were needed, he believed, to redress the injustices that were the underlying causes of the Depression.

When Roosevelt was having difficulty getting some of his New Deal legislation passed because of Supreme Court rulings that his policies were unconstitutional, he planned to "pack the court" with justices favorable to his politics. One aspect of the plan would have expanded the number of justices from nine to fifteen.[8] It is significant that Hiss agreed about the need to politicize the Supreme Court. He wrote: "It is my own belief that the Supreme Court should be politically accountable. I and some other New Dealers had agreed with President Roosevelt's plan to increase the number of justices to ensure a majority with liberal views. Privately, Felix Frankfurter had himself been New Dealer enough to approve of the plan."[9] Hiss's advocacy of bypassing constitutional restraints and his open disregard for both the constitutional principle of separation of powers and for the precedent of an independent, nonpoliticized judiciary are astounding, and symptomatic of his leftist authoritarianism. Using the judiciary as a political instrument of state power is a characteristic feature of both Communist and Fascist regimes.

Hiss felt that "we were entitled to think of ourselves—and we most certainly did—as a select few."[10] This claim by Hiss reflects the recurring elitism of a higher wisdom that is thoroughly embedded in the ideologies of the left: the "enlightened" know best; authoritative leadership is needed to direct the masses; a vanguard is required to advance the revolution; and so on and so forth. Alger saw himself and his colleagues as that vanguard.

British author Dame Rebecca West drew a similar elitist profile of British spies. She pointed to Alan Nunn May, who transmitted atomic secrets to the Soviet Union in the late 1940s, as an example of the scientists who claimed that because of their superior technical knowledge they formed a "special elite" that would enable them to seize power. West went on to indicate that "there is a similarity between the claims of the Nazi-Fascists and Communist-Fascists," claims that "depend on an unsound assumption that the man who possesses a special gift will possess also a universal wisdom which will enable him to impose an order on the state superior to that contrived by the consultative system known as democracy; which will enable him, in fact, to know other people's business better than they do themselves."[11]

West insightfully sums up a basic attribute of the left, namely its belief in itself as an elite group that should impose its own views on the "masses"—Lenin's principle of the role of the vanguard. And it suggests the commonality between Fascism and Communism, which is discussed in chapter 10 below. Whether it is called Progressivism, Communism, Socialism, or Fascism, this elitism on the left seeks to gain power through a centralized government to best serve its goal to control society and to dictate and carry out how society ought to be organized and ruled.

When the stock market crashed in October 1929, Hiss did not realize what the impact would be, but he said he was intent upon the daily round of life; this kept him from any foresight. (This statement is probably true—his personal letters bear this out.) According to Hiss, the worsening of the economy confirmed the

liberal outlook he had acquired as a student and that was strengthened and given focus at Harvard Law School. The spirit of reform
was symbolized by Felix Frankfurter and his championing of Sacco
and Vanzetti.[12]

Through research at law school on labor unions, Hiss had become aware for the first time of the long fight for industrial reform,
which sometimes produced pro-labor action. However, gains often
were canceled out, Hiss felt, by bias against labor prior to 1933.
According to Hiss, most committed New Dealers distrusted business ethics and blamed the 1920s era of Big Business, with all its
excesses, for the economic crisis that led to the Great Depression.[13]
Therefore, the need for government action and intervention seemed
obvious to them. They believed that donations, charity, and other
forms of relief should be a public concern and the duty of the
government, not a concern of private charities. For example, Hiss
seemed to feel somewhat betrayed at one point when Frankfurter
was trying to obtain private donations from wealthy businessmen
and bankers for the underprivileged. Hiss was convinced that only
large-scale government intervention was needed, not private chari-
table activities.[14]

Hiss identified a few of the Young Turks in his memoir: his
brother Donald, Lee Pressman, Abe Fortas, John Abt, Telford
Taylor, Nathan Witt, Francis Shea, and Margaret Bennett, among
others. Hiss announced, "We were the shock troops."[15] He then
described how Harry Hopkins, Roosevelt's closest senior advisor,
was "the complete New Dealer," involved in all the relief programs.
Hiss looked forward to working with Hopkins, whose goals "ex-
emplified that element of the New Deal that causes many to look
back upon a period as one of shared aspiration and comradely
cooperation rather than hard times."[16] Although Alger was proud
of his days as a New Dealer, he still was able to assess realistically
and objectively the New Deal's limitations in his memoir, written
years later: the New Deal program, he wrote, "did not cure the Depression, though it ameliorated its distress. Only the industrial and

agricultural demands created by World War II eliminated unemployment and farm surpluses."[17]

Hiss's first job in the government was a position offered to him by Jerome Frank, the general counsel of the AAA. The AAA was a former U.S. government agency established in the Department of Agriculture under the Agricultural Adjustment Act of 1933 as part of Roosevelt's New Deal program. Its purpose was to reduce crop surplus so as to effectively raise the value of crops, thereby giving farmers relative stability again. The farmers were paid subsidies by the federal government for letting a portion of their fields remain uncultivated. The money for these subsidies was generated through an exclusive tax on companies who processed farm products. The act created a new agency, the AAA, to oversee the distribution of the subsidies. Hiss was concerned with legal matters, ensuring that the AAA law was constitutional and the contracts drawn up under it were legal and enforceable.[18] Hiss headed up a section, composed of about twenty-five lawyers, that drafted contracts for paying farmers to reduce their production.[19] Hiss's responsibilities at AAA did not include questions of policy but he became involved in disagreements when policy and the law overlapped.

In 1935 Frank was dismissed, along with all the other lawyers in his office (including Pressman), but not Hiss, who had been detailed to the Nye Committee at the time and escaped the purge. The farm-wing administrator of AAA, Chester Davis, removed them. In *Perjury*, Weinstein suggested that the Chester Davis purge was prompted by a pro-sharecropper opinion on a cotton contract that the farm "interests" opposed. Ironically, Hiss was the active force behind the opinion, according to Weinstein. Years later, Frank observed that the opinion was Hiss's and that he, Frank, just signed off on it. He questioned why Davis fired the other people but not Hiss. Both Frank and Davis declined to testify as character witnesses at Hiss's trial, despite requests from the defense.[20]

In 1936 the Supreme Court declared important sections of the AAA invalid, but Congress promptly adopted in that same year the

Soil Conservation and Domestic Allotment Act, which encouraged conservation by paying benefits for planting soil-building crops instead of staple crops. The Agricultural Adjustment Act of 1938 granted the AAA, during prosperous years, to make loans to farmers on staple crop yields and to store the surplus produce, which it could then release in years when the yield was low. In World War II the AAA focused on increasing food production to meet wartime needs. It was renamed in 1942 the Agricultural Adjustment Agency, and in 1945 its functions were taken over by the Production and Marketing Administration.

Hiss was detailed from the AAA in July 1934 to assist the staff of the Senate Special Committee under the chairmanship of Senator Gerald Nye, to investigate the role of the munitions industry in World War I. The goal was to introduce legislation to control international cartels dealing in armaments and to prevent profiteering in wartime.[21] A year later, in August 1935, Hiss accepted a position as a consultant with the Department of Justice and was assigned to the solicitor general's office, headed by Stanley Reed.

After a brief time in the Office of the Solicitor General, where he helped to defend New Deal legislation from constitutional challenges, Hiss joined the Department of State in September 1936. Chambers, who was "running" (an espionage term for agent handling) Hiss at this time, maintained that Soviet Military Intelligence (GRU), which directed Chambers and his network of assets, sought to move some underground Communist members out of New Deal agencies, such as the AAA. Chambers admitted these were agencies "which the Party could penetrate almost at will," but the new objective now was to "gradually infiltrate 'old-line' departments, with the State Department having priority."[22] A position at the State Department would enable Hiss to influence U.S. foreign policy as well as have access to classified documents.

In 1975 Alger Hiss agreed to an interview at Columbia University; the result of this discussion was a 282-page document titled "The Reminiscences of Alger Hiss," which is included with the

Hiss family papers at New York University as well as in the Columbia University Center for Oral History. The interview contains some interesting insights into Hiss's political beliefs about Communism.[23] Initially he made comments on how some of the domestic excesses of the Cold War could have been avoided if Roosevelt had lived or if Truman had been a "different kind of person." He went on to say that one reason New Dealers were subject to McCarthy's attacks and why he, Hiss, "was singled out" was that they (and he) were Roosevelt's "surrogates" and by attacking them, "it could lessen Roosevelt's appeal and stature."[24] Of course this had been the standard rationale of the Hiss defense for years. An attack on Hiss was an attack on Roosevelt, on the New Deal, and on Yalta and the UN.

The interviewer later asked Hiss, as a curiosity, what he found wrong with Communism. Hiss replied that as an individual he would be unhappy in China because of lack of free speech and the inability to read and travel whatever and whenever he desired, for example. However, he continued, for the millions of Chinese "it is better than what went before." Illnesses and drudgery were mitigated. And when asked about the millions massacred, Hiss answered that he "doubts very much if they're in the millions." He claimed that many Chinese were killed in battle and many (in the Kuomintang) who were opposed to Communism left the country, so "the problem of liquidation which Mao would have undertaken must have been minimized." (Was Hiss really suggesting that Mao killed fewer people because there were less available to kill?) Hiss said the same could be said for Cuba, where many fled the country in air and boat lifts.[25]

With regard to the Russian Revolution, Hiss maintained that for the peasants and workers the "situation had not worsened since Czarist times." Again, he noted that he personally would miss the "pleasures of intellectual pursuits" but still would rather be a Russian than a black in South Africa. The situation is all about relativism, he suggested. And Hiss pointed out that to talk about major upheavals on the scale of revolutions (French, Russian, Chinese, and American) in terms of "only those who suffered during the period of disequilibrium is not necessarily the best way to judge its human value or potential."[26]

These observations speak for themselves. Even at this late date in his life, Hiss continued to marginalize and justify the crimes of Communist systems as a necessary means to achieve their ends. He viewed the systems as acceptable and an improvement for the people trapped in them, yet he admitted he would not be happy living in one, because of their lack of freedoms.

VI:

THE WARE GROUP

At First No One Believed the Ware Group Existed

I T IS CLEAR that Alger Hiss's transition from member of a New York law firm to member of the Communist Party and Ware Group took place; what is still unclear is exactly how it happened.

Between 1933 and the early part of 1934, Harold Ware (1890–1935) was standing up Washington's first covert Communist Party cell. Whittaker Chambers wrote that Ware organized within the United States government one of the most threatening fifth columns in American history. Ware was a member of the Communist Party; in the early 1920s he set out for the Soviet Union with a group of radicals to develop a collective farm, the so-called Kuzbas colony in Kemerovo Oblast, in the Altai Mountains.[1] He had worked in the Soviet Union organizing collective farms at Lenin's invitation.[2]

Ware returned to Washington at Moscow's direction to organize farmworkers. In 1933, at the onset of the Roosevelt administration, Ware began recruiting young New Dealers for the Communist Party. Communists who were recruited into the Ware Group had to end their public party activities if they had any, and go "underground"[3] as covert operatives. Moscow saw the need to keep intelligence-gathering and party organizational work separate. For example, when Soviet military intelligence, the GRU (then called "the Fourth Department" of the Red Army's General Staff), decided to recruit Whittaker Chambers, who was at the time an open party member and editor of the Communist journal the *New Masses,* for underground work "running" the Ware Group, Chambers had to dissolve all public connections to the open Communist Party and end his career as a journalist.

According to Chambers, the Soviet espionage apparatus in Washington, D.C., was in constant contact with the national underground of the CPUSA, in the person of its chief, a Hungarian Communist called J. Peters. J. Peters was an "illegal"—in the United States under false documentation, totally separated from any official diplomatic presence. Chambers claimed that during his entire six years in the Soviet underground, Peters had been the official secret contact man between a succession of Soviet apparatuses and the CPUSA.[4]

The Ware Group originally was identified by some as being a Marxist study group that discussed theory, Communist literature, and major economic issues of the day, and where party dues were collected. This view was held by Nathaniel Weyl, a charter member of the Ware Group, and Josephine Herbst, ex-wife of John Herrmann, Ware's chief assistant in the underground from 1933 to 1935. An investigator during the Hiss trial said the Group engaged in "low-grade espionage work" and some sort of information gathering took place.[5] The Group did hold discussions on Marxism-Leninism and read party literature. J. Peters occasionally gave a lecture on the theory of Leninism and dues were collected. However, Chambers said that its primary function was not as a study group; its primary mission was to infiltrate the U.S. government in the interests of the Communist Party.[6] The purpose of the Group was not primarily espionage at the time, but certainly it was one of its eventual objectives, according to Chambers.

J. Peters introduced Chambers to Harold Ware in New York

City in the spring of 1934 as "Karl," his underground name. During the meeting, Alger Hiss's name came up, as "an exceptional Communist and a member of the Ware Group for whom Peters had a high regard."[7] Then, in midsummer 1934, Chambers met with Hiss for the first time, along with Peters and Ware, in Washington, D.C. It was a brief introduction, allowing Chambers to make contact with Hiss, since he was about to take over "running" him. Following this initial meeting, "Karl" made several calls at Hiss's home, where he also met Priscilla. Hiss was highly intelligent but without real Communist experience, Chambers observed; Alger was "gracious in the way which is his peculiar talent."[8] In a development not favored in the underground, Chambers gradually formed a close friendship with Alger Hiss and it extended to their families.[9]

The Ware Group initially consisted of young lawyers and economists hired by the AAA, an agency that reported to the secretary of agriculture but was independent of the Department of Agriculture bureaucracy. Chambers maintained that when he first made contact with the Ware Group in 1934 he did not know how many of the members of the Group already had been Communists or how many were recruited by Ware. The Ware Group consisted of a leading committee of seven members (1934–35) who met weekly or fortnightly. Meetings at first were held at Ware's wife's music studio, and subsequently at the apartment of Henry Collins, a Ware Group member, at 1213 St. Matthews Court in northwest Washington, D.C.—a mews between M and N streets, NW, just off Connecticut Avenue. It remained the Group's headquarters until sometime in 1936–37, when it then moved to the house of John Abt, who by then had become head of the Ware Group and was an assistant to the attorney general of the United States.[10] After Ware died in 1935 in an automobile collision, the Group's leader was Nathan Witt, then John Abt.

All the members of the Ware Group were dues-paying members of the Communist Party and J. Peters considered this group (along with his Hollywood underground network) as one of his major sources of income.[11] Ware Group members regularly paid 10 percent of their salaries to the Communist Party. J. Peters emphasized to the Group that "since its members were intellectuals without Party experience, it was extremely important to their feeling of Communist solidarity that they make exceptional money sacrifices for the Communist Party." Moreover, Lenin had stressed the importance of dues as a test and a binder of party loyalty.[12]

The Ware Group initially was not a spy ring in the technical sense. Its functions did include recruiting new members into the underground; staffing of government agencies with Communist Party members; and most importantly, influencing, from the most strategic positions, the policies of the U.S. government.[13] Chambers was the first person to disclose the existence of the Ware Group. He identified its organization and membership to the assistant secretary of state in charge of security, Adolf A. Berle, as early as September 2, 1939, during a private meeting at Berle's home.[14] (See chapter 8 for a full discussion of the Berle-Chambers meeting.) At the time of the congressional hearings and Hiss trials (1948–50), Chambers testified publicly about the existence of this covert apparatus supporting Soviet intelligence in the U.S. government and identified eight officials who belonged to it when he was introduced to its members: Lee Pressman, Nathan Witt, John Abt, Charles Kramer (born Krivitsky), Henry Collins, Victor Perlo, Donald Hiss, and Alger Hiss. Alger Hiss was a leading member of the Ware Group.

Another Ware Group member, Nathaniel Weyl, came forward in 1950 and stated that in 1934 he had been a Communist and was part of the Ware Group. Weyl now corroborated Chambers's account of the existence of the Group. Weyl left the Group shortly before Chambers took it over, sometime in mid to late 1934. Subsequently, in 1951, Lee Pressman, a charter member of the Ware Group,[15] testified under oath before the House Committee on Un-American Activities (HUAC) that he, Nathan Witt, John Abt, and Charles Kramer had been Communists and members of the Ware Group,[16] thus also corroborating Chambers's testimony on the existence of such a group, but only identifying four of the eight members cited by Chambers.

While Chambers was being trained in underground tradecraft, Ware and J. Peters were organizing individuals into this secret Communist group. Ware found a large number of incipient or registered Communists already in the AAA. However, J. Peters wanted to position some of them in other agencies, where they could influence foreign policy. In time, probably as many as seventy-five Communists were recruited into the Ware Group and in a number of its subcells.[17] It was Chambers's task to move career Communists into the old-line agencies, particularly the Department of State. Some former Ware Group members moved into Elizabeth Bentley's KGB espionage network.

Chambers was instructed by J. Peters to set up a "parallel apparatus" with the Ware Group, and Hiss was to be the first man in his new apparatus. The new cell was organized as a spin-off of the Ware Group. Among other new agents who entered Chambers's GRU network in 1935–36 were Treasury Department official Harry Dexter White, George Silverman (a government statistician later employed in the War Department),[18] and State Department official Julian Wadleigh. The objective, emphasized by Colonel Boris Bykov, whom Chambers knew as "Peter" (a GRU officer operating out of New York who was Chambers's superior), was to penetrate U.S. government agencies that were in a position to make foreign policy.[19]

At this same time, Hiss was getting ready to leave the AAA and move to the Nye Committee. Senator Gerald Nye was a progressive Republican from North Dakota and a Roosevelt and New Deal supporter. This new detail to the Nye Committee (1934–35) would give Hiss access to some classified information. There is disagreement on whether or not Hiss took classified material from the Nye Committee. Chambers said this is why Hiss was recruited into the apparatus, to steal such documents, and that he did, and Chambers claimed he had photographed them, and then they were presumably passed to Soviet intelligence. Hiss denied this charge. According to Allen Weinstein, the Nye Committee's work interested the USSR's military and industrial espionage elements because of its access to files of some of the leading U.S. arms manufacturers.[20] At the time, the State Department's liaison with the Nye Committee, Joseph C. Green, stated that the department had never given the Nye Committee secret documents. But, according to Weinstein, the State Department did give the committee copies of a number of confidential documents, particularly those dealing with negotiations on the sale of munitions with foreign governments. Years later Nye told the FBI investigators that he believed Hiss was a Communist during his time on the committee.[21]

There was concern by Secretary of State Cordell Hull, as well as by President Roosevelt, that this congressional committee could endanger foreign relations by mishandling diplomatic exchanges. In fact, a record of complaints existed, made by the State Department, about periodic release of such sensitive documents, including communications in diplomatic codes. According to Weinstein, John Wiltz, a leading scholar of the Nye Committee's work, maintained that in Hiss's own defense files there is evidence confirming the Nye Committee's use of secret government documents. But Wiltz said the record does not clear up the discrepancy between Green's position and available documents. When interviewed by Wiltz, Gerald Nye, who presumably had a vested interest in defending his committee, said he believed Hiss had used his position on the committee for espionage, as Chambers had stated.[22]

Nathaniel Weyl (1910–2005) was the first person to corroborate Chambers's testimony on the existence of the Ware Group. He was not identified by Chambers, because he had left Washington and the Ware Group shortly before Chambers arrived. He did not testify during the Hiss trials but in November 1950 he did speak to the FBI and told them Hiss was a Communist and a member of the Ware Group. Weyl then came forward publicly in February 1952, testifying before the U.S. Senate Internal Security Subcommittee (McCarran Committee) that early in 1934 he had been a Communist and a member of the Communist cell the Ware Group, along with Alger Hiss. Subsequently, in a 1953 interview, Weyl acknowledged publicly that he was a member of the Communist Party beginning around January 1933 in New York City, before coming to Washington, D.C., until sometime in 1937 or 1938. He said he actually broke with the party in 1939 over the Nazi-Soviet Pact.[23] The pact, officially titled the Treaty of Non-Aggression between Germany and the Soviet Union, was an agreement signed in Moscow on August 23, 1939. It was a nonaggression pact between the two countries and pledged neutrality by either party if the other were attacked by a third party. It remained in effect until June 22, 1941, when Germany invaded the Soviet Union. In addition to stipulations of nonaggression, the treaty included secret protocols dividing parts of Europe into German and Soviet spheres of influence.

Weyl, whose father was a founding editor of the *New Republic*, had joined the Socialist Party at age eighteen, in 1928, during his second year at Columbia University. He also studied at the London School of Economics. After graduation from Columbia, he joined the Communist Party and wrote for the Communist press. Weyl said that he believed capitalism was dying. At the time, "I thought the alternatives before the world were socialism or fascism . . . and like many of my contemporaries, I thought of socialism as a political and economic order that would bring security, equality, freedom, peace, etc."[24] Weyl lived long enough to witness, however, that it brought poverty, misery, dependence, slavery, and death.

While Weyl was a secret member of the underground, he said he was not aware that espionage was involved in Communist activity until he read about the Canadian spy ring in 1945. He felt there was a sharp distinction between having been a Communist and having been a spy. Weyl stated that he was never a spy. He said he was an economist in the AAA. About three months after Harold Ware approached Weyl, Ware identified himself as a representative of the Communist Party Political Bureau and told Weyl he was there to organize a group that was to consist of men who were expected to have promising careers in the government. The group was being organized completely independent of other Washington Communists and set up on the basis of the strictest secrecy. Ware ordered all members not to associate with other Communists. Weyl said he was instructed to join the Group by Ware, after he came to Washington, D.C., from New York City.[25]

As he testified before the Senate Internal Security Committee in 1952, Weyl claimed that the people present at the Ware Group meetings in the 1933–34 time frame included Harold Ware, Lee Pressman, John Abt, Alger Hiss, Charles Krivitsky (aka Charles Kramer), Henry Collins, Nathan Witt, and Victor Perlo. Weyl did not mention Donald Hiss but did include John Donovan. Otherwise it was the same list of men that Chambers had identified. According to Weyl, "they all knew they were part of a revolutionary organization. The unit was thought of as a revolutionary political party. They were there because they believed in revolution. They thought the capitalist system was dying and would have to change over to a socialist form of organization." And Weyl maintained that it was easy to set up Popular Fronts if the program was anti-Fascist and in line with the New Deal.[26]

Unlike Lee Pressman, Weyl stated in a 1953 interview that Alger Hiss was a member of the Communist Party. He said Hiss attended Ware Group meetings regularly; he was seldom absent at meetings. "We all paid dues. I saw Hiss pay dues at the meetings," said Weyl. Hiss was "pleasant, but also aloof and withdrawn. . . . He was a devoted Communist. . . . He was not likely to come out with original thoughts. I would say his aim was to conform, to do what was wanted." In comparing Hiss with Pressman, Weyl suggested that Pressman was very popular, very well liked, and more exuberant than Hiss, "less careful about saying the right thing." He was also less "solemn and reverential toward Communism and the Communist Party" than Hiss.

Every member of the Ware Group was a Communist Party member, Weyl said. "No outsider or fellow traveler was ever admitted." Weyl claimed he resigned from the government to get out of the unit. "I found the secrecy uncomfortable and disquieting." Later in the same interview, Weyl said the basic reason he left was the new loyalty program of the government. "I wasn't willing to perjure myself. Therefore I would have had to tell the story about Pressman, Hiss, and the rest. I didn't want to do that, so I resigned." Moreover, Weyl continued, once the United States was at war in Korea and "it became (Korean) Communism, it had to be considered simply as treason."[27] Weyl acknowledged he was not willing to give up the names of those who worked with him in the party in Washington, D.C. "I wasn't prepared to be an informer. Nor did I know that espionage was involved, or suspect that. . . . I was called before the HUAC in 1943 and testified falsely that I had never been formally a member of the Communist Party, but that I had followed Communist discipline." Weyl didn't testify at the Hiss trials; he did not go to the FBI until 1950. "The Korean War very definitely made me do that."[28]

Weyl believed that Hiss's challenge to Chambers drew attention to Alger's life. According to Weyl, it was a double life, and the web of deception was certain to be a weak spot, causing the Hiss narrative to break down. Weyl stated he believed Hiss maintained his innocence because he was still a Communist and Moscow wanted him to stand firm. Weyl said they all "consciously accepted evil means to do good because to be effective in the world, you must use the tools of power."[29]

Lee Pressman (1906–69) was on the *Harvard Law Review* and graduated from the law school with Alger Hiss. He worked on the IJA in New York City with Hiss as well. He and Hiss left New York for Washington, D.C., to become New Dealers. Pressman was appointed assistant general counsel of the AAA in 1933 by

Secretary of Agriculture Henry A. Wallace. In 1935, after Pressman was fired in the Chester Davis purge, he took on two other government positions. He left government service in 1936 when John L. Lewis made him chief counsel for the Congress of Industrial Organizations (CIO) for the Steel Workers Organizing Committee. Pressman was forced out of this position in 1948, reportedly after losing a power struggle with anti-Communist leader Walter Reuther.[30] He became a close advisor that year of American Labor Party–Progressive Party presidential candidate Henry A. Wallace. In his 1948 testimony before the HUAC, Chambers identified Pressman as a Communist and member of the Ware Group. Initially Pressman refused to answer questions, citing potential self-incrimination. In interviews with the FBI in 1950, and the HUAC in 1951, however, Pressman admitted that he and John Abt, and Nathan Witt and Charles Kramer, were all members of the Ware Group. But he denied that Hiss was a member of the Group during his time as a member.[31]

John Abt (1904–91) graduated from the University of Chicago, Phi Beta Kappa and summa cum laude, and from its law school. He spent most of his career as chief counsel to the CPUSA.[32] He practiced corporate law before going to Washington in 1933. Abt was chief of litigation for the AAA from 1933 to 1935. Following that, he was assistant general counsel of the Works Progress Administration (WPA), then chief counsel to Senator Robert La Follette Jr.'s Civil Liberties Committee from 1936 to 1937 and special assistant to the U.S. attorney general from 1937 to 1938.[33] He worked with the Progressive Party of former vice president Henry A. Wallace.[34]

Abt was a member of the Ware Group, as was his sister Marion Bachrach. After Harold Ware died in 1935, Abt married Ware's widow, Jessica Smith. Smith was editor of the *New World Review* magazine, then *Soviet Russia Today*. The FBI opened an investigation of Abt in late 1943. In 1951 when Lee Pressman identified Abt as a member of the CPUSA and the Ware Group in HUAC testimony,[35] Abt took the Fifth Amendment, invoking the privilege against self-incrimination, and would not testify. Over a decade later, Abt won a unanimous Supreme Court ruling in 1965 that individuals may invoke their constitutional privilege against self-incrimination and refuse to register with the government as members of the Communist Party. Abt considered this his greatest legal victory. At his eightieth birthday celebration, Abt admitted that he had been a member of the Communist Party for fifty years. "I am sure that this announcement will surprise no one here tonight," he said.[36]

Nathan Witt (1903–82) graduated from New York University and Harvard Law School. He was on the IJA with Hiss and Pressman and went with them to Washington, D.C., to join the AAA and the Ware Group. In 1933 he was an attorney on the staff of the AAA; he then moved to the National Recovery Administration (NRA); in 1936 he transferred to the legal staff as assistant general counsel of the National Labor Relations Board (NLRB); in 1937 he was its secretary.[37] After he resigned from the board in 1941, he became a partner in the New York law firm of Witt & Cammer. He also had been counsel to many unions and in 1955 gave up his law practice to become full-time counsel to the International Union of Mine, Mill and Smelter Workers. When that union merged with the United Steel Workers of America in the 1960s, Witt became associate counsel for the union's Mine, Mill and Smelter division. He retired from that position in 1975.[38]

Henry Collins (1905–61) was the Ware Group treasurer and collected the Communist Party dues during each meeting. He gave them to Chambers, who turned them over to J. Peters. Collins, a childhood friend of Hiss from his Baltimore days, remained an intimate friend throughout the 1930s and 1940s and met the Hisses frequently at their home. He graduated from Princeton and Harvard Business School. In 1933 Collins worked for the NRA, and he had positions after that in the Agriculture Department and the Labor Department. In 1938 he attempted to recruit Laurence

Duggan, a State Department official, into the Communist Party, according to Duggan's FBI testimony.[39] Duggan said that Collins wanted him "to assist in furnishing information . . . to the Soviets." Duggan said he turned down the request.[40]

Collins had made several attempts to get into the State Department to serve the party[41] and finally landed a position in 1946. He worked for several weeks on a Senate subcommittee, but was forced to resign when an inconclusive FBI report on him was given to the committee. By 1948 he was executive director of the American Russian Institute in New York City, cited by the attorney general as a Communist front organization.[42] Collins was subpoenaed to appear before a grand jury in December 1948. He denied all of Chambers's charges of Communist involvement by him or Abt, Pressman, Witt, or Ware (!)—the latter being openly known as a Communist. John Herrmann's letters to his wife, Josephine Herbst, showed that he had moved his operations to Collins's apartment on St. Matthews Court in Washington, D.C.; Herbst also said Collins was aware of all the 1934 activities. Victor Perlo's estranged wife, Katherine, sent an anonymous letter to the FBI in 1944, listing Collins as a member of Perlo's (see below) underground group.[43]

Charles Kramer was born Charles Krivitsky in 1906 in New York. He attended New York University and received bachelor's and master's degrees in economics. Kramer was a Ware Group member (then later a Perlo Group asset) and on the staff of the AAA in 1933. Members of the CPUSA underground helped each other advance in the government when possible. For example, some assisted Charles Kramer in getting positions in the government. John Abt hired Kramer for the Senate Civil Liberties Subcommittee (the La Follette Committee); Nathan Witt helped him get a job within the NLRB before World War II. Victor Perlo signed Kramer's job performance rating at the Office of Price Administration during the war and was listed as a job reference.[44]

Kramer eventually moved to the Perlo Group, which was run

by the KGB. His wife was a committed Communist who served during the 1930s as a courier for the KGB's New York *residentura*. Kramer held various posts on the Hill, eventually joining the staff of Senator Harley Kilgore of West Virginia, whose committee was focused on wartime economic mobilization. Victor Perlo unsuccessfully put increased pressure on Kramer to intensify his collection of documents and information for Soviet intelligence.[45] Kramer also had been an advisor to Senator Claude Pepper (D) of Florida. When Elizabeth Bentley, a former courier for Soviet intelligence, exposed Kramer in 1948, Pepper publicly stood by him. Subsequently, Kramer worked for Henry A. Wallace and the Progressive Party until the early 1950s. He then moved to Oregon and "faded from public sight."[46]

Victor Perlo (1912–99), like Weyl, was an original member of the Ware Group. He graduated from Columbia University in 1933 with bachelor's and master's degrees in mathematics and statistics. Perlo served the Roosevelt administration in various agencies, including the NRA. He left government in 1937 to work for the Brookings Institution, then returned in 1939, working for Harry Hopkins at the Department of Commerce. In 1940 Perlo moved to the Office of Price Administration and by 1943 he was chief of the Aviation Section of the War Production Board. After the AAA purge in 1935 and Ware's death, the Ware Group re-formed under the leadership of John Abt, then Victor Perlo. Mrs. Katherine Perlo, the estranged wife of Victor Perlo, confirmed the existence of the Perlo Group in an anonymous letter to the White House as well as the FBI in 1944, naming Abt, Collins, Kramer, and Witt, and others, as members of the Group.[47] In addition, Perlo was named as a Soviet agent by Elizabeth Bentley.[48] When he was called before congressional committees investigating Soviet espionage in the 1930s and 1940s, Perlo invoked the Fifth Amendment and refused to provide answers.[49] From the 1960s until his death, Perlo served as the chief economist of the Communist Party in the United States. He was also a board member of the party.[50]

Donald Hiss (1906–89) was a member of the Communist Party and Ware Group, according to Whittaker Chambers and KGB archival material,[51] but Chambers claimed that he never passed secret information. In his HUAC testimony, Donald denied ever being a Communist Party member or a member of the Ware Group. Chambers testified before the HUAC that he had a formal relationship with Donald, unlike his brother Alger, with whom he developed a very close friendship. Chambers said he collected dues from Donald at Alger's home, which raises the question of why this did not happen at St. Matthews Court during the Ware Group meetings.[52] Did Donald not attend those meetings? If not, why not?

During a meeting with Colonel Bykov, Chambers, and Alger Hiss, Bykov informed them it was critical that Moscow know what information the State Department had with regard to possible Fascist war plans, Chambers wrote. Bykov requested Alger's help in obtaining actual documents, especially those relating to Germany and the Far East. Alger agreed, according to Chambers, but took a different position with regard to his brother. Bykov asked if Donald, a legal advisor to the newly created Philippines Division of the State Department, could also bring out classified material. Alger essentially said no to Donald passing classified material.[53] In a statement by Chambers during the 1948 Baltimore deposition (related to the Hiss libel suit), he said Alger was not sure that his brother was "sufficiently developed" yet for that function.[54]

Apparently Alger wanted to protect his brother in some way, or perhaps he really thought he was not ready for the risky work of espionage. There was also some concern that Donald's wife, who was not a Communist, could cause a problem. In any event, Chambers said he never received any stolen classified material from Donald Hiss. David Murphy, in his book *What Stalin Knew: The Enigma of Barbarossa*, made the interesting comment that "the Berlin residency had a source, code-named Yun, covering the American Embassy there. Little is known of this source except that he was in contact with Donald Hiss, embassy first secretary [Donald Hiss worked for the State Department at the time]; L. M. Harrison, second secretary; J. Patterson, first secretary; and Colonel B. P. Payton, air attaché. On April 9 and 10 he reported that these officers were convinced that, soon after the end of the war with Yugoslavia, Germany would invade the USSR." [55] Murphy had no further data available on Donald's role in Germany.

In addition to the Ware Group and Chambers's parallel apparatus there were other networks operating inside the U.S. government. Nathan Gregory Silvermaster (1898–1964), an economist with the War Production Board during the war, headed a large network of Communists that had penetrated the U.S. government. He was identified as a Soviet agent in the cables from the Venona program (the U.S. Army intelligence program responsible for analyzing decrypted high-level Soviet intelligence messages intercepted during and immediately after World War II).[56] He was also identified independently by Soviet defector Elizabeth Bentley. Chambers revealed that "by 1938, the Soviet espionage apparatus in Washington, D.C., had penetrated the State Department, the Treasury Department, Bureau of Standards, and the Aberdeen Proving Grounds in Maryland."[57] It had active sources, individuals who supplied the apparatus with secret information in the form of official U.S. government documents to be microfilmed.

To cite just a few of the more well-known names Chambers mentioned: Harry Dexter White in the Treasury Department was an assistant to Secretary of Treasury Henry Morgenthau Jr. Chambers identified White as a fellow traveler who passed him classified information but was not actually a member of the Communist Party.[58] At Aberdeen it was Vincent Reno, working on the top-secret Norden Bombsight. Reno confessed in 1948 to his espionage activities on behalf of Soviet military intelligence. Reno was also listed in the Gorsky Memo as Number 118. (For a discussion of the Gorsky Memo see chapter 16.) At the State Department, in addition to Hiss, Julian Wadleigh was a Soviet intelligence source.[59] Chambers maintained that Wadleigh was never a member of the Communist Party but a "very close fellow traveler" who turned over documents to him to be photographed.[60]

Aside from Hiss, probably one of the most influential and important members of Chambers's group until Chambers's defection, then under Silvermaster's ring during the war, was White. Harry Dexter White (1892–1948) was born in Boston to immigrants from Lithuania. He attended Columbia University, served in World War I, and obtained bachelor's and master's degrees from Stanford and a Ph.D. at Harvard. He quit his economics teaching job and joined the Roosevelt administration. He quickly became the number-two man at Treasury, assistant to Secretary of Treasury Morgenthau.[61] According to Chambers, White was a fellow traveler committed to the Communist cause who used his office to advance Soviet interests.

In February 1942, for example, Congress passed a bill to lend Chinese Nationalist leader Chiang Kai-shek $500 million. White stalled the payments, despite Morgenthau's promise to the Chinese minister of finance, H. H. Kung, that he would expedite them. And two White subordinates (Solomon Adler and Frank Coe, both Soviet agents, code-named "Sachs" and "Peak," respectively) tried to undermine efforts to support Chiang with the loan.[62] In addition, Harry Dexter White's handwritten memo on American foreign policy toward Japan dated 1938 was passed to Chambers and was among the "Pumpkin Papers," a stash of secret documents and microfilm Chambers had kept over the years to protect his family and himself after he defected. There were four sheets among the Papers that were in White's handwriting and given to Chambers.[63]

White passed to Moscow sensitive policy memoranda of the U.S. Treasury Department on the plans and thinking of Morgenthau and Roosevelt on wartime economic issues.[64] White was the official who encouraged the deindustrialization of Germany; this became known as the "Morgenthau Plan." Roosevelt and Churchill eventually rejected it.[65] Elizabeth Bentley testified that the plan, whose real author was White, was aimed to reduce Germany, after the war, to a "fifth-rate power," which would be to the advantage of the USSR.[66] And finally, Senator William Jenner's conclusion in his 1953 hearings on subversion in government departments said: "White's name was used as a reference by other members (of the Party) when they applied for government service. He hired them, promoted them, and gave them raises. He transferred them and vouched for their loyalty."[67]

White (who had three code names: "Jurist," "Lawyer," and "Richard") was referenced fifteen times in the Venona files. He was "highly regarded" by Moscow.[68] His efforts were deliberate attempts to advance the interests of the Soviet Union at the expense of U.S. national interests. Yet some have seen White as a dedicated New Deal internationalist who enacted government policy that favored the Soviet Union during World War II in order to maintain good relations with Moscow.[69] This includes the author R. Bruce Craig, who describes White in his biography as a utopian who believed in a Soviet-American partnership, who saw no dichotomy in being a committed New Deal progressive and an internationalist cooperating with Stalin's regime in the service of world peace.[70] This was how some commentators saw all New Dealers. They confused the "why" of these men, whose personal views of idealism led them to support Stalin's Russia, with the "what" they did—commit espionage against their own country. White died on August 16, 1948, of a heart attack, three days after testifying before the HUAC.

In Hiss's collection of papers at New York University's Tamiment Library, there are handwritten notes from devoted New Dealers suggesting that any opposition to them was unreasoning. Many of them viewed the McCarthy era as an ugly period of national hysteria and believed that the "red scare" was erected to obstruct New Deal reforms. Some of the notes suggested that in the 1940s, "arrogant nationalism and super patriotism were the order of the Day." Others claimed that the "outlook of America's self-congratulating citizens encourages a provincial assumption that its accomplishments are unique."[71] This anti-American view has not died; it is evident today, in the form of attacks on "American exceptionalism."

While crusading against Communism in the 1950s, Senator Joseph McCarthy, a Republican from Wisconsin, caused the anti-Communist movement in the United States a large amount of unnecessary difficulty because of his overstatements and at times unbalanced rhetoric. His hyperbole was sometimes made worse by heavy-handed tactics of some security officials and congressional investigators. For his part, Whittaker Chambers feared that McCarthy would impair or even destroy a serious anti-Communist movement in the United States, that McCarthy would discredit the whole anti-Communist effort. For this reason, Chambers said, he could not endorse William F. Buckley and L. Brent Bozell's book, *McCarthy and His Enemies,* which was a defense of Senator McCarthy.[72]

That being said, McCarthy's detractors did in fact turn a blind eye to the actual issue—the extensive Soviet infiltration inside the U.S. government—and used McCarthy's excesses to deride the issue of Communist infiltration and to smear him to such an extent that his name is to this day synonymous with *witch hunt.* Political biases and McCarthyism aside, the fact is that the U.S. government during the 1930s and 1940s was seriously penetrated by Soviet intelligence. Not only were Soviet agents embedded in the State and Treasury departments and AAA but also in the War, Navy, and Justice departments, as well as in the OSS.[73] This was a counterintelligence failure of the first order. And when Soviet code clerk Igor Gouzenko defected in Canada in September 1945, he turned over at least one hundred Soviet classified documents that proved the existence of extensive espionage networks in both Canada and the United States.[74]

As British historian Robert Conquest noted, Richard Nixon and some other members of the HUAC were accused of being "mean, partisan, unjudicial, tricky, driven by ambition." Conquest goes on to say that while such points are undoubtedly legitimate, they should not be allowed to obscure the main issue. "Was Nixon right? He was."[75] Some Hiss defenders like to suggest that the Hiss case was a "watershed" that turned the country away from the New Deal to McCarthy's crusade of anti-Communism. This formula is simplistic, historically. McCarthy was active in his crusade only from 1950 to 1954, when he was censured by the Senate. What turned the country away from the New Deal's pro-Russian position to anti-Communism were not some indiscriminate exaggerations of one senator, which had an effect for a few years, but the unfolding Soviet policies of total domination of Eastern Europe, the Berlin blockade, the Soviet-backed Korean War, the purges, man-made famines, and the gulag, where millions of innocent people died—to name a few.

Another British writer, Gordon Brook-Shepherd, pointed to the lack of comprehension and awareness in New Deal America of the ambitious Soviet networks for espionage, propaganda, and subversion inside the United States at the time. This deficiency, he claimed, resulted in such counterintelligence failures as the total ineptitude in handling crucial sources like Soviet defectors Alexander Orlov and Walter Krivitsky. The KGB intelligence officer Alexander Orlov testified in 1957 before a congressional committee that when he defected in 1938, the United States had been placed on equal footing in intelligence terms as Great Britain and France. This meant the KGB alone (not counting the GRU) and only legal operations (not counting "illegal" operations) was "running" at least eighteen spy rings. In the intervening years, only two networks were exposed—those spy rings connected to Bentley (KGB) and Chambers (GRU).[76] Brook-Shepherd went on to point out that "coming in 1957, all this information about Soviet penetration was merely a sobering catalog for the record." But, he continued, had it been revealed in 1938, and acted upon, "it might have gone some way toward saving the West from President Roosevelt's fateful illusion that the Soviet Union, with its spunky, commonsense leader, Uncle Joe, was the only proper country for America to do business with in sorting out the postwar world."[77] And when the United States finally awoke to the Communist threat, Brook-Shepherd observed, what resulted was the McCarthy hysteria of the 1950s, which over-shadowed the real menace.[78]

George Kennan, former ambassador to the Soviet Union, wrote in his *Memoirs* that the penetration of the U.S. government by Communists in the late 1930s "was not a figment of the imagination of the hysterical right-wingers of a later decade . . . it really existed . . . and it was quite extensive."[79] Kennan recognized there was a subversion problem in the United States in the 1930s and during the wartime alliance with Moscow, and that the Roosevelt administration addressed it ineffectively.[80] The British government also experienced massive penetration by Soviet intelligence, especially from the Cambridge and Oxford espionage spies.[81]

Even Moscow eventually acknowledged the fact of Soviet infiltration into the U.S. government. The Russians admitted this was the case in a *Red Star* (*Krasnaya Zvezda*) article by Vladimir Lota on May 5, 2006. Lota revealed that Soviet intelligence sources during World War II "obtained information from nearly 70 American ministries, departments, directorates, committees, and subcommittees in the governmental structure of the USA." As just one example, *Red Star* cited a meeting that the chief of the OSS station in Bern, Switzerland, Allen Dulles, had with a German SS commander in northern Italy that was duly reported back to Moscow.[82]

J. Peters, head of the American Communist Party underground in the United States, commented to Chambers on the size of party infiltration: "Even in Germany under the Weimar Republic, the Party did not have what we have here." The party could recruit agents within the U.S. government by scores because in the 1930s, the revolutionary mood had become so acute due to the Depression. Chambers maintained that Communists and fellow travelers who "staffed this Fifth Column" were dedicated revolutionists whose primary allegiance was to international Communism, not the United States.[83]

Will this solid, well-established, corroborated, multisourced record of Soviet intelligence infiltration of the United States government in the 1930s and 1940s put to rest the argument that McCarthyism was nothing more than right-wing fantasies about Communists having insinuated themselves into the American government? Probably not.

VII.

WHITTAKER CHAMBERS

A. The Witness

Chambers: I know that I am leaving the winning side
for the losing side, but it is better to die on the losing
side than to live under Communism

WHITTAKER CHAMBERS WAS Alger Hiss's "handler" for Soviet military intelligence in the 1930s. He was born Jay Vivian Chambers in Philadelphia on April 1, 1901, and subsequently changed his name to Whittaker, after his maternal grandfather.

Whittaker Chambers came from a troubled family. He had an absentee father, Jay Chambers, a graphic artist at the *New York World*, who was bisexual. His grandmother, who lived with the Chambers family, was mentally ill. A younger brother, Richard, was psychologically disturbed and eventually committed suicide. Following Richard's birth, the family moved to Brooklyn. However, Jay's wife, Laha, decided to leave Brooklyn and resettle in the suburbs. She reportedly disliked New York City, missing the openness of her origins in Wisconsin. Whittaker's father did not want to move from Brooklyn, given its proximity to the elevated subway, with easy access to his Manhattan office and the galleries and theaters he frequented. But his mother, insistent and strong-willed, prevailed. The family moved in 1904 to Lynbrook, on Long Island's south shore. The house at 228 Earle Avenue was suitable "for Laha to regain the 'paradise' of upper-middle-class respectability she had known in childhood."[1] For his part, Chambers viewed himself as coming from an ordinary middle-class family.

Whittaker's maternal grandfather, Charles Whittaker, immigrated with his family to Milwaukee from Scotland in 1845, when Charles was five years old. He became a language teacher and principal in Milwaukee's public schools. He married Mary Blanchard, a descendant of Huguenots. She spoke fluent French and later taught it to her grandson, Whittaker. After many business losses, Charles moved his family, first to Chicago and then to New York City. They lived very meagerly in New York, in a small apartment over a lunch counter they ran on West Twenty-Third Street. There was no money with which to send Laha, their only child, to college, so she started an unsuccessful stage career.

Soon after, Laha moved back home with her parents and was a cook and waitress in the luncheonette. Charles died in 1899, leaving his wife and daughter a twelve-dollars-a-month Civil War pension, some kitchen utensils, and a couple of hundred books.[2] Laha had met Jay Chambers by then; he used to eat at the luncheon counter. He was five years her junior, a recent graduate from Philadelphia's Drexel Institute of Art, Science, and Industry. Jay was in New York to accept a job at the *World* that he obtained through his father, James Chambers, a well-known journalist. Jay and Laha married in January 1900. Jay's mother, Dora, opposed the marriage on the grounds that Laha was unworthy of her only son.[3] They had two children, Whittaker and Richard.

In her effort to achieve acceptability in the Lynbrook community, Laha joined the local mother's club and was elected president; she also was on the committee that founded and staffed the village's first library. Whittaker was raised an Episcopalian (but later in life became a Quaker). Yet the Chambers family did not seem to "fit in" with the local community. Whittaker, who felt he was an unwanted child, thought of himself as an "outcast."[4] According to Sam Tanenhaus, who wrote a definitive biography on Chambers, when he began grammar school he felt that he did not fit in with the other boys; he never played with them and remained a loner. He was shunned by schoolmates.[5] Moreover, the Chamberses' marriage was crumbling. Jay moved out in 1908 and went back to Brooklyn. He was there for a year, during which period his family did not see him. At this time, Whittaker remembered, his mother developed a fear of prowlers and slept with an ax under her bed. Seven-year-old Chambers himself was soon keeping a knife under his pillow. His father sent them eight dollars a week; Laha had to supplement that with various activities such as selling her baked goods. It was years later that Whittaker understood his mother's unhappiness; her husband, Jay, was bisexual.[6]

During his high school years, Chambers studied various languages by himself, at home. Besides learning German, Italian, and Spanish, and mastering French, he "began a correspondence with a famous philologist, George Frazier Black, at the New York Public Library. With Black's help, Chambers began studying Arabic, Persian, Hindustani, and the Assyrian of the cuneiform inscriptions." Black helped Chambers pick up a smattering of gypsy dialects as well.[7] At nights Chambers worked on translating the works of two famous Germans: the philosopher Lessing and the writer Goethe.

Also during his high school years, Chambers studiously followed the battles of World War I, with maps mounted on his bedroom wall. After the Russian Revolution he began studying the Russian language, memorizing hundreds of words. Chambers said his language studies proved very useful later in life. He was able to earn a living as a German and French translator during the years when he worked for the Communist Party as a journalist for meager wages.[8] For example, *Bambi*, the story made famous by Walt Disney, was originally a 1923 Austrian novel written by Felix Salten. The first English edition of *Bambi* was translated by Chambers from the German and released in 1928. His translation of *Bambi*, which became a classic, was an instant success. "I suddenly found myself an established translator," Chambers wrote.[9]

In June 1919, Chambers graduated from South Side High School. He wrote years later in his autobiography, "Few boys run away from happy homes."[10] Following graduation, he left home with his friend Tony Muller and traveled to Washington, D.C., getting a job replacing railroad tracks, within blocks of the Capitol. The physical work as a day laborer kept him exhausted. But he met workmen from a variety of European backgrounds; he also became particularly friendly with a large group of Latin Americans. Working with these foreigners provided Chambers with an opportunity to try out the many languages he had taught himself. When the job was over in September, the two boys traveled to New Orleans. Chambers found it difficult to get work at the shipyards and wound up living in cheap flats in the French Quarter. Chambers remarked in *Witness* that the workers in New Orleans were not like those in Baltimore and Washington, who were the factory proletariat. The workers in New Orleans, he said, were "that passively rotting mass" that Marx had called the "lumpenproletariat"—"the wretched of the earth," the lowest level of laborer.[11] After four months, he wired home for money, which his father sent. He gave some of the money to Muller, who had decided to enlist in the Marines, and the rest he used to purchase a ticket back to Lynbrook.

When Whittaker returned he agreed to start university in the fall; until then he was a mail clerk at a midtown Manhattan advertising agency where his father recently had become a director. Working in the same office as his father, he saw another, warmer, friendlier side of him, he said. They traveled together to and from work every day; Tanenhaus wrote that the job brought father and son closer together.[12] After six months, Chambers applied to Williams College in Massachusetts, to accommodate his mother's choice of colleges; Whittaker lasted on that campus all of three days. He left Williams and enrolled at the school of his choice, Columbia University, class of 1924. The family lacked money, and thus admission to Columbia was advantageous because it enabled

Chambers to live at home in Lynbrook, commuting each day by subway and by Long Island Rail Road.

During the 1920s, Tanenhaus observed, Columbia, under President Nicholas Murray Butler, had become a "model of a twentieth century urban university." Its faculty included the likes of John Dewey, philosopher, psychologist, and educational reformer, and Franz Boas, father of American anthropology. According to Tanenhaus, professors encouraged students "to think for themselves, rather than simply absorb facts."[13] Chambers's classmates at Columbia included, among others, Meyer Schapiro, Lionel Trilling, Louis Zukofsky, Mortimer J. Adler, and Clifton Fadiman. Some of these became Chambers's trusted friends. Most were Jewish. He knew few Jews in Lynbrook and was in awe of their brilliance and the extent and depth of their knowledge. These *ernste Menschen* (serious men), as Chambers called them, helped shape his ideas. Under their influence, he read Tolstoy, Dostoevsky, Ibsen, Chekhov, Strindberg, Hauptmann, and others.[14] Chambers was to become a man "so incurably bookish" that he could spend hours waiting outside a federal grand jury room in 1948 reading Dante.[15]

As a political conservative, Chambers had many arguments with his peers about politics and philosophy. But they also gave him his first understanding of Bolshevism, and the Russian radical tradition of Marx, Bakunin, Nechaev, Prince Kropotkin, and the Narodniki—intelligentsia from the upper and middle classes in Russia who left the cities for the villages (in other words, "going to the people"), to teach the peasantry their moral imperative to revolt.[16]

In his second year, Chambers took up residence at Columbia. When he enrolled at Columbia University as a freshman, he had been assigned a faculty advisor, Mark Van Doren, at the time a young instructor in the English Department. Chambers quickly developed a friendship with him. He started sending him poems he had been writing. Although Van Doren rejected most of them, he encouraged Chambers to continue writing, leading Chambers to believe he had a calling as a poet. Van Doren also was impressed with Chambers's prose, which he thought was equally as good as his poetry. In fact, Van Doren rated Chambers the "best" of all the undergraduates he knew in the 1920s.[17] And following one of Chambers's oral exams for an advanced seminar for upperclassmen, Mortimer J. Adler, one of the examiners, actually applauded, saying, "Chambers was simply brilliant."[18] That adjective has been used often to describe Chambers's intellect and writing abilities.

During his second year at Columbia, Chambers was elected editor in chief of the campus literary magazine *Morningside*. He had published in it an atheistic play, *A Play for Puppets,* under the pseudonym John Kelly, which caused somewhat of a scandal. A student delegation denounced it as "filthy, sacrilegious, and profane." Some faculty members called for Chambers's expulsion. The controversy spread beyond the campus to the *New York Times* and the *Tribune,* both of which covered the story. Despite the support he received from Van Doren, Chambers became despondent over the very negative reaction to his play and dropped out of Columbia in January. He was not expelled, as some have claimed.[19]

Van Doren suggested that Chambers might want to go to Soviet Russia, telling him that "the Russian Revolution is like Elizabethan England. All the walls are falling down. You should go and see it."[20] Van Doren said Chambers could go as a relief worker for the American Friends Service Committee, which was administering Quaker relief in the Russian famine areas. Chambers met with the Quaker group; however, when they found out about the atheistic play he had written, their reaction was very ugly. Chambers said "it was an invisible turning point in my life." He felt a "stinging sense of rejection" and asked "where in Christendom is the Christian?"[21]

So instead Whittaker went to Europe in June 1923 with friends Meyer Schapiro and Henry Zolinsky (aka Zolan), a student poet at City College of New York. Surprisingly, Chambers's father gave him money for the boat ticket. The three travelers spent most of their time in Berlin, politically volatile in this time between the wars. They saw Weimar Germany in a state of turmoil—months after the French occupied the Ruhr valley and months before Hitler's unsuccessful Munich putsch in November. Chambers also traveled to Paris for a couple of weeks. When he returned to Lynbrook, he went back to Columbia briefly, but dropped out a second time, voluntarily, for the express purpose, he said, of joining the Communist Party in reaction to the many problems he had seen in postwar Europe. Chambers had entered Columbia as a self-described political conservative and Christian Scientist.[22] But by the time he left he was no longer a conservative or religious. At this same time, in 1924, Chambers's "sexuality had become a new and troubling question for him . . . he barely understood it."[23] He had become conflicted about his sexual identity and bisexual leanings.

In the early spring of 1925, Chambers joined the CPUSA. (During his HUAC testimony on August 3, 1948, Chambers erroneously had remembered this year as 1924.) Chambers said no one recruited him. He was a paid functionary of the Communist Party, writing at first for the *Daily Worker*, then for the *New Masses*. By now Chambers believed Communism alone could save the world. William F. Buckley, reflecting on Chambers at the centennial of his birth, said he came to understand why Chambers "resigned as editor of the Communist *New Masses*, where he had earned an international reputation as a writer, to go scurrying about the streets of Washington, Baltimore, and New York, carrying pocketfuls of negatives and secret phone numbers and invisible ink." In a letter to Buckley, Chambers revealed: "I came to Communism . . . above all under the influence of the Narodniki [Russian populists from the middle class who were adherents of an agrarian socialist movement, active from the 1860s to the 1890s]. They have been deliberately forgotten, but, in those days, Lenin urged us to revere the Narodniki . . . Unlike most Western Communists, who became Communists under the influence of the Social Democrats, I remained under the spiritual influence of the Narodniki long after I became a Marxist. In fact, I never threw it off. I never have. And, of course, it was that revolutionary quality [in me] that bemused Alger—mea culpa, mea maxima culpa."[24]

Later on, Chambers wrote that "the dying world of 1925 was without faith, hope, character.... Only in Communism had I found any practical answer at all to the crisis, and the will to make that answer work. If it was the outrage, it was also the hope of the world."[25] The Depression was still several years away; Chambers spent the time as a journalist for the Communist Party. He continued to work on the *Daily Worker*; then he had a brief break with the party. He returned as an editor of the *New Masses,* the Communist Party's literary magazine. He also took an evening job at the New York Public Library; it was an undemanding position and gave him time to read as well as an opportunity to supplement his income. Even though he left Columbia, Chambers continued to send poems to Van Doren, some of which his former professor had published.

Chambers's brother Richard, two years younger than Whittaker, had enrolled at Colgate University. Whittaker said his brother was happy as a boy. He went to Colgate with a group of his close friends from high school. Richard was good-natured, very popular, uncomplicated, Chambers wrote. He was on the baseball and track teams. But while at Colgate, Richard had failed to make a fraternity that his close friend and roommate had made. His mother was worried but Chambers thought it was a "silly" concern. Later Chambers realized his mother was correct; "this social rejection to which his sociable nature made him vulnerable, for which nothing in his past prepared him, and which he lacked the human resources to resist, was the starting point of his disaster."[26]

Richard left school and became more and more depressed, saying that life was worthless and meaningless. He became an alcoholic, married briefly, and eventually, after several attempts, killed himself by drinking a quart of whisky and placing his head on a pillow inside an oven. Chambers was convinced that his brother had committed suicide largely out of despair with the world, a despair he himself soon came to share.[27] In the wake of this tragedy,

Chambers's father died, in 1929. His mother, Laha, died many years later, in June 1958 at age eighty-six. In her last years, she kept up a busy schedule of social activities such as lunches and club meetings. As Tanenhaus reported, Laha enjoyed the brief celebrity of the Hiss trials in the 1940s when journalists came out to Lynbrook to interview her.[28]

Whittaker moved to a cottage in Long Island with a "Communist girl," Ida Dailes, in what he described as a "Party marriage." They lived together until 1930. Ida got pregnant and Chambers pressured her into an abortion. Chambers had begun another relationship, with Esther Shemitz, a young artist he had met in 1926. She was Russian-born, had studied at the Rand School, and was a pacifist. Esther had traveled to Boston to protest the Sacco and Vanzetti executions, and she was briefly enrolled in the Socialist Party. Though she was politically engaged, she was more interested in art.[29] On April 15, 1931, Chambers married Esther at the Manhattan Municipal Building. They had two children, Ellen and John, born in New York City in 1933 and 1936, respectively.

In 1932 a staffer on the *Daily Worker*, John Sherman, instructed Chambers to "go underground."[30] (Chambers described Sherman as one of those "figures whose relationship to the *Daily Worker* was rather erratic or mysterious, and who wandered in and out of that little universe, like comets, at unpredictable intervals."[31]) That is, he was to become part of the covert Soviet intelligence network in the United States. This meant he had to sever all contact with the open party and its newspapers. Years later, Chambers wrote, he found out that when he went underground in 1932 he was assigned to the Fourth Department of Soviet military intelligence (the GRU). No one told him this information at the time.[32] GRU stands for Glavnoye Razvedyvatel'noye Upravleniye, the Main Intelligence Directorate (of the General Staff of the Armed Forces).

Chambers was at first a courier in New York City. He then was assigned to establish himself in Washington, D.C., to "learn the setup of the Ware Group," and assume "running" it. He was then to "separate out some members of the group," forming a "parallel apparatus" that would eventually penetrate the upper reaches of government.[33] One story during this time period remains unclear. According to Allen Weinstein, Chambers and Esther (whose underground name was "Liza") went to Moscow on fraudulent passports in April 1933. If so, he was most likely in the USSR for training as an agent at the Lenin School and for briefings by the GRU, since he recently had been assigned to covert operations for Soviet military intelligence. Weinstein referenced the postcards Chambers sent from Moscow to friends Jacob Burck and Meyer Schapiro during that time.[34] Chambers denied that he and Esther ever went to the Soviet Union, although at the time he was the one who actually started the story, presumably to impress his friends, according to Sam Tanenhaus. Tanenhaus maintained that the record does not support the claim that Chambers and his wife went to Russia. The timing of his movements and other people's memory of seeing him during 1933, along with Esther's pregnancy, indicate this story was a myth.[35]

In 1934, J. Peters introduced Whittaker Chambers to Harold Ware in a New York City automat. They discussed Chambers's new role associated with the Ware Group. Ware made arrangements to see Chambers in Washington. As previously noted, sometime in mid-1934, Whittaker Chambers met in a Washington restaurant with Harold Ware, J. Peters, and Alger Hiss for the first time. As Chambers later related the story, very soon after this first introductory meeting, he visited Alger and Priscilla Hiss at their home. They thought he was Russian and Chambers did not correct them. And they knew him as "Karl." While he was with the apparatus, Chambers wrote, everyone thought he was European, maybe Russian or German, by the way he spoke.[36]

In his memoir, *Witness,* Chambers described the very close and deep relationship that he developed with Alger Hiss.[37] Chambers was a constant visitor at the various Hiss homes in Georgetown. The Chambers family even shared an apartment with the Hisses on

P Street for a short period of time. Later, Chambers and his family moved to Baltimore. Chambers recalled that he and Alger had a friendship as close "as a man ever makes in his life."[38] Of course, in the intelligence world, a "handler" developing a close relationship with a source was contrary to good tradecraft. Because the first Ware Group member to be set apart as the first person of the parallel network was Alger Hiss, Chambers believed that his close friendship with Hiss was necessary to help offset any underground isolation Hiss may have felt.

Chambers wrote that Alger had a "mildness, a deep considerateness, and gracious patience." Rarely did Hiss show a streak of cruelty. Chambers did, however, record the few times he had: when he was telling Hiss that he and his wife, Esther, found Baltimore charming, Hiss referred to the "horrible old women of Baltimore." Hiss also indicated his contempt for Roosevelt as a "dabbler in revolution who understood neither revolution nor history" (Chambers said this was the common view of Roosevelt among Communists) and made "brutal references to Roosevelt's physical condition as a symbol of the middle-class breakdown." Chambers also saw cruelty in Hiss's many lectures to him about the terrible condition of his teeth.[39]

Chambers developed a system for transmission of stolen government documents. Starting in early 1937 and through April 1938, Chambers testified during the Hiss trials, he went to Hiss's home regularly every ten days to two weeks between 5 and 7 P.M. to pick up documents and copies of documents from Hiss.[40] Chambers took the documents and microfilm obtained from Hiss and other Soviet spies in his apparatus from Washington to Baltimore to have them copied by Felix Inslerman, a photographer for the apparatus; he returned to Washington so his assets could replace the stolen original documents by the next day of business, and then he transferred the copies to his Soviet superior in New York, GRU colonel Boris Bykov.[41]

In 1936, Hiss began feeding classified material to Chambers.

"He would bring home a briefcase containing documents from the State Department," explained Chambers. "I would then take the documents to Baltimore to be photographed, returning them to Alger Hiss late the same night or the next morning."[42] In the case of Harry Dexter White, who was a fellow traveler but not a Party member, official documents from the Treasury Department were passed to George Silverman, who acted as the go-between. Silverman took documents from White and then passed them to Chambers. In the case of Wadleigh and Abel Gross, David Carpenter was the go-between for them and Chambers.[43]

Chambers said that sometime between 1935 and 1937, Moscow had decided to recruit new people into the Soviet intelligence apparatus. According to Chambers, Hiss was an assiduous talent spotter, constantly looking for recruits. He invited prospects to dinner parties.[44] Two individuals whom Hiss had worked on at various times to recruit were State Department officials—Noel Field and Laurence Duggan.[45] Alger and Priscilla began a series of social visits with Field and Duggan. At one dinner, as Hiss was trying to recruit Noel Field, he learned that Field already was attached to another Soviet intelligence apparatus, a KGB network run by Hede Massing.[46]

When Chambers broke with the party, he went through a moral and psychological crisis. He was summoned to Moscow several times but did not go; years later he said he considered himself lucky that he extricated himself from the underground without being assassinated, as was Stalin's practice with some other defectors. In April 1938 he fled from Washington with his family and hid out for a month in a cottage near Daytona Beach, Florida. He would stay by the window all night, with gun in hand, for fear he would be tracked down and attacked.[47]

After his return to Washington, Chambers went to Hiss's house on Volta Place in Georgetown to see Hiss and try to convince him also to leave the party. It was Christmastime 1938. He wrote in *Witness* that he had dinner with Alger, Priscilla, and Timmie,

Priscilla's son by her first husband. After dinner, when they were alone, he tried to explain to Alger why he broke from the party. "I began a long recital of the political mistakes and crimes of the Communist Party," Whittaker wrote. In his words, these were:

- the Soviet government's deliberate murder by mass starvation of millions of peasants in the Ukraine and the Kuban;

- the deliberate betrayal of the German working class to Hitler by the Communist Party's refusal to cooperate with the Social Democrats against the Nazis;

- the ugly fact that the German Communist Party had voted in the Reichstag with the Nazis against the Social Democrats;

- the deliberate betrayal of the Spanish Republican government, which the Soviet Government was only pretending to aid while the Communists massacred their political enemies in the Spanish prisons.[48]

Chambers continued, "This gigantic ulcer of corruption and deceit had burst, I said, in the great Russian purge when Stalin had consolidated his power by massacring thousands of the best men and minds in the Communist Party on lying charges." Chambers said he begged Hiss to break with the party, too. Hiss's response, an angry one, was "What you have been saying is just mental masturbation."[49] That was his sole response. When Chambers left, Hiss had tears in his eyes, he said. As Chambers was leaving, Hiss gave him a Christmas present that Priscilla had purchased for his young daughter, Ellen, a petty little gift, Chambers wrote. It was a little wooden rolling pin from the five-and-dime store, worth about a nickel.[50]

Hiss's response to Soviet crimes was predictable for a committed Communist. J. B. Matthews's 1938 book, *Odyssey of a Fellow*

Traveler, provides an important insight into this type of reaction. Matthews, a self-proclaimed Marxist, was in the Ukraine in the summer of 1932 and was an eyewitness to the horrors of the famine. His instinct, he said, was to explain the nightmare as a legacy of czarist rule, which Stalin's second five-year program would correct. (Blame it on the predecessor.) He then compared it to India where poverty was worse. (The relativist argument.) This was "the orthodox answer to every scene of misery and horror. Of course there was no famine! My will was set to believe there was no famine." To admit the truth, Matthews wrote, would result in being denounced as a "betrayal of the working class."[51] This went beyond having a blind spot—this was total blindness. Matthews subsequently broke out of the cultural trance, faced the reality of Stalin's crimes, and became a staunch anti-Communist.[52]

To understand the Hiss response to Chambers's defection one must also understand the core evilness of Marxism-Leninism, where any crime was acceptable in order for Communism to retain power. Lenin believed that for the revolutionary, everything is moral that serves the revolution, and iron discipline is necessary for the sake of achieving the revolutionary purpose.[53] Documents from the Lenin archives, brought forth in Richard Pipes's *The Unknown Lenin,* include a revealing March 19, 1922, letter from Lenin to Molotov for Politburo members. Lenin wrote: "One wise writer on matters of statecraft (i.e., Machiavelli, *The Prince,* chapter 8) rightly said that if it is necessary to resort to certain brutalities for the sake of realizing a certain political goal, they must be carried out in the most energetic fashion and in the briefest possible time because the masses will not tolerate prolonged application of brutality."[54]

Subsequently, in *Witness,* Chambers pointed again to difficulties he had with remaining a Communist. He saw the great purges as massacres reminiscent of Oriental despotism. In the purges, he said, "millions were massacred, including those Communists who made the Russian Revolution (Rykov, Bukharin, Kamenev, Zinoviev, Piatakov, Rakovsky, Tukhachevsky et al.). As Communists, Stalinists were justified in the purges; from their viewpoint they could not have taken any other course. The purges, like the Nazi-Soviet Pact, were the true measure of Stalin as a revolutionary statesman. That, I saw as the horror of the purges—acting as a Communist, Stalin acted rightly. In that fact laid the evidence that Communism is absolutely evil."[55] In his book Chambers recalled approaching Hiss about the Soviet purges and the character of Stalin. Alger only replied, "Yes, Stalin plays for keeps, doesn't he?"[56] In other words, revolutionary purpose was all that mattered; this belief was perhaps what sustained Hiss as he lived half his life in deceit and deception.

Probably the essential reason Chambers quit the party was that his Communist faith in man was replaced by his religious faith in God. Whittaker Chambers made his final break with the Communist Party in April 1938. After the murder of a GRU defector in Europe, Ignace Poretsky (aka Ignace Reiss), Chambers was worried about the safety of his family and himself. When Poretsky had defected, he announced his break with the party in a defiant letter to Moscow opposing the great purge. He was assassinated in Switzerland in 1937. The General Staff of the Soviet Army was undergoing a purge, and GRU operative Walter Krivitsky, a close friend of Poretsky, was concerned for his welfare, as well. And of course Leon Trotsky was a prime target for Stalin and was assassinated in Mexico in August 1940. Alexander Foote, a member of a spy network in Switzerland working against Germany during the war, expressed the same concern when he defected. He stated, citing Krivitsky and Trotsky, that the Soviet system knew only one penalty for traitors—death.[57] Chambers's fears for his own and his family's safety were not unfounded.

Poretsky's murder prompted Krivitsky to defect the following month. Krivitsky was subsequently found dead inside a Washington, D.C., hotel in February 1941. The District of Columbia police ruling of the death as a suicide remains controversial to this day. According to author Gary Kern, who investigated the death, there were clues that could indicate that rather than death by voluntary suicide, Krivitsky could have been killed.[58] Chambers's wife, Esther, and the children were spending the winter in New Smyrna Beach, Florida. Fearing for the safety of Krivitsky's wife and son, Chambers had them join his family in Florida immediately following the funeral.[59]

Juliet Poyntz, who had been a member of the Daughters of the American Revolution, was a founding member of the CPUSA. After resigning from the party, Poyntz disappeared in June 1937 in New York City, never to be seen again. Some sources believed she also was assassinated by the KGB.[60]

Chambers, in response to these events, asked his wife's nephew to hide what he called his "life preserver," a packet of document copies, handwritten memos, and microfilm that implicated top-level Soviet assets in the U.S. government, and he made it known he would have these American spies exposed if anything happened to him or his family.[61] All of this material became known as the "Pumpkin Papers."

Following his defection, Chambers was hired in 1939 by Henry Luce as a book reviewer for *Time* magazine. Over the next decade, Chambers eventually attained the post of senior editor. He directed the foreign news and book sections, and wrote numerous cover stories. *Time*'s obituary of Chambers mentioned one article in particular by him that was published on March 5, 1945, shortly after the Yalta Conference. In the article, titled "The Ghosts on the Roof," Chambers predicted a "ruthless, imperialistic Russia about to launch an offensive to conquer the world."[62] The subsequent expansion of Soviet power proved his assessment to be accurate.

During the House Un-American Activities Committee hearings on August 25, 1948, Chambers tried to explain to the committee why such respectable men in the New Deal joined the Communist Party. They sought a moral solution in a world of moral confusion. Marxism-Leninism offered an oversimplified explanation of the causes, and a program for action. Chambers went on to ponder how it was possible that so many Communists were able to operate so freely in the U.S. government. Men who hated Communism were pursuing the same aims as Communists and they were unable to distinguish one from another. Since they could not see that their firm beliefs of liberalism added up to socialism, they obviously could not be expected to see what added up to Communism. They could not grasp the differences between them. So Chambers believed that the Communists were able to stay firmly entrenched because a move against them was felt by liberals as a move against themselves.[63]

In his memoir, Chambers also weighed in against the New Deal. New Dealers did not take the New Deal seriously as an end, he claimed. "They regarded it as an instrument for gaining their own revolutionary ends. It was not a reform movement. The New Deal was a revolution seeking to replace the power of business with the power of politics. But whether revolutionists prefer to see themselves as Fabians who seek power by gradualism or Bolsheviks who seek it by dictatorship—either way it is a struggle for power." As Chambers saw it, the New Deal was not a genuine revolution but simply a change within power relationships in the country. Chambers declared the New Deal was a "revolution by book keeping and lawmaking" and was made by "Congressional acts and Supreme Court decisions, but not by tanks."[64]

After the Hiss perjury trials, both Chambers and Hiss wrote their books to present their stories to the public. Whittaker Chambers's book, *Witness,* published in 1952, was an immediate and huge success. When the preface of *Witness* appeared as a feature in the *Saturday Evening Post,* that issue of the magazine sold an astonishing half-million extra copies on the newsstand.[65] Hiss wrote his book, *In the Court of Public Opinion,* published in 1957, after he was released from prison. A review of Hiss's book in the *Observer,* by Dwight Macdonald, compared it to *Witness.* The critic did not particularly like the "aura of the sentimental, coarse-grained, egotistical" in *Witness* but still thought "it was a completely authentic human document." Hiss's book, on the other hand, had "no human voice at all"; the book was "only the drone of a legal machine geared to special pleading."[66] *In the Court of Public Opinion* in fact read like a legal brief and was devoid of any human story; it was not successful.

In the remaining years of his life, Chambers stayed mostly on his Pipe Creek Farm, in Westminster, Maryland. For a short period of time he worked again as a journalist for the *National Review*. He would travel to the magazine's offices on East Thirty-Fifth Street in New York for a couple of days to meet with publisher, editor in chief, and good friend William Buckley and other editorial staff before publication of each edition. He reveled in this activity. Many on the magazine's conservative staff were highly intelligent, deeply cultured former radicals such as James Burnham, Frank Meyer, and Willmoore Kendall. Chambers started to have some differences with this group, however. For example, members of the conservative staff of the *National Review* were champions of *The Road to Serfdom*, by F. A. Hayek, whereas Chambers was talking up *The Affluent Society*, by John Kenneth Galbraith.[67]

Chambers also took a stand on a controversy that erupted in 1958 when the Supreme Court struck down the State Department's rule that denied passports to U.S. citizens based on political (in other words, Communist) beliefs. Chambers came down in favor of this ruling, which allowed Alger Hiss to receive a passport.[68] Chambers also broke with Buckley over his support for McCarthy, a difference reflected in Buckley's 1954 book, *McCarthy and His Enemies*. Nevertheless, aside from these few specific issues, Chambers had an immense influence not only on Buckley but on the incipient conservative movement Buckley was leading. And this strong and deep influence extended for many more years, to Ronald Reagan.

Soon the commuting schedule to New York became too strenuous for Chambers, who had developed a serious heart disease and had had several heart attacks. So his short career with the *National Review* ended. From his farm in Maryland, Chambers wrote an occasional piece for the magazine. In 1959 he did manage to fulfill two of his goals. He took Esther to Europe. She had always dreamed of such a trip, especially to Paris. And during the trip Chambers rendezvoused in Austria with his good and highly esteemed friend Arthur Koestler, the ex-revolutionary famous for his sublime book *Darkness at Noon*. Chambers's poor health forced them to cut their trip short by a month, and he returned to his Westminster farm to recuperate.

In a few months, Chambers was on the move again, to fulfill his second goal. He decided to return to school to complete his formal education. He enrolled at Western Maryland College, located near his farm (and now known as McDaniel College). For the last two years of his life, he took courses not only in romance languages and Greek but also in biology and economics. Chambers stopped writing for *National Review* due to lack of time, since he was a full-time student. This too became a strenuous routine and he suffered his final heart attack. He did manage to live long enough to see both his children marry. His daughter, Ellen, had married several years earlier to Henry Into and was living in Augusta, Georgia; she gave birth to a son in 1954.[69] Whittaker attended his son John's June wedding, which took place in Washington, D.C., the month before he died in 1961.

Time wrote: "Chambers died in July 1961 at age 60 of a heart attack at his 300-acre farm in Westminster, Maryland. Chambers joined *Time* as a book reviewer, rose steadily to the post of senior editor, directed the foreign news and books sections, and wrote numerous cover stories on divergent personalities ranging from Marian Anderson to Reinhold Niebuhr to Albert Einstein. A man who loved self-dramatization, Chambers attracted a group of fiercely loyal friends with his nonconformist personality, his brilliant—though often high-flown—writing style, the surprising spread of his scholarship, and, more important, his apocalyptic view of the world, which saw all mankind as threatened by moral decay."[70]

The following editor's note appeared in the August 6, 2001,

issue of *National Review,* regarding the centennial of Chambers's birth in April 1901: "The White House convened a full house (140 guests) at the Executive Office Building on July 9, 2001, to remember Whittaker Chambers. Chambers' son was present and brought in to display the Medal of Freedom awarded posthumously to Chambers by President Reagan in 1984. Also displayed, borrowed from the Library of Congress, was a copy of a 'pumpkin paper' on which the case against Hiss turned." Moreover, Chambers's Maryland farm was designated a National Historic Landmark. The speakers, introduced by presidential assistant Tim Goeglein, were William F. Buckley Jr., Sam Tanenhaus, Robert Novak, and Ralph de Toledano.[71]

Chambers claimed that he started to repudiate Marxism-Leninism when experience and the record had convinced him that Communism was a form of totalitarianism. It represented a "spiritual night to the human mind and soul." Chambers prophesied, "I know that I am leaving the winning side for the losing side, but it is better to die on the losing side than to live under Communism."[72] In 1938 Chambers quit the party because, he explained, his Communist faith in mankind had been replaced by a religious faith in God as the only force that could reform society.[73] Chambers's impact was reflected in an article in *World Affairs*: "Standing alongside the testimonies of Koestler, Andre Gide, Ig[n]azio Silone, and others whose god of Communism failed, Chambers' odyssey would become the gold standard against which the experience of future generations of rank-breakers would be measured."[74]

B. The GRU

The Main Intelligence Directorate of the General Staff of the Soviet Armed Forces

In the mid-1930s, the main Soviet espionage networks in the United States were run by the GRU, rather than by the KGB.[75]

After Chambers's defection in April 1938, Stalin started to transfer intelligence operations from the GRU to the KGB.[76] KGB operations in the United States during the mid-1930s were run by an "illegal" *rezidentura* (station) whose leader was Boris Bazarov. Bazarov was succeeded as the KGB's "illegal" *rezident* (station chief) by his former deputy, Iskhak Akhmerov.[77] However, Akhmerov was soon recalled back to Moscow. "For the first time, the center of NKVD [i.e., KGB] operations in the United States was moved, after Akhmerov's recall, to the KGB legal *rezidentura* headed by Gaik Badalovich Ovakimyan."[78] Akhmerov returned to the United States in December 1941 to reestablish the "illegal" *rezidentura*, based in New York. He then moved to Baltimore to run the network in Washington, D.C., which included most prewar agents who were successfully reactivated, such as Larry Duggan and Harry Dexter White. Akhmerov used a furrier and clothes shop as a "cover" occupation.[79]

The defection of Chambers caused much disruption to GRU operations in Washington.[80] During this turmoil, Hiss continued to work, but it is unclear who was "running" him. Vasili Mitrokhin, a KGB defector and a former KGB archivist, made transcripts of highly classified KGB files that he brought out when he was exfiltrated from Russia in 1992 by the British Secret Intelligence Service. Mitrokhin claimed that the KGB used the Chambers defection as a pretext to take over most of the military intelligence (GRU) networks involved in foreign intelligence, "with the notable exception of Alger Hiss."[81] It is unclear why Hiss was allowed to remain with the GRU. It also is not known whether, while remaining with the GRU, Hiss was run for a period of time by the KGB "illegal" *rezident* Akhmerov during the war years, as Gordievsky maintained.[82]

As the KGB took over GRU operations, it would assume control of agents. For example, according to Mitrokhin, nuclear physicist Klaus Fuchs, recruited by the GRU in late 1941, went to the United States in 1943 as part of the British team taking part in the

Manhattan Project,[83] a program conducted during World War II to develop the first atomic bomb. The project was led by the United States and included participation from the United Kingdom and Canada. At that time, without his awareness, Fuchs was transferred from GRU to KGB control. After his arrest in 1950, Fuchs claimed he never knew which branch of Soviet intelligence he was working for.[84] And in the 1930s, Harry Dexter White was originally GRU-controlled through its "illegal" *rezident* in New York, Boris Bykov. Bykov was recalled to Moscow during the purges and control of White shifted to the KGB.[85] During the war years White was run by the KGB's Akhmerov, according to Mitrokhin.[86]

But the KGB did not take over every GRU operation, and not all GRU operations stood down following the various defections. In November 2007, then Russian president Vladimir Putin posthumously awarded Zhorzh (George) Abramovich Koval a gold star marking him as a Hero of the Russian Federation and publicly identified Koval by his code name "Delmar." Koval was a GRU agent who had worked at top-secret nuclear laboratories in Oak Ridge, Tennessee, and Dayton, Ohio, during the war. John Earl Haynes, a historian at the Library of Congress and scholar on Soviet espionage in the United States, said "we knew next to nothing about the extent of the GRU's operation against the Manhattan Project until the Koval thing came up."[87] Actually, the United States knew next to nothing about overall GRU operations in the United States during the 1930s and 1940s. Little information is available on this subject, even to this day. GRU files have never been made available, as were some KGB files.

Koval was born in Iowa in 1913 to Russian parents; in 1932 the Koval family moved back to the Soviet Union, settling in the Siberian town of Birobidzhan. After he graduated from a university in Moscow, Koval returned to the United States as a deep-cover "sleeper agent" for the GRU—a trained spy for military intelligence. He joined the U.S. Army in 1943 and after basic training was accepted into the Army Specialized Training Program. Koval was sent to City College of New York to study electrical engineering. By 1944 he was selected to be a part of the Manhattan Project and assigned to Oak Ridge. After the war, he fled the United States and returned to the USSR; he died in 2006. At the time of his award, the Defense Ministry newspaper *Red Star* (*Krasnaya Zvezda*) disclosed that when the USSR detonated its first bomb, a plutonium weapon, in August 1949, their accelerated achievement was due to "the initiator for that bomb which was prepared to the 'recipe' provided by military intelligence agent Delmar—Zhorzh Abramovich Koval."[88] This statement from Moscow's Defense Ministry not only reveals that the GRU was operational in the United States during the war but also highlights the successful contribution of espionage to Russia's nuclear program development.

Unlike its sister organization, the KGB, scant information is available about the GRU in open sources. The following data is from Owen A. Lock's essay on chiefs of the GRU.[89] Established in 1918, the GRU was headed for eleven years (1924 to 1935) by General Jan Berzin. Prior to that posting, Berzin, a Latvian, served in the VCheka (KGB) Special Section and then was deputy chief of the GRU from 1921 to 1924. Domestic turmoil, including purges and defections over the next decade (1935 through 1946), resulted in changes in the leadership of the GRU no less than eleven times. The GRU had a dual system for collecting information: "illegals" for the most sensitive clandestine work, and the military attaché system, where officers had valid documentation and were protected by diplomatic immunity. During his tenure, Berzin increasingly used agent recruits as "illegal" *rezidenti* abroad to supervise the work of technicians, couriers, and agents who were generally native to the target country. He believed that using falsely documented agents with no ties to the official Soviet presence in-country would minimize the chance of detection. GRU agents at that time typically were not Russians but rather European Communists with knowledge of foreign languages and familiar with Western customs.

By 1929–30, Berzin's GRU was quite successful, with a sizable number of networks that drew upon the Communist Party's resources of personnel. However, as internal political problems grew in Moscow, and networks collapsed, the strain between the GRU and the KGB increased. According to Lock, once the KGB's arm of military counterintelligence (Third Chief Directorate) was tasked with security inside the GRU, the struggle for foreign intelligence supremacy was a fait accompli. The GRU was actually subordinated to the KGB for a year, 1937–38. It was at this time that KGB chief Nikolay Yezhov "disemboweled" the GRU, recalling most of its intelligence officers and purging them, Lock wrote. This was also the time when the major wave of defections began, including Barmine, Krivitsky, Massing, Poretsky, and Orlov.

The Washington network was revived by Nathan Gregory Silvermaster; Harry Dexter White did not actually join the group but supplied intelligence to Silvermaster during the war. The courier for the Silvermaster Group from 1941 was Elizabeth Bentley, a KGB operative based in New York, who was the contact between the KGB and the Silvermaster and Perlo networks.[90] Following the purges, and because these networks were compromised, Stalin transferred most of foreign intelligence operations and collection over to the KGB and away from the GRU, which during the 1920s and 1930s had been the main player in intelligence operations overseas.[91] Since then, the KGB had remained the lead organization for collection of foreign political and economic intelligence, while the GRU has focused on collecting specifically military intelligence.

VIII

THE STATE DEPARTMENT BUREAUCRAT

Hiss Becomes a Target for U.S. Counterintelligence

L ouis Budenz, managing editor of the Communist paper the *Daily Worker* from 1940 to 1945, stated in his book *Men Without Faces* that he was "an active participant in the whole network of conspiracy" in the United States, of which the *Daily Worker* was part. He indicated there were two types of people in the conspiracy: those who committed espionage and those who influenced opinions in the United States. Budenz acknowledged that "not infrequently a select comrade did both."[1] Influence operations to affect policy (as well as media opinions) were carried out by Soviet intelligence services in Western countries and were a significant adjunct to Moscow's foreign policy. In the United States, these operations were designed to influence the behavior and actions of American officials in order to shape U.S. political policies and decisions so that they would favorably serve Soviet objectives.[2]

From his post at the State Department, Alger Hiss was such a select comrade who was in a position both to provide classified material to the GRU and to influence American policy in the 1940s toward China and American postwar policy toward Russia. This was one reason why Hiss, in his post at the State Department, was so important to Moscow. Soviet sources had many espionage successes, especially in the atomic weapons field. And other sources, such as Alger Hiss, had enormous influence over U.S. foreign policy in these decades. Chambers summarized this leverage succinctly: in the postwar period Soviet influence could be felt in the "crash of China" and "Carthaginian mangling of Europe."[3]

When Alger Hiss joined the Department of State in September 1936, his first job was as assistant to Assistant Secretary of State for Economic Affairs Francis B. Sayre, Hiss's former Harvard Law School professor. At the same time that Hiss started work at the State Department, the Soviet GRU sent Colonel Boris Bykov to the United States in the autumn of 1936 as a replacement for Chambers's GRU contact.[4] It was Bykov, the new GRU *rezident*, who revived the earlier idea to fully exploit the network's assets inside the U.S. government for espionage purposes. During the years (1936–38) that Hiss worked for Sayre, Hiss accommodated Bykov's "push" for more and more U.S. classified documents; Bykov especially wanted his sources to procure information on plans for a possible future war by Germany and Japan.[5]

Hiss was completely involved with Whittaker Chambers at this time—passing State Department documents to Chambers, who in turn gave them to Bykov, and developing a strong friendship with Chambers, until the latter broke with the party in 1938. That Hiss was involved in these activities probably explains why there are few if any recollections in his memoir, *Recollections of a Life*, for 1936–38. Similarly, there is also a void during this period in his personal correspondence.

After Sayre left for the Philippines in late 1939 to be the U.S. high commissioner, Hiss transferred to another office to become assistant to Dr. Stanley K. Hornbeck, advisor on political relations and the State Department's expert on Far Eastern policy. Hiss recommended to Sayre that he hire as his replacement Noel Field, a Soviet intelligence source who left the State Department in 1936 to join the League of Nations, despite the fact that Fields's experience was only in European affairs.[6] Because Field had been identified to the State Department as a member of various front groups starting in 1926, and as a Communist Party member in 1925,[7] he did not get the appointment. Sayre later declined to testify as a character witness for Hiss.[8]

From 1939 to 1941, the years of the Nazi-Soviet alliance, Hiss again seemed to lapse into amnesia; he had few recollections of this event and his memoir glides over this time of his life. Actually it is not surprising that he had nothing to say about this momentous political event, which at the time caused shock waves to everyone on the "left," especially those who never saw the commonalities of Fascism and Communism. Many Communists left the party over the Nazi-Soviet alliance. A committed Communist like Hiss remained in the party but probably was numbed by the episode. This was a full-blown blind spot for him. Even from the distance of half a century, when Hiss wrote his memoir, *Recollections of a Life,* in 1988, he airbrushed the Nazi-Soviet collaboration from his mind and his book. He did not even make an attempt at rationalizing the occurrence. The story was thoroughly obscured. Still, the total silence about this crucial event in Hiss's professional and political life is deafening. When the Nazis betrayed the pact and invaded the Soviet Union, Lionel Trilling, a literary critic and anti-Stalinist leftist, reflected that radical intellectuals, progressives, and liberals "would now once again be able to find their moral bearings and fare forward."[9]

Odd bits of information came out of the Hiss trials about this time frame. For example, during the first trial, "testifying to Hiss's pro-British sentiments at the time of the Nazi-Soviet Pact (when Communists opposed aid to England), Stanley Hornbeck related his knowledge of his former assistant" on another subject. Hornbeck said Hiss had favored aiding only the Nationalist government in China and not the Communist insurgents during the war, "a dubious argument" in support of Hiss, stated author Allen Weinstein, because "the Soviet government took much the same position at the time."[10]

During the war years, Hiss was involved in various high-priority policy issues at State, with long-term consequences. In his position in the Far East department from 1939 to 1944, Hiss's primary responsibility was to support China, headed by the Chiang Kai-shek regime, in its struggle against Japan. Hiss spent most of the war years in the Far East department, working the China policy. In mid-1944 he left the department and became deputy director of the State Department's Office of Special Political Affairs (OSPA) and subsequently OSPA director. In this new assignment, Hiss shifted his focus to postwar planning, specifically on the formation of the United Nations (at Dumbarton Oaks in 1944, the San Francisco Conference in 1945, and the London Conference in 1946) and on the Yalta Conference in 1945. He resigned from the State Department at the end of 1946.

In the Far East department, Hiss advised and worked with agencies providing economic and financial aid to China. Hiss said this was a delicate situation; he had to assist the Nationalist government while also supporting the resistance movement that involved the Communist Chinese under Mao Tse-tung. Spirited debates took place in the Far East section at State about the role of Chinese Communists, who many claimed were actively fighting the Japanese military, while others disagreed, claiming the Communists were more interested in fighting the Nationalist Chinese, led by Chiang. Hiss revealed in his memoir: "My own position in this closely contested debate was, I'm afraid, an attempt to carry water on both shoulders." It seemed unproductive, he wrote, to weaken American support of Chiang, but at the same time it "was vitally important to encourage all forces that were actively resisting the Japanese invaders. I therefore hoped continually for a compromise between the two factions."[11]

Eventually, anti-Communist sentiment in the United States led to a hardening of the policy to maintain the Chiang government,

Hiss had concluded, and thus the goal to support the Chiang Kai-shek regime became so "obsessive" that it precluded any future compromise with Mao.[12] Others believed that Mao's regime in Yenan was more interested in and spent more resources on defeating the Nationalists under Chiang and seizing territory that the Nationalists had lost to the Japanese, than it was in collaborating in the defeat of the Japanese.[13] In fact, Mao's focus was on the civil war with the Nationalist Kuomintang government, not fighting the war with Japan.[14]

The policy on China at this time was in a state of flux. Veteran China hands in the Far East division, led by Stanley Hornbeck, who supported loans to China, were resentful of the increasing criticism of Chiang Kai-shek by the pro–Yenan regime liberals.[15] The anti-Chiang group was in favor of what they called the "agrarian reformers" in Yenan, that is to say, the Mao faction. The latter included Solomon Adler, who was a Treasury Department official and part of the Silvermaster spy network, and John Stewart Service, an American diplomat who served in the Foreign Service in China prior to and during World War II; he was considered one of the State Department's "China Hands."[16] Service correctly predicted that the Communists would defeat the Nationalists in the civil war.

Adler and Service both agreed on the need to "get tough" with Chiang. Adler sent a note to Harry Dexter White at Treasury in February 1945 that said the China policy needed "to be given teeth." He proposed to support Chiang "*if and only if* he really tried to mobilize China's war effort against Japan by introducing a coalition government, meaning coalition with Yenan" (emphasis in original). To do this, he proposed to the Treasury Department that it withhold financial aid to Chiang, especially a promised loan of $200 million in gold.[17] Many others aimed at sabotaging Chiang; they wanted to establish direct U.S. contact with Yenan. They played up the "supposed virtues" of the Yenan regime and the corruption and inefficiency of the Chiang regime.

Meanwhile, the Treasury Department was attempting to enforce a policy of "financial strangulation." The veteran journalist and author M. Stanton Evans noted in his book *Blacklisted by History* that "records of this anti-Chiang campaign, including cables, memos, and transcripts of meetings, reveal an astounding cast of players—White, Lauchlin Currie, Harold Glasser, V. Frank Coe, and Alger Hiss among them."[18] During a 1948 HUAC hearing, Representative Karl Mundt, Republican of South Dakota, pursued the Hiss connection. Mundt stated that after looking at Hiss's activities while he was in the State Department, "there is reason to believe that he organized within that department one of the Communist cells which endeavored to influence our Chinese policy and bring about the condemnation of Chiang Kai-shek."[19]

In the spring of 1944, after Hiss became deputy director of OSPA, he was positioned at the center of the postwar planning process. He was named executive secretary of the Dumbarton Oaks Conference, held in Washington, D.C. (August–October 1944), to formulate plans for the organization of the United Nations. Hiss was the official note taker at Dumbarton Oaks. The establishment of the UN was the top priority in Hiss's portfolio. Subsequently, he became director of OSPA. He was assigned to be a special assistant to Secretary of State Edward Stettinius at the Yalta Conference in February 1945. The belief among Hiss and many New Dealers was that internationalism transcended national loyalties. This belief would serve the Russians well at Yalta, which is discussed separately in the next chapter.

In the summer of 1945 the *Amerasia* spy case broke. *Amerasia* was a "left-wing" journal on Pacific affairs and took an especially strong position (anti–Chiang Kai-shek) on the China issue. The editors of the journal had contacts with both State Department officials and with Soviet agents. In June 1945, the FBI raided the *Amerasia* office in New York and seized some 1,800 classified government documents from the State Department, the War Department, the Office of Strategic Services, the Office of Naval Intelligence, and the Office of Postal and Telegraph Censorship.

During the Hiss trials, the *Amerasia* case was briefly raised when the defense suggested, unsuccessfully, that Chambers may have retrieved the Hiss papers he had in his possession from the seized *Amerasia* documents, thus making them tainted evidence.[20]

Following Yalta, preparations for the establishment of the United Nations was Hiss's primary mission. Hiss maintained that because of Roosevelt's intense desire in founding a world organization, an interest shared by Secretary of State Cordell Hull and his successor Stettinius, the United States became the chief architect of the United Nations.[21] From April 25 to June 25 representatives from all over the world met in San Francisco to finalize the draft of the United Nations charter. Hiss was appointed secretary-general of the UN conference. Soviet defector Mitrokhin suggested that the KGB's "regret at failing to wrest Hiss" from the GRU must have intensified when he was appointed to this position.[22] Stettinius, as chairman of the U.S. delegation to the UN conference, was present at its official founding on June 26, 1945. Stettinius resigned in June 1945 as secretary of state to become the first United States ambassador to the United Nations. Molotov was a key figure on the Soviet side throughout the two months of negotiations and drafting of the charter.

On the U.S. side, according to Alger Hiss, Leo Pasvolsky, a State Department official and personal assistant to Secretary of State Cordell Hull, was the principal drafter of the final draft of the UN charter. Hiss claimed Pasvolsky had played a key role in formulating the structure of the UN. Pasvolsky, a "White Russian," anti-Communist émigré, and naturalized American, attended the Dumbarton Oaks talks and the UN conference at San Francisco and presided over the first session of the UN Preparatory Commission in London in January 1946.[23] Yet he did not attend the Yalta Conference. Why not, if he was so key to the UN issue—a critical one discussed at Yalta? Pasvolsky resigned from the State Department in March 1946 and became director of international studies at the Brookings Institution. A former State Department historian and head of the department's Treaty Staff, Bryton Barron, disagreed with Hiss; he maintained that Hiss was the true "architect" of the UN—not Pasvolsky.[24]

With representatives from fifty countries at San Francisco, some U.S. officials saw an opportunity to collect intelligence. On March 19, 1945, OSS chief General Donovan sent a letter to Secretary of State Stettinius that suggested the OSS's sizable group of foreign experts could be made available to do research work that might be needed during the conference. Some of Stettinius's advisors, especially Hiss, strongly opposed Donovan's offer.[25]

Following the San Francisco Conference, back at State, Hiss made an extraordinary proposal. He lobbied within the State Department to create a new post, "Special Assistant for Military Affairs," linked to his Office of Special Political Affairs, and which would have had a far-reaching role in overseeing foreign and military policies. On September 7, 1945, he made this proposal and suggested that a special assistant was needed who would routinely receive information on all aspects of military, diplomatic, and security policies and intelligence. Thus, Hiss, in turn, would have access to information regarding atomic energy, arms procurement, and military intelligence. Hiss also proposed a State Department reorganization scheme, under which he would acquire "working control" over the flow of papers within the department.[26] None of these proposals materialized.

The London Conference was held between January 10, 1946, and February 1, 1946. The U.S. delegation, headed by Ambassador to the UN Stettinius, included his deputy, Adlai Stevenson; Senator Arthur Vandenberg, a Republican from Michigan; James Byrnes, Truman's secretary of state; Leo Pasvolsky; Eleanor Roosevelt; and Alger Hiss, who was a principal advisor.[27] They were in London attending the organizational session of the UN. The Preparatory Commission drafted the bylaws and rules of procedure for the newly created United Nations.

While in London the first half of 1946, Hiss kept up his personal correspondence with Priscilla. His letters to "Thy Pros" and signed "Thy Hill" were very chatty, writing about parties and dinners and social rounds he attended and remarks about "the very fun of writing to thee." One letter boasted about being Eleanor Roosevelt's escort to a formal dinner, an event also recorded in his memoir. One of Priscilla's responses included her concern for her son, Tony, who she wrote was acting negative and unhappy because of Alger's absence. Their letters always expressed concern for their son.[28]

One item on the agenda at the London Conference was the selection of the future UN secretary-general. Soviet ambassador to Washington Andrei Gromyko told Stettinius that "he would be very happy to see Alger Hiss appointed temporary secretary general," which would make him a candidate for the office of the first permanent secretary-general of the United Nations.[29] The Soviets obviously were pleased with their man. Gromyko, who was reiterating a suggestion he had made at the San Francisco Conference the previous April, said he was most impressed with Alger Hiss. Allen Weinstein remarked in *Perjury*: "The endorsement of a leading American official by the Russians remains practically unique in the annals of Soviet-American diplomacy at this time."[30] From Moscow's perspective, Hiss's appointment would have given the Soviet Union an agent of influence in place in the top UN position.

Mrs. Roosevelt, who had long been a favorite of young New Dealers as "Roosevelt's conscience," made a big hit with Hiss at the conference. Hiss wrote in his memoir that he met her for the first time on the voyage over to London on the *Queen Elizabeth*.[31] However, among Hiss's personal papers at New York University there is an invitation from President and Mrs. Roosevelt to the Hisses to a White House reception on December 16, 1937. This invitation came at a time when Hiss was considered a low-ranking government official; it was odd that he received it and it would have been even odder for the Hisses not to accept such an invitation.[32] In any event, during the conference, Mrs. Roosevelt asked Hiss to escort her to a glamorous dinner party. He was thrilled.[33]

"Our mood reflected the hopes of the architects and founders of the United Nations for a new world of peace and international collaboration," Hiss wrote.[34] But Hiss lamented that "by the time the first meeting of the United Nations took place"—the First General Assembly meeting opened on January 10, 1946, in Westminster, London—"the Cold War was already gathering momentum and the hoped-for unity of the Great Powers had substantially faded."[35] This was truly a remarkable statement, coming from Hiss no less, admitting that the Cold War had already started and was "gathering momentum" and allied unity was gone—several years *before* Senator McCarthy, the alleged creator of the Cold War, was on anyone's radar screen.

In 1945, information pointing to Hiss as a Soviet asset came from two significant defections. One was Igor Gouzenko, a cipher clerk at the Soviet Embassy in Ottawa, Canada, who defected September 5, 1945, with more than a hundred documents on Soviet espionage operations in Canada and the United States. The Canadians provided the FBI with Gouzenko's information on September 10, 1945.[36] Gouzenko later told the FBI that the Soviets had an agent in the United States in May 1945 who was an assistant to the then secretary of state, Edward R. Stettinius.[37] The other defector was a former courier for a KGB espionage network in Washington, D.C., Elizabeth Bentley, who in the course of her 1945 debriefings by the FBI mentioned Hiss in connection with members of her network. She had little to say about him directly because she was not GRU—she reported to the KGB and thus would not be aware of his activities. But some of the agents who had switched over to Bentley's group knew Hiss, such as Charles Kramer and Harold Glasser.[38]

As a result of the intelligence now from three sources—Gouzenko, Bentley, and Chambers—FBI director J. Edgar Hoover was no longer hesitant about calling Hiss a security risk. In November 1945, Hoover asked Attorney General Tom Clark to "install technical surveillance" in Hiss's Washington home, which lasted throughout Hiss's final twelve months at State.[39] Shortly after Hiss returned from London in early 1946, the FBI and State security elements, as well as some members in Congress, started to close in on him. Hiss was told about a report that several members of Congress were getting ready to make statements on the floor of Congress that he was a Communist.[40]

According to a March 19, 1946, FBI report, Secretary of State Byrnes wanted to dismiss Hiss. He called Hiss into his office on March 21 and told him that some congressmen were ready to go public with charges and added that this information had come from the FBI. Hiss swore to Byrnes that he was not a member of the Communist Party.[41] Byrnes advised Hiss to go to the FBI and offer himself for a full investigation. He also said it made sense to go straight to Hoover. Hiss tried but never did see Hoover; instead he met with one of his chief assistants, assistant FBI director D. M. Ladd, on March 25.[42] Hiss answered his questions and denied ever being a Communist. Hiss believed the issue was resolved.[43] In *Perjury*, Allen Weinstein wrote that State Department memos declassified during the 1970s show that by spring 1946 "almost all of the State Department's security staff thought Hiss had been involved in some form of undercover Communist work."[44]

A State Department internal security investigation of Hiss in 1946 by Secretary of State Byrnes (made public in 1993) placed restrictions on his access to confidential documents. The investigation revealed that Hiss had procured classified documents that he was not authorized to see.[45] When State Department security officers began to look closely at Hiss in 1946 they discovered he had used his authority to obtain top-secret reports "on atomic energy . . . and other matters relating to military intelligence" that were outside the scope of the OSPA, which dealt largely with UN diplomacy.[46] Hiss also had requested top-secret files from the OSS on British, Soviet, French, and Chinese internal security policies, as well as on Far East policy.[47] His personnel recommendations received careful review.[48] In 1946, Hiss was staffing the UN. He forwarded the résumés of hundreds of people. About fifty showed up later as permanent employees and a couple of hundred in part-time assignments.[49]

Hiss's desk calendar also was being monitored. It is notable that at no time had Hiss ever mentioned knowing or seeing British Embassy official and member of the infamous "Cambridge 5" Donald Maclean, who had been posted to the British Embassy in Washington from May 1944 until 1949. As first secretary, Maclean had access to high-level British policy documents.[50] Yet for September 14, 1946, Hiss's desk calendar (monitored by State Department security for the August–October 1946 period) has an unexplained entry that recorded a meeting with "McLean [*sic*] British Emb." According to Allen Weinstein, none of the State Department's records or Hiss's work or the 1945–46 Office of Special Political Affairs files refers to a meeting with Maclean or any business that would have led Hiss to arrange one. Maclean did not work on UN matters, nor was he Hiss's counterpart.[51] What the meeting was about remains a mystery. It may be of some interest that two days prior to the meeting, on September 12, 1946, *Washington Post* columnist Drew Pearson wrote an article based on a leaked classified U.S. military study of British military operations against the Greek Communist insurgency. The document also contained highly classified material on the British order of battle in Greece. A State Department security inquiry led back to Hiss's office; he denied responsibility.[52]

Chambers related an interesting story in *Witness* that also indicated Hiss was under suspicion at this time. Chambers had two visits from a State Department officer; on the second one, Chambers asked him if he thought Hiss was still a Communist. The State Department official answered as follows: Yugoslav leader Tito (still allied with Stalin in August 1946) had just shot down a U.S. military plane and captured or killed its crew. "I can answer like this . . . we're having Alger Hiss draft the State Department's note of protest, one to put him on the spot, and two, so he will tell the Russians secretly that we mean business."[53]

The U.S. government was warned about Alger Hiss as early as September 1939, after the Nazi-Soviet Pact was signed on August 23. Whittaker Chambers met Isaac Don Levine, a U.S. journalist, who knew Chambers and had put him in contact with another Soviet defector from military intelligence, Walter Krivitsky. Prompted by Stalin's new alliance with the Nazis and resulting concerns that information obtained by Moscow would also wind up in Berlin, Levine maintained that he pressed Chambers to go to Washington and report what he knew about Communist infiltration in the U.S. government, which Chambers had not done after his defection the previous year. Levine stated that at first Chambers was reluctant, because of his own vulnerability, but agreed to a meeting only with Roosevelt and with a guarantee of immunity. Unable to set up a meeting with the president, Levine did get one with Adolf A. Berle Jr., assistant secretary of state and Roosevelt's designated person for security matters.[54] Contrary to Levine's account, in *Witness* Chambers denied he ever asked for immunity.[55]

In any event, on September 2, Chambers went with Levine to Berle's home, Woodley House, the historic landmark estate that belonged to former secretary of war Henry L. Stimson. Based on his understanding that his information would be forwarded to Roosevelt, Chambers identified two covert Soviet intelligence networks operating for years in Washington, D.C., that were stealing classified government documents and turning them over to Soviet couriers. Chambers named State Department officials who knowingly furnished classified documents to Soviet undercover agents, among them the Hiss brothers and Laurence Duggan and Noel Field (who had transferred to the League of Nations by then). He also cited Lee Pressman, Nathan Witt, and John Abt, among others. Chambers said he deliberately left out two names—Assistant Secretary of the Treasury Harry Dexter White, who though not a Communist Party member, Chambers claimed, still collaborated with the Soviet underground and passed material to it; and George Silverman. Chambers said he thought these two, White and Silverman, may have broken from the party after he had visited them in the previous year and had urged them to do so as well.[56] They had not.

Berle was astonished by this information; he wrote up his notes summarizing Chambers's testimony and titled them "Underground Espionage Agent," even though Chambers never used the word *espionage*. Berle claimed he informed the "White House," but to no avail. Information Chambers had given to Berle in 1939 was not welcomed within the administration; it was warned that Hiss was a security risk, but took no action. Berle did not inform the State Department's security office.[57] He did not provide the information about Chambers's meeting to the FBI until June 1943.[58] Official apathy prevailed.[59] Ambassador to France William C. Bullitt also had reported in 1939 to Hornbeck at the State Department that French premier Edouard Daladier warned him "about two brothers named Hiss" who were Soviet agents inside the State Department. Bullitt said Daladier attributed his information to French counterintelligence sources. Reportedly, President Roosevelt also dismissed Bullitt's concern about Hiss.[60] Isaac Don Levine claimed that FDR "brushed off" warnings of Hiss as a security risk from Bullitt and Berle, as well as from labor leader David Dubinsky and New York journalist Walter Winchell.[61]

According to FBI files, Chambers told the FBI in 1942, and in two other FBI interviews, in 1945 and 1946, that Hiss was a member of the Communist Party.[62] However, Sam Tanenhaus writes, "Chambers told the FBI he had never 'participated in a Soviet espionage ring or any branch of Soviet intelligence.' He also claimed to have no 'documentary or other proof' of espionage performed by underground Communists in Washington. He was to pay dearly for these lies."[63] During the Hiss trials, the defense tried to imply that these lies indicated that Chambers's entire testimony also was false.

Raymond Murphy, a State Department security official, questioned Chambers about Hiss on March 20, 1945, at Chambers's farm in Westminster, Maryland. During these interviews with authorities, Chambers did not reveal—or in some cases he denied—that the Communists he had identified were involved in espionage. When Murphy visited Chambers a second time, in August 1946, Chambers continued to insist that Hiss's underground unit "was not a spy ring."[64] Chambers obviously felt a strong need to protect Hiss and the others, including himself, from charges of illegal and criminal activities.

By 1946, so well-known were the Hiss activities and sympathies that the *Christian Science Monitor* could write, "More than one Congressman, whenever the subject of leftist activity in the State Department is mentioned, pulled out a list of suspects that was invariably headed by Mr. Hiss."[65] The investigation by State internal security was completed in November 1946. And as Secretary of State Byrnes was easing Hiss out, two weeks later, Hiss informed John Foster Dulles he was available for the job he had been offered at the Carnegie Endowment for International Peace.[66] Byrnes later would decline to testify as a character witness for Hiss.[67]

Hiss tried to justify leaving the State Department by saying that because of the emergence of the Cold War, policies toward the United Nations would no longer be rewarding. So at the end of the year he accepted the offer (an offer first received in January 1946 from Dulles) to become the president of the Carnegie Endowment. The chairman of its board of trustees, John Foster Dulles, initially proposed Hiss's selection as president.[68] Hiss pondered whether to accept the offer during the whole of 1946. In reality, Hiss was being eased out of the State Department. Hiss remained director of OSPA until he resigned on December 10, the day after the endowment trustees elected him as president. He remained at State clearing up his desk until January 15, 1947. According to Weinstein, at no time did Hiss inform the trustees at Carnegie about the charges of Communist ties, his March discussions with Byrnes, or his FBI interview.[69] Hiss's salary increase was substantial; he was earning $9,000 a year at State and the Carnegie salary was $15,000–$17,000 a year.[70]

Hiss and his family moved to New York City and Hiss assumed his duties as president of the Carnegie Endowment on February 1, 1947. He sold his house on 3210 P Street NW (the only one he ever had bought)[71] and rented a small third-floor, two-bedroom walk-up apartment in Greenwich Village at 22 East Eighth Street. On his appointment as president of the Carnegie Endowment, congratulatory letters to Hiss came pouring in from academia, law offices, banks, high-level government officials (an especially long letter from Dean Rusk), and former colleagues. (One of these was Laurence Duggan, now director of the Institute of International Education. Hiss's response to Duggan was that he looked forward to working together again.[72])

But the brewing scandal of possible complicity in Communist activities followed Alger Hiss to New York. On June 2, 1947, Hiss was interviewed by the FBI about membership in Communist organizations, including the International Juridical Association, and his relationship with various individuals known to be Communists, including Whittaker Chambers. Hiss denied any Communist affiliations and signed an affidavit to that effect. He was careful not to categorically deny he knew Chambers. He would qualify his response by saying "he did not know a man by that name," which was true; he knew Chambers only as "Karl." A federal grand jury in New York, which had been convened from April 1947 to December 1948 to investigate Communist infiltration in the U.S. government, subpoenaed Hiss to appear on March 16, 1948. Hiss was called before the grand jury in the Southern District of New York and denied yet again the charges of being a Communist. "Lacking concrete evidence, the Grand Jury declined to act at this time."[73]

The same lack of concern over Hiss and general apathy toward Communist subversion carried over into the Truman administration, which dismissed Republican charges of Communist influence as partisan politics. Truman thought the attacks against Hiss were really against him and politically motivated. And some no doubt were motivated by partisan politics, but not all. Truman claimed the

Hiss charges were a "red herring." This attitude started to change in March 1947, when Truman issued Executive Order 9835, establishing a loyalty program to clean up Communist influence in the U.S. government. The order also called for the attorney general to compile a list of organizations deemed subversive.[74] Then the government prosecuted Hiss and the Rosenbergs. Even Walter Reuther, a socialist, purged the Communists from the CIO.[75]

The refusal to believe Hiss's guilt went beyond partisan politics. Tennent "Pete" Bagley, a former CIA chief of Soviet bloc counterintelligence, in his book *Spy Wars*, drew an analogy between Alger Hiss and Kim Philby, the British spy, where the same blindness was at work. Bagley stated that MI6 refused to believe that Philby was a spy, and it took the flight of Maclean and Guy Burgess eight years after the first suspicions to halt Philby's way up to the top of MI6. Even then they kept him on. He was finally dropped for errors of judgment, not treason. Bagley noted that Philby was even rehired by MI6, who set him up as a journalist in Beirut. Many of his colleagues did not believe he was a Soviet agent—the Soviets could not penetrate their ranks! Bagley wrote that "their brains filtered out perceptions they did not desire." He exclaimed that "the veil was finally lifted from their eyes when Philby surfaced in Moscow." Bagley observed that "Alger Hiss was another beneficiary of such willful neglect of the obvious."[76]

The penetration into the U.S. government achieved by Moscow was being realized slowly. Soviet intelligence had reached close to the heart of the U.S. government with Harry Dexter White, assistant secretary of the Treasury, and Alger Hiss, director of the Office of Special Political Affairs at the State Department. They both did not just steal documents for Soviet intelligence; they also influenced foreign policy to serve the interests of Moscow. The damage done was not only at specific times, such as Yalta and the Morgenthau plan for the industrial destruction of Germany (which was credited to Harry Dexter White), but also on many of the day-to-day issues.[77] Furthermore, it was of great value to the

Soviets that they were able to use the Hiss documents to break the State Department codes and tap into American diplomatic traffic. Sumner Welles, undersecretary of State (1937–43), testified that the documents Hiss gave to Chambers were critical to U.S. security and were particularly valuable to Moscow's effort to break U.S. diplomatic codes.[78]

The activities of Alger Hiss and Harry Dexter White also had longer-term effects. Hiss was a key player in the establishment of the United Nations. White drafted the concepts for postwar financial stabilization. His idea of a new international financial order was realized in July 1944 at the UN Monetary and Financial Conference, also known as the Bretton Woods Conference, with the creation of the International Monetary Fund and parts of the World Bank. Without going into the merits or deficiencies of the UN and the IMF and the World Bank, the fact of the matter is that two men committed to Communism, two men who turned over U.S. government secrets to the Soviet Union, and two men whose internationalist goals transcended their national loyalties, Hiss and White, laid the foundations for the political and economic global organizations still in operation today. The outcome of Moscow's influence operations in this instance was a long-lasting triumph. Perhaps that explains Hiss's serenity for a half a century. He believed he had won.

IX.

YALTA

FDR: Russia Will Become a Constructive
Force in World Affairs

O N AUGUST 14, 1941, Roosevelt and Churchill agreed to
the "Atlantic Charter," a statement explicitly affirming
that "no territorial changes" would take place without
the "freely expressed wishes of the people concerned" and that
sovereign rights and self-government would be restored to all
countries following the war. Decisions about borders should await
the end of the war. It took only a few months for realpolitik to
trump the idealism of the Atlantic Charter. In December 1941,
according to British foreign secretary Anthony Eden, during a
trip to Moscow Stalin told Eden that he wanted eastern Poland.
As Eden noted in his memoirs, this was a breach of the Atlantic
Charter as well as the British commitment to support Poland.[1]
Moscow also conveyed to Eden its demands for the three Baltic
states.[2]

In early 1942, after discussions about the USSR and the Polish
question, Roosevelt and Churchill essentially agreed the Atlantic
Charter was not to apply to Poland. They thought that Russia, now
an ally, should not be denied the frontiers she occupied in 1939–41
during the Nazi-Soviet Pact. Yet earlier, Roosevelt was giving

General Sikorski, prime minister of the Polish government-in-exile in London, assurances that were reflected in the Atlantic Charter. Months later, Roosevelt and Churchill decided to cede almost half of Poland to the Soviet Union without the consent of or consultation with the Polish government. Churchill did forewarn Sikorski that while Poland must be independent, her eastern frontier would have to be revised in Russia's favor, but she would be compensated in the west with former German territory.[3] This dialogue and decision concerning Poland occurred before the Yalta Conference even took place.

At the Tehran Conference (November 29–December 1, 1943), which set the stage for Yalta, Stalin was able to obtain major concessions. At a private meeting between Roosevelt and Stalin at Tehran on the last day of the conference, the fate of the Polish frontier was sealed. Notably, the minutes of the meeting showed Roosevelt's concern over domestic U.S. elections in 1944 and how six million Polish-Americans in the United States would respond, and that he did not want to lose their votes.[4] This domestic concern of course had no effect on Stalin. A second meeting on Poland was held a few hours later, and included the British (Churchill and Eden, among others) and an addition to the U.S. delegation, Harry Hopkins. U.S. secretary of state Edward Stettinius said that he and Alger Hiss worked together to assist Roosevelt in the formulation of his views on the Polish eastern frontier and to assist in any possible future constitutional issues or legal problems that might arise with the U.S. Senate.[5]

A Stalin victory at Tehran, which would be confirmed at Yalta, was the official recognition by the Western Allies of the Curzon Line as Poland's future eastern border. Also at Tehran, a firm promise was given to Stalin that a second front would be opened in France by May 1, 1944. Stalin also won recognition of his claim to Koenigsberg, which historically never had belonged to Russia. Roosevelt also won a victory—Stalin's agreement to declare war on Japan no later than three months after the end of the war in

Europe. Therefore, according to some historians, by the time the leaders met at Yalta, there wasn't much room to maneuver.[6]

On the other hand, historian S. M. Plokhy, in his recent book, *Yalta: The Price of Peace,* implies that during the three-day U.S.-British layover at Malta, prior to Roosevelt and Churchill arriving at Yalta, there was still room to maneuver. Plokhy wrote that Roosevelt avoided any discussion with the British prime minister, who wanted to use the occasion of the Malta stopover to discuss a common strategy for the upcoming Yalta Conference. However, Roosevelt purposely arranged his schedule to leave no time for substantive talks with Churchill. Roosevelt did not want to be committed to a common agreement with the British; he wanted to be free to negotiate as he saw fit.[7]

U.S. president Roosevelt, British prime minister Churchill, and Soviet marshal Stalin—the so-called "Big Three"—finally met at Yalta in the Crimea from February 4 to 11, 1945, to coordinate military strategy to defeat Hitler, redraw the map of Europe, and continue with plans to establish the United Nations. According to two Soviet scholars, Mikhail Heller and Aleksandr M. Nekrich, by the end of the conference "the United States and Great Britain gave de facto recognition at Yalta to the formation of the Soviet Empire."[8] This may not have been the intended goal but it was in fact the outcome. There were a series of circumstances that caused this to happen.

The first and most important cause was Roosevelt's preconceived notion that he could trust Stalin, which turned out to be wrong. He went into the February conference with that mind-set, that preconception. This misreading of Stalin was remarkable, given that Stalin had been Hitler's ally from 1939 to 1941 and switched sides only when the Germans invaded the Soviet Union and he then needed Western support to survive the Wehrmacht onslaught. Moreover, Stalin kept control of the territory that the Soviet Union had acquired in the secret protocols of the 1939 Nazi-Soviet Pact (the Molotov-Ribbentrop Pact).

Following the German invasion of Poland on September 1, 1939, and the Soviet Red Army invasion of Poland days later from the east, the Nazis and Russians divided Europe into what became zones of occupation. Russia's share included eastern Poland; Bessarabia (incorporated into the Moldavian SSR), which Romania had appropriated in 1918; northern Bukovina (transferred to the Ukrainian SSR), which had never belonged to Russia and was not part of the secret deal in the 1939 pact;[9] and finally, the three Baltic states (Estonia, Latvia, and Lithuania), whose incorporation into the USSR was a unilateral Soviet action. One state in the Soviet sphere of influence remained independent—Finland. Its resistance led to the Winter War of 1939–40, from which Finland emerged with reduced territory but still sovereign.[10]

In the United States during the war years, domestic political views shifted about Russia and in general were optimistic. After all, it was said, Russia was now an ally in the war (nearing its end but still being waged during Yalta) and was helping the United States defeat Nazi Germany at such great cost to itself. Former undersecretary of state Sumner Welles argued that the chances of a harmonious postwar era were good for the two powers that would emerge from the war, the United States and the USSR. He stated that "the maintenance of world peace and the progress of humanity" is going to depend on the two countries working together in a "positive and constructive" manner.[11] Roosevelt set the tone at Yalta for this hopeful view by suggesting that if the Allies were patient and understanding, the Soviet Union would take part in the new world organization (the United Nations) and become a constructive force in world affairs.[12] This assessment was wrong.

The second major determinant to the successful outcome for the Soviet Union at Yalta was the military reality on the ground. Several months before the Yalta Conference, the Soviet Union essentially already controlled the fate of most of eastern and central Europe and the Balkans. "The presence of 6.5 million Soviet soldiers" in those areas reinforced Soviet claims at Yalta. "By the end of January 1945, one week before the Yalta Conference, Soviet forces had reached the Oder-Neisse line, were approaching Frankfurt-am Oder and Küstrin (Kostrzyn), and had taken Schneidemuhl (Pita). The Red Army was only 65 kilometers from Berlin."[13] This was the territorial reality, and both Roosevelt and Churchill understood it and accepted it.

Geography was the third major factor that influenced the results at the Yalta Conference, which Churchill had designated Operation Argonaut. Churchill "categorically" opposed Stalin's proposal to hold the conference in the Crimea, because he feared that Stalin would gain "a great advantage" from being on his home turf.[14] At Roosevelt's insistence, Churchill reluctantly agreed to accept Stalin's plan to meet at Yalta. The location of the conference was not favorable to the West but Stalin refused to leave his own territory. Roosevelt, sick and dying, traveled six thousand miles; after a transatlantic voyage on the U.S.S. *Quincy* and the flight from Malta to Sevastopol, the American delegation still had to undertake a rough six-hour jeep ride up and down the mountainside to Yalta. The physical strain of the trip on Roosevelt is evident in the photographs taken of him at Yalta. It should be noted that at the Tehran Conference the year before, in December 1943, where concessions to Stalin were made, Roosevelt was not sick.

Roosevelt, along with the American delegation, stayed at Livadia Palace, the czar's former summer residence. Churchill and the British delegation headquartered at Vorontsov Palace, several miles away. Stalin and the Russian delegation resided at Koreis Villa, an estate once belonging to Prince Yusupov, located between U.S. and British headquarters.[15] The "Big Three" meetings and plenary sessions took place at Livadia Palace. A vast amount of damage had been done to these palaces; the German army had occupied Yalta and when the Soviets recaptured it in April 1944 the palaces required a great deal of restoration—quickly, before the conference was to begin in February. Because the meeting was on Russian territory, some historians have argued that "Stalin was in complete psychological control of the situation." With "his political skills, and his military in control, it was his conference." [16]

If all that were not enough, a fourth aspect of Stalin's advantage, and probably one of the most decisive ones, was the intelligence he received from his espionage networks. Foreknowledge of the U.S. and British negotiating positions greatly enhanced Stalin's ability to plan and adjust his strategies and tactics. While many, including Alger Hiss, have praised Stalin's negotiating skills at Yalta, and while Stalin may indeed have had good negotiating abilities, he also was able to rely on the vast amount of intelligence he was receiving about the American and British negotiating positions. For example, a document obtained by the KGB *rezidentura* (station) in London "gave Stalin a complete account of Churchill's intentions" and "spelled out the British positions on all major issues, from the partition of Germany, to Poland, as well as the voting formula to be adopted in the UN Security Council and the proposed membership of Soviet republics in the United Nations." [17]

Donald Maclean and Guy Burgess, two of the Cambridge 5, were both officials in the British Foreign Office and supplied hundreds of classified documents to Soviet intelligence on military and political secrets impacting the conference. In 1944 Maclean was posted to the British Embassy in Washington, D.C., and had access to sensitive documents that he turned over to Soviet intelligence. Nearly a dozen Venona messages included the extent of intelligence that Maclean had provided to the KGB. He passed information regarding the closing phases of the war, to include a summary of discussions between Roosevelt and Churchill in Quebec City in 1944, and other secret correspondence between Roosevelt and Churchill on issues related to postwar strategies and even on disagreements between the two allies. [18] Having this intelligence in advance gave Stalin an immeasurable advantage to achieve his objectives.

According to KGB defector Pavel Sudoplatov, a Soviet intelligence official who was appointed chief of the special team set up in preparation of Yalta, Soviet spies provided intelligence to Stalin and Molotov that allowed Stalin to realize the Allies did not have a comprehensive or joint plan for postwar Europe, and that the United States was ready to compromise.[19] Moreover, Stalin had his intelligence services prepare psychological profiles of each member of the American delegation.[20] In addition to the advanced intelligence Stalin received, the U.S. and British residences at Yalta, according to KGB defector Oleg Gordievsky, were "comprehensively bugged"[21] and thus contributed to Stalin's information on U.S. and British internal discussions each day. KGB defector Ilya Dzhirkvelov, who had been part of a KGB security detail at the Yalta Conference, claimed that the telephone cables also were "bugged."[22] Years later, Dzhirkvelov and a senior Department of Defense intelligence official met privately in the United Kingdom in the mid-1980s to discuss the history of the KGB. Dzhirkvelov recounted how, as a member of the State Security detail assigned to the Yalta Conference, he had been privy to the security arrangements for a secret award ceremony for Alger Hiss in Moscow after the Yalta meetings.[23]

At Yalta Stalin had in his midst, embedded in the Western delegations, some Soviet sympathizers (that is, New Deal internationalists who did not believe the USSR was a threat to the United States but rather a future partner). Top advisors in the Roosevelt administration "were so partial to the Stalin regime that they did not have to be recruited."[24] Moreover, there was present at Yalta at least one recruited Soviet intelligence asset—Alger Hiss—who most likely made the negotiating positions of the United States available to Stalin for each of the plenary sessions. He could have provided insights into U.S. intentions and changing positions, probably on a daily basis, to the GRU, whose presence at Yalta was known.[25]

Roosevelt had vetoed James Dunn, chief of the European Division, who was on the list of State Department personnel for inclusion in the U.S. delegation to Yalta, because of Dunn's open opposition to his liberalism and pro-Russian policies.[26] According to Hiss, Stettinius proposed him (Hiss) for Yalta because of his work on the UN charter, which included his service as secretary of the Dumbarton Oaks meetings.[27] However, it was the president, according to Stettinius, who tapped Alger Hiss to go to Yalta. Stettinius told Harry Hopkins that the purpose of his January 2 meeting with the president was to "bring with him people who will be involved in the forthcoming conferences." The president, Stettinius explained, "did not want to have anyone accompany him in an advisory capacity, but he (FDR) felt Messrs. Isaiah Bowman [President of Johns Hopkins University and an expert on international organizations] and Alger Hiss ought to go."[28]

It is unclear why, in January 1945, Alger Hiss, not yet a senior staffer and who never dealt directly with the president, was approved by Roosevelt to go to Yalta, despite warnings that FDR had allegedly received as far back as 1939 about Alger Hiss being a potential security risk. Who would have suggested that choice to Roosevelt? Roosevelt approved Hiss to be a chief assistant at Yalta and secretary-general at the founding conference of the United Nations, to be held in San Francisco. Roosevelt either did not take security concerns seriously or didn't receive them. It is at least plausible to assume that Lauchlin Currie, a White House staffer, identified as a Soviet asset in the Venona cables,[29] may have intercepted Berle's memo claiming Hiss was a Soviet agent. Stettinius, for his part, claimed that he "never heard of any questioning of Mr. Hiss's loyalty from anyone inside or outside the State Department or from the FBI during my time of service in the Department."[30]

Prior to the Yalta Conference, the State Department prepared, and Hiss had access to, a series of "black books"—the position papers for Roosevelt on U.S. strategy involving issues to be discussed at Yalta. Hiss knew the U.S. positions on unresolved issues such as the future of Poland, the USSR entry into the war against Japan, and the role of France in the occupation of Germany.[31] Even before Yalta, Secretary of State Stettinius and his staff (Hiss, Director of

European Affairs H. Freeman Matthews, and Wilder Foote) had lengthy discussions at stops in Marrakech and later Naples, before they arrived at Malta, on such key issues as the Polish question, the treatment of Germany, the political and economic situation in Italy, and China.[32]

Contrary to conventional wisdom that Hiss was a mere note taker or concerned only with UN issues at Yalta, he played a major role in all nonmilitary, substantive issues at the conference. Stettinius's private papers reveal that he relied heavily on Hiss for his expertise on a variety of issues. Stettinius's diaries and private papers also show Hiss during meetings authoritatively weighing in on the "United States" or "State Department" position.[33] Hiss's involvement at Yalta went well beyond his portfolio on the UN; Hiss was participating in and central to all the relevant substantive issues. In fact, only days after Hiss was selected to go to Yalta, according to the official Yalta compilation provided by the State Department, at a January 10 staff meeting Stettinius stated that "all memoranda for the President to take to the meeting of the Big Three" should be "in the hands of Mr. Alger Hiss not later than January 15."[34] Moreover, Stettinius stated the memoranda should not only be background but contain policy guidance as well.[35]

State Department historian Bryton Barron, who initially was in charge of compiling the Yalta papers, stated that an effort to minimize Hiss's role at Yalta was traceable to partisan politics and old loyalties within the department. Barron revealed that the papers Hiss had in his possession included documents that covered issues far beyond the UN. For example, they included papers on the Soviet proposal on German reparations and the U.S. position paper on the status of Poland.[36] And Barron drew attention to a February 10, 1945, memorandum in the Yalta papers on page 920, initialed by Stettinius and intended for Roosevelt. It recommended that the three powers encourage Kuomintang-Communist unity in the war effort against Japan. Across the document in Hiss's handwriting and initialed by him is the following notation: "Bohlen [Charles

Bohlen, a senior State Department official who was Roosevelt's interpreter at the Yalta Conference] says 'the President has already taken this up with Stalin with satisfactory results.'"[37] Barron stated that the State Department made it difficult to appreciate Hiss's full involvement at Yalta because the voluminous account of the Yalta Conference in *Foreign Relations of the United States* has a misleading index with respect to Alger Hiss and "fails to include some of the most important references to his activities."[38]

Hiss worked with Stettinius on the issue of Poland's new boundaries. In his diaries, Stettinius maintained that at a pre-Yalta meeting on February 1, with the Americans and British (including Prime Minister Anthony Eden), Hiss—not the secretary of state— raised the question of China, stressing the importance the United States placed on support for an agreement between the Comintern and the Chinese "Congress" in order to further the war effort and prevent civil strife.[39] On the morning of February 4, Alger Hiss—at the time a midlevel State Department official—was included at the meeting with Roosevelt, Stettinius, Averell Harriman (U.S. ambassador to the USSR), Charles Bohlen, and State's expert on European affairs, Matthews, to review the U.S. proposals for the conference agenda.[40] At another subsequent contentious plenary meeting over a trusteeship for French Indochina, there was a short intermission, during which Stettinius asked Hiss to do a quick summary of the State Department's memorandum on the trustee-ship issue. Stettinius used the Hiss summary to resolve the issue when the meeting resumed. Hiss was obviously well-informed on all the issues raised at Yalta and was able to provide timely input.[41]

During the Yalta Conference, Hiss also worked on plans for the future United Nations. He was deeply involved in drafting the language for such issues as veto power for members of the Security Council.[42] He also had an added task of note taking at the plenary sessions.[43] In photographs of these sessions Hiss can be seen sitting almost directly behind Roosevelt. There was no single official record of the meetings, nor any stenotypist recording of what was said. Each delegation kept its own minutes. Charles Bohlen was the official note taker for the United States and also its interpreter. Each of the three countries had records of the meetings that varied in their descriptions, although the language of the final protocol was identical. Hiss, who was still an active Soviet asset in 1945, in his role as advisor to Secretary of State Stettinius at Yalta, attended not only plenary sessions but also the foreign ministers' meetings. After these sessions and the dinners following them, Stettinius met with Bohlen, Matthews, Hiss, and Foote to confer on the sessions' topics. The group also met with Roosevelt the morning before the first session to review U.S. proposals for the conference agenda.[44] In short, as previously noted, Hiss was an integral part of all the non-military, substantive issues discussed at Yalta.

Hiss's likely contact at Yalta would have been General Major Mikhail Milshtein (cover name "Milsky"), a GRU officer who served undercover as Soviet vice consul in New York from 1935 to 1938 and may have been one of Hiss's control officers at that time. General Milshtein stated in his memoir that he had been in New York for four years, until 1938, when he returned to the USSR.[45] In the spring of 1944, his assignment, he wrote, was to obtain information about: What stand would the United States take after the war? What would the U.S. policy be toward the Soviet Union? What would happen to the U.S. armies after victory over Nazi Germany and its satellites (in Eastern Europe)?[46] Milshtein was English-speaking, and dressed in civilian clothes undercover as a military advisor to the Soviet delegation at Yalta. At the time he was, in fact, head of the GRU's first directorate, in charge of overseas espionage.

In their book *Sacred Secrets,* the Schecters wrote that based on their confidential anonymous sources of retired GRU officers and their relatives, Hiss met regularly at Yalta with Milshtein.[47] Svetlana Chervonnaya, a Soviet commentator, interviewed Milshtein before he died in 1992. Chervonnaya and author Kai Bird confirmed that Milshtein not only had been at Yalta but had been in contact with a high-level source during the conference (who they thought was another member in the U.S. delegation, Wilder Foote—not Hiss).[48] The oral testimonies revealed by the Schecters have not been corroborated by documentary evidence, since GRU files, unlike some KGB files, have never been opened. Nonetheless, given Milshtein's own testimony that he was involved in collecting intelligence relevant to Yalta, that he was a GRU officer, that he was at Yalta, that he reportedly was in contact with an asset during the conference, and that Hiss was a GRU source who was present at Yalta, it is at least plausible that Milshtein was Hiss's contact there.

In his *Recollections of a Life,* written four decades after Yalta, Hiss reflected on his experience at the conference. He said that after forty years what stood out—"strikingly"—were the "surprising geniality as host and the conciliatory attitude as negotiator of Joseph Stalin, a man we know to have been a vicious dictator."[49] He observed that Stalin was short and stocky and usually wore a freshly laundered khaki military tunic with no medals. Stalin, he wrote, reflected "pride and had a natural air of authority." By contrast, Hiss wrote, Churchill was "stooped and paunchy in rumpled garb." Yet he had "superb eloquence." For Hiss, however, Roosevelt had the greatest presence: grace, charm, serenity, his posture of "regal composure." Hiss commented, "He radiated goodwill, purpose, leadership, and personal magnetism." Hiss found Harry Hopkins, Roosevelt's closest advisor, equally impressive. At Yalta, Hopkins took part in decisions of policy; "his was the primary voice of conciliation and patient negotiation."[50]

Hiss stated in his memoir that Stalin was calm and restrained, courteous and soft-spoken. Yet he reacted quickly to what he considered weakness or inconsistency on the West's part. He was a skilled negotiator. Hiss then observed that Stalin killed and tortured millions of his fellow citizens; he conducted a rule of terror and would not allow any dissent. Hiss said the "deep contradiction between those abominations and his rational demeanor at the Conference puzzled and fascinated us." Stalin, he felt, was an enigma.[51] Hiss pointed to Stalin's "flexibility and agreeableness" at Yalta. He wrote that that was not Stalin's mood at Tehran and Potsdam.[52] Preoccupied with his reflections on Stalin, Hiss continued, "We knew of his many crimes against his people" and that "he was like a tyrant out of antiquity." But he also had skill as a negotiator and success as a war leader. "The personal characteristics he displayed at Yalta were at odds with his image as a dictator: he was calm; humorous; considerate and well-mannered and genuinely conciliatory, abandoning his position at times with grace."[53] For example, Hiss noted, Stalin accepted with reluctance French participation in the control of occupied Germany, which he had vigorously opposed.[54] Hiss maintained that Stalin cut an impressive figure at Yalta.

At the end of Yalta, Hiss said, "I believed there was a real possibility of a 'correct' relationship between us and the Russians." Unfortunately, Hiss continued, Roosevelt died and then "after years of brinkmanship and confrontation, Kennedy and Nixon were able to bring off their policies of peaceful coexistence and détente."[55] It is interesting to note that Hiss gave credit to his nemesis, Richard Nixon, for policies that validated the hopes of Yalta that Hiss had harbored.

The role of Harry Hopkins in Roosevelt's administration, as the president's most trusted advisor, remains controversial after more than a half century. Hopkins advised Roosevelt on foreign policy in general, and specifically at Tehran and Yalta. According to KGB defector Colonel Oleg Gordievsky, the KGB regarded Hopkins as its agent.[56] Gordievsky said he later came to the conclusion, personally, that Harry Hopkins was an unwitting agent of influence for the Soviet Union.[57] Gordievsky claimed he was the first to reveal that Akhmerov was Stalin's personal representative to Harry Hopkins.[58] Iskhak Abdulovich Akhmerov joined the KGB in 1930 and transferred to the foreign intelligence arm of the KGB in 1932, serving in Turkey and China. In 1935 he entered the United States as an "illegal" and served until 1939. Akhmerov returned in 1942 and was the KGB "illegal" *rezident* in the United States during World War II.[59]

Over the decades, scholars and historians have disagreed over Hopkins's status. Many believed he was a Soviet agent; some claimed he was a fellow traveler; others thought of him as an agent of influence and unwitting source, or, to use (allegedly) Lenin's term for such sources, a "useful idiot." Others have agreed with Hopkins's own view: that he was an American patriot and not a Communist, though totally sympathetic to the Soviet Union. Hopkins's unqualified support for Russia during the war, the argument goes, could have had more to do with defeating the Nazis than a commitment to Communism. Never hiding his position, Hopkins said both in private and in public that Russia was the decisive factor in the war and must be supported. According to Gordievsky, Hopkins, unlike Roosevelt and the State Department, had concluded that the United States must come to terms with the fact that the Soviet Union would "without question . . . dominate Europe on the defeat of the Nazis" and that "Soviet-American friendship held the key to the postwar world." Thus Hopkins encouraged Roosevelt to establish a personal rapport with Stalin.[60]

Hopkins accurately assessed the future Soviet domination of Europe, and apparently had no problem with that development, in that he advised Roosevelt to accept the fact. Given this background of Hopkins's views and his influence with Roosevelt, the favorable results for Moscow at Yalta should have come as no surprise. One question that remains unanswered to this day about Hopkins is why he didn't communicate his positions, which he made public, with official Russian foreign ministry personnel. Hopkins had a back-channel contact with Akhmerov, the KGB "illegal."[61] The question remains: why was he not communicating with overt high-level officials in the Soviet Embassy in Washington, D.C.? He was contacting Akhmerov, who was not only a KGB officer but an "illegal" one at that—in the country under false documentation, and with no official ties to Moscow. Having a high-level official, such as presidential advisor Hopkins, be in contact with the Soviet "illegal" *rezident* in the United States was highly irregular and perhaps even unprecedented.

With regard to substantive issues, military matters and end-of-war strategy were discussed at Yalta's first plenary session. Then Stalin raised the German question, insisting the term *dismemberment* be inserted into the surrender instrument that already had been approved by the European Advisory Commission.[62] Next on the agenda was the issue of war reparations to be paid by the Germans. Stalin wanted the Germans to pay $20 billion, half of which would go to the Soviet Union. The British rejected Stalin's demands for exorbitant German reparations; they were too severe. Churchill pointed out that it was the extensive reparations after World War I that led to the rise of Hitler. Eventually the topic was abandoned and the representatives agreed to refer the matter to a reparations commission that would subsequently meet in Moscow.[63]

Churchill raised the issue of France, one of his most important concerns. He wanted France to have a share in the occupation of Germany. The United States agreed to help restore France as a major power. They had a difficult time convincing Stalin. "Although thoroughly contemptuous of France's contribution to victory, Stalin finally became amenable to Churchill's proposal."[64] He agreed that France would receive an occupation zone but not a seat in the Allied Control Council,[65] the military occupation governing body of the Allied Occupation Zones in Germany. The three members of the organization, based in Berlin-Schöneberg, were the United States, the United Kingdom, and the Soviet Union. France was later given a seat on the commission with a vote, but it had no duties.

Roosevelt became the first to raise the sensitive and crucial issue of Poland. (Poland was discussed in seven of the eight plenary sessions.[66]) Roosevelt said he generally favored accepting the Curzon Line as Poland's eastern boundary (as he already had agreed to at the Tehran Conference in December 1943), but that the Poles would like East Prussia and part of Germany. Roosevelt continued that "it would make it easier for me at home if the Soviet government could give something to Poland." He reminded all that there were 6–7 million Poles in the United States. He raised the issue of giving the Poles Lvov (he brought it up at the Tehran Conference as well). And he added that the oil lands in the southwest of Lvov might be given to them also. Roosevelt said, "I am not making a definite statement but I hope Marshal Stalin can make a gesture in this direction."[67] That opening line, in effect saying he was requesting but not insisting on concessions, was a gift to Stalin. Churchill was firm on one aspect of the Polish issue, saying that the British conceded Stalin's territorial demands (the Curzon Line) but he would insist on political guarantees to allow for a new provisional government to replace the unrepresentative, pro-Soviet Lublin government, and insist on a Russian pledge to hold free elections.[68]

Red Army troops had control of most of Poland; so Churchill's strategy was to give in on the territorial issues and eventually agree to the Curzon Line as Poland's future eastern border, and no longer insist on the return of Lvov to Poland, and recognize Stalin's claim to Koenigsberg[69]—but to emphasize the political issue. They discussed drawing the western frontier of Poland from the town of Stettin (which would be Polish) and then southward along the river Oder and the western Neisse.[70] Poland's western border was actually decided at the Potsdam Conference (July 17–August 2, 1945). All prewar German territory east of the line (23.8 percent of the former Weimar Republic lands, most of them from Prussia) went to Poland, and a large amount of its German population was expelled by force. Giving East Prussia to Poland meant the forced resettlement of six million Germans, but that was seen as compensation for lost territories to Russia on Poland's eastern border. Churchill claimed that the form of government, "a strong, free, and independent Poland, was much more important than particular territorial boundaries."[71] Roosevelt and Churchill extracted a promise by Stalin to hold free elections in Poland. Stalin never kept it.

Not surprisingly, on this main issue, the Polish question, the Soviet view was adopted: London Poles in exile in England would join the provisional Lublin (Communist-controlled) government, to form a national unity government. And the Soviets agreed to hold elections as soon as possible. However, it was not long before members of the non-Communist Polish leadership were purged, imprisoned, or killed.[72] In his 1957 book, *The New Class*, Yugoslav Communist Milovan Djilas revealed that "at an intimate party in 1945 Stalin said: 'In modern war, the victor will impose his system, which was not the case in past wars.'" Djilas pointed out that Stalin's statement about imposing the Soviet system (that is, on the countries of Eastern Europe) was made before the war was over, "at a time when love, hope, and trust were at their peak among the Allies."[73]

When reviewing Stalin's actions toward Poland for the five years leading up to Yalta, it is difficult to identify the basis for the Allies' hope. As Stalin told Eden in 1941, he wanted eastern Poland. Stalin viewed the Polish government-in-exile in London as an obstacle to redrawing Poland's borders. According to historian Plokhy, Russia's battlefield successes emboldened Moscow to "push" the Poland issue. Days after the Red Army success of the encirclement of the German Sixth Army at Stalingrad in November 1942, Stalin abolished thirty-six offices of the Polish Embassy in the USSR responsible for Polish citizens deported or evacuated to the Soviet interior. In January 1943, Moscow revoked a provision of its treaty with the London-exiled Polish government recognizing Polish citizenship of ethnic Poles in Soviet territory after September 1939. They now would be treated as Soviet citizens.[74] A battle of words continued between the London Poles and Moscow. On March 5, 1943, the Polish government-in-exile in London stated the Curzon Line was an armistice boundary, not a state border, which stance further exacerbated the situation with Moscow.

The next critical event, in April 1943, provided insight into inherent Soviet intentions toward Poland. The Germans discovered the bodies of more than 4,500 Polish officers buried in mass graves in Katyn Forest, near Smolensk, Russia—the liquidation by the Soviets of almost all the Polish officer corps taken prisoner in 1939 when the Soviet Union invaded eastern Poland. The total number of Polish prisoners of war killed was about 22,000, which represented the decapitation of Poland's elite. Beginning as early as September 1939 in eastern Poland, KGB squadrons rounded up the cadres of a national resistance—active and reserve officers, some fifteen thousand men, half in uniform the other half lawyers, doctors, teachers, professors, journalists, priests, and intellectuals who would have been a future problem for the Soviets, who had just absorbed about half of Poland in the division of the country under the Nazi-Soviet Pact. They were distributed among three Soviet concentration camps: Ostachow, Kozielsk, and Starobielsk. All those sent to Kozielsk—just under five thousand—were assassinated in April 1940 in the Katyn Forest, each with one shot in the back of the head. The fate of the other ten thousand Poles remains unknown to the West.[75]

The Polish government-in-exile in London insisted on an investigation of the Katyn massacre by the International Red Cross; the Nazi Germans agreed but the Russians did not. The Red Cross Commission, along with two other independent groups (Polish and German), investigated and concluded, based on forensic evidence, that the massacre occurred in April or May 1940, a date that ruled out Nazi responsibility—that would be after the signing of the 1939 Nazi-Soviet Pact and prior to the 1941 Nazi invasion. Stalin accused the London Polish government of collaborating with Nazi Germany and maintained that the Germans were responsible for the massacre after they invaded Poland.

It was not until 1990, under Mikhail Gorbachev, and later on the occasion of a visit by Boris Yeltsin to Warsaw in 1992, that the Russians finally fully acknowledged that Stalin's Politburo had sole responsibility for the 1940 massacre at Katyn and the cover-up of the tragedy.[76] On October 14, 1992, President Yeltsin made public the document containing the Soviet Communist Party Politburo's decision, signed by Stalin on March 5, 1940, ordering the shooting of 26,000 Poles interned in the USSR after the Soviet attack on Poland in September 1939.[77] More recently, in April 2010, Russia published on the Internet documents proving that Soviet secret police massacred Polish officers at Katyn Forest in 1940, a crime the USSR long attempted to cover up. Katyn "was a very dark page. . . . It is not just those abroad who allow history to be falsified. We ourselves have allowed history to be falsified," Russian president Dmitri Medvedev said in a May 7, 2010, interview with *Izvestiya*. Following this interview, on November 26, 2010, Russia's national parliament, the Duma, for the first time officially condemned the mass murder of Poles at Katyn and admitted that Stalin ordered this crime.[78]

In the summer of 1944, Stalin announced that he broke diplomatic relations with the Polish government in London and started a campaign to get the Western Allies to recognize the alternative pro-Soviet Polish government he had established in Moscow, the Polish Committee of National Liberation.[79] Roosevelt was "hopeful" the two Polish sides could form a single government, according to the British ambassador in Washington, Lord Halifax. In his January 6, 1945, meeting with Roosevelt, on the eve of Yalta, Lord Halifax said Roosevelt suggested that "all Poles must be brought to see that they could only exist by the good favor of Stalin."[80]

Stalin resumed negotiations with the London Poles, promising them support for their planned attack against the German occupation in Warsaw. The London Poles set off an insurrection in Warsaw led by the Home Army, wanting to defeat the Germans alone, but realized that they required military assistance from Stalin, which they were promised but did not receive. The result was the 1944 Warsaw uprising and massacre—in sixty-three days approximately 200,000 military and civilians were killed. Thousands of these were Poles in the underground resistance and clandestine military units.[81]

During the battle for Warsaw, Churchill suggested, to no avail, that the Allies help the Poles. After six weeks of German bombardment of Warsaw, the Soviet Red Army was sitting on the outskirts of the city. The uprising was crushed in October by the Germans. The Polish Communist forces under Soviet orders fought their way to the suburbs of Warsaw, but went no further. Soviet Red Army troops occupied the suburb of Praga, and also went no further. In his memoir Churchill described Soviet intentions: "They wished to have the non-Communist Poles [fighting in Warsaw] destroyed in full by the Germans, but also to keep alive the idea that they were going to their rescue."[82] The Soviets did not enter Warsaw until January 1945.

The events involving Poland that led up to the Yalta Conference, taken collectively and considered objectively, show clearly that going into Yalta the Allies must have known—or should have known—Stalin's motives and intentions toward Poland and that the Soviet position on Poland was nonnegotiable. It is difficult to understand how Roosevelt's trust in Stalin survived his acts of treachery with regard to Poland. This was a deep-seated delusion.

In recalling the events of Yalta in his memoir, Alger Hiss said his view on the Polish question was that Stalin resisted tenaciously— and successfully—the U.S. and British positions designed to liberalize the future Polish regime. Hiss said that the United States and Great Britain had no real bargaining power, however, since the Red Army occupied most of Poland. In short, Hiss's position was that the West did not surrender anything in Eastern Europe that the Red Army could not have taken. And the Allies, still at war, wanted to show solidarity. Hiss wrote, "We thought we had done as well as can be expected under these circumstances on the subject of Polish elections and the structure of the new government."[83] That is to say, nothing was actually achieved by the United States and Britain that supported a free Poland.

Roosevelt's two main goals at Yalta were to have Russia enter the war in the Pacific and to join the United Nations.[84] Stalin agreed to both. Therefore, from Roosevelt's perspective, Yalta was a win-win. For a promise to enter the war against Japan within two or three months after Germany surrendered, Roosevelt accepted at face value Stalin's false historical territorial claims. But for Roosevelt, ending the war in the Far East was critical. His military advisors predicted that without the Soviet Army's help, it would take another eighteen months after the end of war in Europe before Japan could be defeated, and they calculated it would cost one million American lives.[85] Former State Department historian Bryton Barron, in his book *Inside the State Department,* contested this view. He drew attention to a paper on page 2,916 of the 1951 congressional hearings regarding General MacArthur and the military situation in the Far East. The document, introduced into the record by Senator Bridges, dealt with the findings of a group of intelligence officers in early 1945 that the United States and the British could defeat Japan, and that therefore concessions to Russia were not necessary, nor was it advantageous to get Russian help.[86]

On the subject of the founding of the United Nations, Moscow had floated an incredible idea the previous year at the Dumbarton Oaks Conference. Soviet Ambassador to the United States Andrei Gromyko said the Soviet Union was to have sixteen seats in the UN—one for each Soviet republic, even though they were not sovereign countries. At Yalta, Stalin reduced the demand to three, in addition to Russia—the Ukraine, Byelorussia, and Lithuania; he then dropped it to two, eliminating Lithuania.[87] Roosevelt initially objected to giving Moscow any extra seats; Stettinius and Hiss at first also opposed.[88] Hiss circulated a memo on February 8, 1945, that provided arguments against inclusion of Soviet republics, on the basis that they were not sovereign states under international practice. It was Hiss who actually led the opposition in the American delegation to Stalin's proposal to give the USSR two additional seats in the UN General Assembly. Hiss's motivation to insist on no extra seats for the USSR remains unclear. It was certainly an anomaly. Perhaps it was a distraction, a feint from everything else that was compromised in Stalin's favor. For Stalin, whether he received two or three seats in some future organization arguably was not as critical to him as controlling eastern and central Europe.

Eventually, Moscow was successful; it was granted two extra votes, when the Ukraine and Byelorussia were allowed to join the UN as independent members. Stettinius maintained in his memoir on the Yalta Conference that Roosevelt told him Stalin felt his position in the Ukraine was "difficult and insecure," and that a vote for the Ukraine was "essential for Soviet unity." Stettinius continued that while Roosevelt strongly objected to sixteen votes, one for each Soviet republic, from the point of view of geography and population the Russian proposal for two extra votes, for the Ukraine and White Russia, "was not preposterous." Roosevelt claimed the real power would be in the Security Council, not the Assembly, and there everyone would have only one vote.[89] From Stalin's perspective, this was a Soviet concession, since Gromyko had demanded sixteen seats at Dumbarton Oaks. The actual concession was on the U.S. side, which lobbied hard for only one seat, since the Ukraine and Byelorussia in fact were not sovereign states. The opening date of the conference to draft the text of the United Nations charter was agreed on: April 25, 1945; the site, San Francisco.

Stalin's pattern of demands continued for the Far East. At the Tehran Conference, Roosevelt and Stalin had reached a secret agreement: in exchange for joining the war against Japan, the USSR would receive southern Sakhalin and the Kuril Islands. They also agreed to joint participation in a forty-year trusteeship over Korea. In addition to these Japanese holdings, Stalin was also seeking concessions at the expense of China, to include recognition of Soviet rights to the Chinese port of Dairen and to place Manchurian railroads under joint Chinese-Soviet administration.[90] China later protested that it was not informed of these decisions concerning its territory and that its sovereignty was infringed. The

United States and Great Britain agreed to recognize the autonomy of Outer Mongolia as well as an independent Mongolia. Subsequently, Stalin included in the agreement the restoration of Port Arthur, Manchuria, to its status as a Russian naval base prior to the 1904–1905 Russo-Japanese War. The agreements on Asia at Yalta were top secret and not part of the official public protocol of the conference.[91]

In his book on Yalta, historian Plokhy noted that the State Department was strongly opposed to the southern Kuril and Sakhalin islands being turned over to the USSR. Stalin knew about State's position from his spy networks. A copy of the State Department memo on the Kurils was found in the Russian archives after the collapse of the USSR. However, the State Department's memo never made it into the Yalta briefing books, so, according to Plokhy, there is no indication that Roosevelt was familiar with State's recommendations about these Japanese territories.[92] Roosevelt had given in not only on the Polish question but on territorial demands in the Far East.

For his part, Churchill rationalized that Stalin, having promised to expand the Lublin Communist government in Poland to include non-Communist Polish leaders and allow free elections, had thus made major concessions. And Churchill was successful on having France included as a major power. But for Stalin, success was far-reaching. The Soviet empire expanded to both the east and west, blocking the West from restricting Stalin's freedom of action in Poland and throughout Eastern Europe, and obtaining territory in Asia as well.[93]

In his book, *Recollections of a Life,* Hiss's assessment of Yalta was optimistic. In diplomatic talks, he wrote, the Allied leaders negotiated agreements on the occupation of Germany but disagreed on Poland, by far the most contentious issue at Yalta. Still, "conflicts were submerged because of the necessity for continued military unity" to end the war. In a series of rationalizations, Hiss stated "the fact was that it was the United States that had sought commitments on the part of the Russians; except for the Russian demand for reparations, all the requests were ours. And except for Poland, our requests were finally granted on our own terms. In agreeing to enter the war against Japan, Stalin asked for and was granted concessions—but the initiative was ours."[94] Hiss wrote that "it was we, not Stalin, who came bearing requests."[95] This is an amazing assessment. Stalin demanded German reparations, which were eventually accepted; he demanded the forced repatriation of Russians, including thousands of Cossacks repatriated against their will, which the United States and Great Britain felt obligated to honor;[96] he demanded that his entire position be accepted on Poland's borders and future government (it was, on both counts); he demanded three extra seats at the UN (he received two); and he demanded territory in the Far East (and was awarded it)—not to mention retention of the three Baltic nations and Bessarabia (Moldova), which were incorporated into the USSR as Soviet republics, and all of Eastern Europe and the Balkans as Soviet spheres of influence.

Roosevelt and Churchill obtained what they considered vital for their interests: agreement on a general policy regarding defeated Germany and its division into four sectors; recognition (only verbal on the Soviet side) of the dissemination of democratic principles in the liberated countries of Europe; approval of the UN; and Soviet agreement to enter the war against Japan. With regard to the latter, the United States dropped atomic bombs on the Japanese cities of Hiroshima on August 6 and Nagasaki on August 9, which effectively ended the war; on August 15, 1945, Japan surrendered. Between the dates of the two bombs being dropped, the Soviet Union entered the war—for about one week. It turned out to be a small price to pay for the territory and influence Stalin received in Asia.

Given the domestic political situation in the United States, pro-Soviet sentiment in the West, and the military situation on the ground, it is unlikely, according to some historians, that the United States and Great Britain could have achieved anything more.[97] In other words, Yalta was clearly a victory for Stalin. The USSR's European borders now stretched from the Baltic in the north to the Adriatic in the south and in the west to the Elbe and the Werra.

Roosevelt's reluctance to antagonize Moscow and wish to ensure Stalin's support was evident in all his actions. His tactics at Tehran and Yalta were meant to accommodate Stalin. A small but notable example of this deference was when OSS officers bought unidentified Soviet cryptographic documents from émigré Finnish cryptanalysts in late 1944, on the eve of the Yalta Conference. Secretary of State Stettinius wrote in a December 27, 1944, memorandum for the president that the papers would be returned to the Russians, and OSS chief William Donovan "promptly obeyed a White House order to return them to the Soviet Embassy."[98]

Shortly after Yalta, Churchill was concerned that Stalin was not honoring his commitment for free elections in Poland. Stalin had barred Western observers and was not following through on the issue of a national government of unity. Churchill wrote to Roosevelt several times; finally Roosevelt replied that he also had been watching with anxiety and concern the development of the Soviet attitude since Yalta.[99] Within weeks after Yalta, Stalin had failed to accept the principle of "free, unfettered elections" and had imprisoned sixteen leaders of the Polish Resistance.[100]

The first few postwar years brought a flurry of events. As the war in Europe was ending in May 1945, the Soviet Union quickly consolidated its control over Eastern Europe. The Red Army was influencing postwar elections by intimidating voters and changing the voting lists as they desired. Although non-Communist candidates could still gain some votes, most of the votes went to the Communists. Coalition governments that were formed immediately after the war were largely dominated by Communists, and key ministries, such as Defense, were always under Communist control.

Stalin started to expand his control beyond Eastern Europe. He began to encourage Communists to take an active part in the immediate postwar elections in Western Europe. In late 1946, the

French and Italian Communist parties were becoming the most powerful parties in their respective countries. In 1947, Moscow created the Cominform (replacing the Comintern, which had been dissolved in 1943) to consolidate the forces of international Communism and to "coordinate the efforts of the Communist parties in a struggle for power." The French Communist Party was attempting to gain power in 1947.[101] In February 1946 Stalin announced in a public speech a five-year arms buildup in anticipation of an inevitable military conflict with the West. On January 19, 1947, rigged elections in Poland gave the majority to a coalition under the control of the Communists.[102] In February 1947 the British foreign secretary, Labor Party member Ernest Bevin, advised Washington "privately" that Britain could no longer give much-needed financial and military aid to the Greek government, which was in danger of being overthrown by Communist guerrillas.[103] Greece had been liberated from German control by Anglo-American troops in 1944, but after the liberation, Communist guerrillas, receiving military aid from Yugoslavia and the USSR, threatened to overthrow the Greek government.

On March 12, 1947, the Truman Doctrine was announced; the essence of the doctrine was that "it must be the policy of the United States to support free peoples who are resisting attempted subjugation by armed minorities or by outside pressure." This was clearly an anti-Communist doctrine and in effect amounted to an American declaration of an end to the New Deal policy of accommodating the Soviet Union.[104] President Truman followed his speech with massive military and economic aid to Greece. The Communist guerrillas in Greece were defeated in 1948.[105] An attempted takeover of Greece, a Communist coup in Czechoslovakia in February 1948, and the beginning of the Berlin blockade in June finally confirmed Stalin's true intentions in Europe.

Western political leaders attempted to maintain Anglo-American-Russian cooperation after the war, but finally they could no longer ignore Stalin's policies of aggression. In response to Stalin's policies,

Churchill gave his Iron Curtain speech in Fulton, Missouri, on March 5, 1946, and U.S. diplomat George Kennan advised the State Department not to expect an era of peaceful coexistence with the Soviets.[106] In response to actions taken by Moscow, the United States launched the Marshall Plan; the Truman Doctrine; the North Atlantic Treaty Organization (whose creation was in large part the result of the threat from Soviet military action against Turkey and Iran[107]); and a nuclear buildup to counter Soviet expansion.[108] On September 22, 1949, Truman announced that the Soviet Union had exploded an atomic bomb.[109]

Asia also was at risk. General George Marshall was sent to mediate between Chiang and Mao. He reported China was "lost" to Communism.[110] In 1949, Mao's Communist forces defeated the Nationalist government in China. At the end of the war, following Japan's surrender, Korea, which had been ruled by Japan, was divided along the 38th parallel. United States troops occupied the south and Soviet troops the north. The failure to hold free elections intensified tensions on both sides, including cross-border raids. The situation escalated into the start of the Korean War when North Korean Communist forces invaded South Korea on June 25, 1950. The Cold War had clearly begun.

When Roosevelt returned from the Crimea to Washington, D.C., and gave his speech to Congress on Yalta and the UN, about securing a permanent peace, was this the consummate politician who knew better, trying to put the best face he could on the agreement? After Roosevelt got back to the White House, Berle apparently reviewed the Yalta agreements "with a scathing eye." Roosevelt said to Berle, "Adolf, I didn't say the result was good. I said it was the best I could do."[111] And his secretary of state, Stettinius, wrote that Roosevelt (and Churchill) "for the peace of the world" had to "make every effort to test the good faith of the Soviet Union."[112] This they both did, but the Soviet Union failed that test.

Alternate views existed. William C. Bullitt, a distinguished diplomat and America's first ambassador to the Soviet Union, tried to argue with Roosevelt about the nature of the Soviet Union. Roosevelt disputed him because the president had already learned about Russia from Harry Hopkins. Bullitt wrote in 1948: "At the close of a three-hour discussion of a memorandum setting forth my objections to his course, which the President had asked me to prepare, he said: 'Bill, I don't dispute your facts, they are accurate. I don't dispute the logic of your reasoning; I just have a hunch that Stalin is not that kind of a man. Harry [Hopkins] says he's not and that he doesn't want anything but security for his country, and I think that if I give him everything I possibly can and ask nothing from him in return, noblesse oblige, he won't try to annex anything and will work with me for a world of democracy and peace.' I reminded the President that when he talked of noblesse oblige he was not speaking of the Duke of Norfolk but of a Caucasian bandit whose only thought when he got something for nothing was that the other fellow was an ass, and that Stalin believed in the Communist creed which calls for conquest of the world for Communism."[113] However, Roosevelt's preconceived notion of Stalin blinded him to any alternative views.[114]

X.

FASCISM AND COMMUNISM

An Essential Congruity Existed Between the Two Ideologies

ALGER HISS WAS one of many individuals caught up in the emerging philosophy of the political left that swept across the twentieth century. During the 1930s, thousands of Americans embraced Communism; some, like Hiss, crossed a line and went further, by spying for the Soviet Union. For committed Communists like Hiss, Leninist ideology became their worldview. Hiss developed a single-minded attachment to an ideology that he committed espionage to support, an ideology that claimed to answer all questions of life, turning a blind eye to alternative arguments. Hiss believed capitalism to be dying and that the only viable alternative was a Communist political and economic order that would bring about equality and social justice, even if it meant, in the process, the murder of millions of people by Stalin's regime. He viewed Communism as the way to save the world in a time of crisis, and at the same time he was able to ignore the human cost experienced in the Soviet Union. Hiss believed it was the hope for a new world of peace and international collaboration. He was blind to the inhumanity of Communism; he saw only utopia.

One of the beliefs perpetrated by the "left" during the twentieth century was that Fascism was an ideology on the "right" of the political spectrum; that Fascism was the antithesis of socialism and Communism or any other ideologies on the "left"; that Fascism was a development out of capitalism, even though the essence of capitalism is the free market and Fascism certainly is not about free markets. This false belief has been used to justify support for socialism and Stalin's Russia, especially during the Hiss years of the 1930s and 1940s. In the 1930s, radical left-wing politics and Communism were given a certain amount of prominence and acceptability in the United States because of the Depression. Many Communists felt comfortable and at home in the Roosevelt administration because of the ideological overlap between the New Deal and Communism.[1] For many intellectuals, the Depression was a result of the collapse and failure of capitalism, and they turned to socialism to address that failure. The result was New Deal policies that were advanced to support the never-defined "public interest."

The second main reason for tolerance of the "left" during the Hiss era was the rise of Fascism. John Ehrman, a former CIA official, wrote that the CPUSA was respected by many American liberals because liberals and Communists "made common cause to promote unions and civil rights for black Americans." He claimed that "Moscow's prestige among liberals and intellectuals increased further when, unlike the Western democracies, it seemed to take a firm stand against the spread of Fascism."[2] Many on the left, in fact, felt this argument gave them "cover," especially when the United States was at war with Nazi Germany. As a result, during World War II progressives viewed Moscow's intentions as benign and advocated reaching an accommodation with the Soviet Union.[3] Perhaps this was one reason why Moscow and the "left" in the United States depicted Hitler as a "right-winger" and made Fascism seem to be a rival to Communism and socialism. The belief prevails to this day. Calling a political opponent a "fascist" has become the ultimate epithet weapon for the "left," a term synonymous with absolute evil and used for someone on the "right" of the political spectrum.

But Fascism is not an ideology of the "right." It arose out of the Marxian milieu. It emanates from the "left"—from Marxian revisionists, many of whom felt that Marx underrated nationalism, wrote A. James Gregor, professor of political science at the University of California, Berkeley. Fascism has its roots in Marxism; it is no accident that Hitler called his movement "National Socialism." "The first fascists were almost all Marxists—serious theorists who had long been identified with Italy's intelligentsia of the 'left.'" Mussolini himself had been a leader of the Italian Socialist Party and was an acknowledged leader among Marxist intellectuals. "It was Italy's intervention in the First World War, not right-wing versus left-wing dispositions, at first, that divided Italian Marxists."[4] The myth of Fascism as "right-wing" is embedded in the false notion, promoted by Communists, that Fascism is conservative, according to Gene Edward Veith Jr., professor at Concordia University Wisconsin. This notion obscures its true meaning. Veith states that "Marxism defines Fascism as its polar opposite. If Marxism is progressive, Fascism is conservative; if Marxism is left-wing, Fascism is right-wing; if Marxism champions the proletariat, Fascism champions the bourgeoisie; if Marxism is socialist, Fascism is capitalist."[5]

Of course these comparisons are fiction, Veith continues. While Communism and Fascism have been rival brands of socialism, it is their commonalities that have defined them. Both strongly opposed the bourgeoisie.[6] (The Nazis scorned bourgeois democracy as decadent.) Both attacked conservatives; both developed into mass movements; both favored a strong, authoritative, centralized government; both practiced a controlled economy and opposed free markets; both practiced strict control over their populations; both rejected the notion of individual liberty; both placed the state above the individual; both had dictatorial regimes that were extralegal and extraconstitutional; both had "leadership cults" surrounding their rulers; both practiced the pervasive use of propaganda, official censorship, and terror; and both committed massive crimes against humanity. In his gripping history, *Bloodlands: Europe Between Hitler and Stalin*, author Timothy Snyder, in discussing the mass murders each was responsible for, states: "Hitler and Stalin thus shared a certain politics of tyranny: they brought about catastrophes, blamed the enemy of their choice, and then used the death of millions to make the case that their policies were necessary or desirable. Each of them had a transformative utopia, a group to be blamed when its realization proved impossible, and then a policy of mass murder that could be proclaimed as a kind of ersatz victory."[7]

While Fascism and Communism were bitter and deadly ideological enemies at times, they were also contemporary regimes flying the socialist banner. Some differences were: Marxists claim that the history of civilizations can be explained only as the struggle of classes, while Fascism denies "class struggle" as the agent for social change; Fascism, unlike Communism, views the "State" as a spiritual and moral fact, and is opposed to Communism's antinationalism. "But their opposition to each other should not disguise their kinship as revolutionary socialist ideologies."[8] So, however different Marxist-Leninist systems were from Fascism, Gregor asserts that given their different histories, "the family traits are evident."[9] At their core, Fascist and Communist ideologies are both antidemocratic and opposed to individual freedom. They view individual rights as conditional, not inalienable.[10]

During the era of the Hiss case, the political lines were so thoroughly drawn in the United States that many on the "left" refused to see any treason in the service of the Soviet Union—especially with regard to Hiss and the Rosenbergs. Attempts at investigation into possible espionage were dismissed as part of the McCarthy witch hunt. McCarthy was responsible for some distortions and false accusations, and McCarthyism remained "a potent myth" in intellectual circles. Robert Conquest said: "In fact, it figures in many historical tests in universities as a major matter in American history—with accounts of the realities of Soviet penetration of U.S. agencies omitted."[11]

Conquest pointed to the common beliefs of Fascism and

Communism: "The overwhelming claim of the collective to the individual's allegiance thus emerged as the basis not only of Communism but also of Fascism and National Socialism. All three, once in power, subordinated the individual to the State, as representing the Community." It was argued that the individual best expressed himself as part of a mass experience.[12] National Socialist ideology was more than its crude racialism, Conquest maintained. "The central message . . . was the new identification of the German individual with the nation and state." Conquest wrote that the late Hugh Seton-Watson, dean of British Sovietology, noted that Nazis were "the fanatics . . . who rejected not only Christianity but also traditional morality as such." Seton-Watson added "moral nihilism is not only the central feature of National Socialism but also the common factor between it and Bolshevism."[13] People passed with ease from Communism to what were in theory its most virulent enemies, Fascism and National Socialism. Moreover, Conquest asserted that Hitler himself said Communists far more easily became Nazis than Social Democrats did. Conquest noted that Hitler also claimed that the "reds we had beaten up became our best supporters."[14]

According to J. B. Matthews, "In the early months of Hitler's triumph in Germany, the Communist International officially viewed Fascism as a sort of unwitting ally of Communism in their common goal of democracy's destruction." The Communist Party "made its position clear in its official publication, the *Communist International*. It declared: 'The establishment of an open fascist dictatorship, by destroying all the democratic illusions among the masses, and liberating them from the influence of social-democracy, accelerates the rate of Germany's development towards proletarian dictatorship.'" Matthews continued, "Nothing could be clearer than that. In August 1931, when the Nazis called for a plebiscite in Prussia with a view to overturning the social democratic government, the Communist International ordered the Communists of Germany to vote with the Nazis!"[15]

The German-Jewish political theorist Hannah Arendt's classic

1951 book, *The Origins of Totalitarianism,* traced the roots of Stalinist Communism and Nazism in both anti-Semitism and imperialism. She examined the two ideologies, Communism and Nazism, from the perspective of their political structures and maintained that both formed totalitarian political systems. An essential identity existed between the two phenomena, she argued. Arendt did not view the political spectrum in linear terms—left and right. Rather she conceived political systems in a circle, whereby totalitarian regimes such as Fascism and Communism met at the top of the circle. At the other end of the circle was their opposite—anarchy. As one traveled around the circle, one passed into constitutionalism, then to participatory democracies, then into anarchy, and continuing around the circle, into despotic regimes, dictatorships, and finally back to totalitarian systems at the top of the circle. If Arendt was presenting her ideas in linear fashion she would place both Fascism and Communism on the "left." With the signing of the Nazi-Soviet Pact of 1939, the convergent nature of these two totalitarian systems was revealed. Germany and Russia established totalitarian systems that were party-states beyond the law, ruled by the will of their leader, through ideology and terror.

The French historian François Furet, following Hannah Arendt and others, considered Communism and Fascism to be "totalitarian twins," since both had their origins in socialism and antiliberal convictions. Furet claimed that "the concept of 'totalitarianism' is not a recent invention of Cold War propagandists seeking to discredit the Soviet Union by identifying it with Nazi Germany, which had been banished from humanity by the Nuremberg trials."[16] Rather the term can be traced to the 1920s, when it was first propagated by Italian Fascism. Furet suggested that one reason why many failed to include the Soviet Union with Germany as a totalitarian state was that Germany was "militarily crushed by a coalition that ended up with the Soviet Union in the camp of the democracies, and German Nazism and Italian Fascism alone were cast in the role of enemy of liberty."[17]

Furet maintained that World War I gave rise to the events and trends that led to "three tyrannies"—Lenin, Mussolini, and Hitler. Lenin and Mussolini came from the same political family—that of revolutionary socialism.[18] In the pre-1914 socialist movement, Lenin and Mussolini shared the same hatred for reformists, the allies of the bourgeoisie. Both "made a radical distinction between the proletarian cause and bourgeois democracy."[19] But the war divided them; Lenin opposed the war by using class struggle, while Mussolini wanted to make war abroad to take advantage of its domestic effects.

To understand the relationship between Hitler and Stalin, Furet declared, "We may start with what has become an accepted observation:[20] Stalinized Bolshevism and National Socialism constitute the two examples of twentieth-century totalitarian regimes. Not only were they comparable, but they formed a political category of their own, which has become established since Hannah Arendt."[21] Both regimes destroyed the civil order in their countries by the submission of individuals to the ideology and the terror of the party-state.[22] Hitler wanted to destroy democracy not in the name of class but of race. For Hitler the role of history was the domination of the Aryan race, and for Bolsheviks it was the emancipation of the proletariat. Hitler said in 1934 that "There is more that binds us to Bolshevism than separates us from it." He said, "The petit bourgeois Social Democrat and the trade union boss will never make a National Socialist, but the Communist always will."[23] Fascism and Communism had a common goal: to crush liberal democracies. Both were opposed to social democrats. Both also embodied the rule of a party over the state, and the total domination of that party by one man—Hitler in one case, and Stalin in the other.

Furet captured the essence of the similarities between the two regimes: Hitler accomplished Lenin's totalitarian promise better than Stalin and Mussolini. The latter left the monarchy intact as well as the church and civil society. "It was in Nazi Germany that Bolshevism was perfected: there political power truly absorbed all spheres of existence, from the economy to religion, from technology to the soul. The irony, or tragedy, of history was that both totalitarian regimes, identical in their aim for absolute power over dehumanized beings, presented themselves as protection from the dangers presented" by each other.[24]

In his classic study, *The Road to Serfdom,* F. A. Hayek maintained that the intelligentsia was blinded to the conflict that existed between the basic principles of socialism and liberalism, while noting the "extraordinary similarity" in many respects of Fascism and Communism. He wrote that these tyrannies clashed frequently before 1933 (Germany) and before 1922 (Italy) because they "were competing for the same type of mind," and they were the outcome of the same tendencies. Hayek claimed that the connection between the two systems had become increasingly obvious. He then quoted several others with the same view. The writer Max Eastman, Lenin's old friend, said Stalinism was worse than Fascism; it was "superfascism." "Stalinism is socialism . . . a political accompaniment of nationalization and collectivization." The American correspondent W. H. Chamberlin said, "socialism . . . is the road to dictatorship." British writer F. A. Voigt claimed that "Marxism . . . in all essentials is Fascism and National Socialism." Finally, the Austrian writer Peter Drucker observed that Russia was traveling the same road toward a totalitarian society that Germany had been following.[25]

The Black Book of Communism: Crimes, Terror, Repression is a comprehensive attempt to catalogue and analyze the crimes of Communism against humanity for more than seventy years. The contributors include scholars and historians from various European countries (four from France, one from the Czech Republic, and one from Poland). This book offered the first attempt to determine the actual magnitude of what occurred in all Communist systems, by systematically detailing crimes, terror, and repression from 1917 to 1989. The authors concluded that Communism was "in truth a tragedy of planetary dimensions," with a grand total of victims variously estimated at between 85 million and 100 million. The Communist record offers the "most colossal case of political carnage in history." Class genocide resulted from Stalin's Gulag, Mao Tse-tung's Great Leap Forward and Cultural Revolution, and Pol Pot's Khmer Rouge. With regard to Nazism, an estimated 25 million were killed as a result of race genocide.[26] The authors take note that a dual perception of these two totalitarian systems exists. The status of Nazism as an "absolute evil" is entrenched, while the crimes of Communism have been marginalized over the years by many in the U.S. media and academia.

The Black Book observed that Hitler and Nazism are a constant presence in the media and television in the West, whereas Stalin and Communism are rarely discussed or seen in films. It added that there is no stigma attached to the status of ex-Communist, while past contact with Nazism, no matter how marginal, or remote, "confers an indelible stain."[27] Alain Besançon, French historian and sociologist, stated that murder is murder whatever the ideological motive; and this is undeniably true for the equally dead victims of both Nazism and Communism. Hannah Arendt echoed this absolute equivalence in *Origins of Totalitarianism*: "both systems massacred their victims not for what they *did* (such as resisting the regime) but for whom they *were*, whether Jews or kulaks."[28] But to some, there was a difference in the evil of the two ideologies: Nazism offered only "unabashed national egoism"[29] while Communism made a claim and a commitment to egalitarian goals and social justice, a claim that seduced millions of people. Its mass murder took place in the name of noble ideas, thus worsening its evilness.

The central thesis of *The Black Book* is that the history of Communism's criminal regimes that committed mass violence against their own people has been ignored or minimized for decades, from New Dealers in the 1930s, to apologists during the 1940s who held up Russia as a wartime ally, to the present. A celebrated comment on the crimes of the Soviet Union and the need to look the other way was made by Jean-Paul Sartre: "that one should keep silent about Soviet camps 'pour ne pas desesperer Billancout' (in order not to throw the auto workers of Billancout into despair). To which his onetime colleague, Albert Camus, long ago replied that the truth is the truth, and denying it mocks the causes both of humanity and of morality."[30]

Stéphane Courtois concluded in *The Black Book* that after a half century of debate, no matter what the facts and evidence are, "degrees of totalitarian evil will be measured as much in terms of present politics as in terms of past realities." So he suggested that there will always be a double standard as long as there is a "left" and "right." No matter how much the Communist failure and its mass murders are documented, there will always be reactions such as the following: "a Moscow correspondent for a major Western newspaper, after the fall of the USSR, could still salute the Russians with 'Thanks for having tried.'" Courtois also believed that any reporting highlighting the history of Communist criminality will be smeared as "anti-Communist rhetoric."[31] In this context, given this reaction on a systemic level, it comes as no surprise that on the level of one person—Alger Hiss—the same reaction by some had occurred: no matter what the facts and evidence, he could not be guilty; the charges were all merely anti-Communist rhetoric.

The voices denouncing Stalin's crimes had been slowly rising from the ranks of European scholars and historians. Milovan Djilas, a Yugoslav Communist dissident, stated in his book *Conversations with Stalin* that "every crime was possible to Stalin, for there was not one he had not committed. . . . to him will fall the glory of being the greatest criminal in history."[32] And similar condemnations came from Moscow, not only from dissidents, such as the Sakharovs and Solzhenitsyns, but from the Kremlin itself. Soviet party leader Nikita Khrushchev began the revelation process in 1956 with his secret speech selectively denouncing the crimes of Stalin against the party. In 1992, Russian president Yeltsin acknowledged, providing archival proof, the slaughter of thousands of Polish officers and civilians by the KGB in 1940 in the Katyn

Forest. Most unprecedented was the recent May 7, 2010, interview in *Izvestiya* with President Dmitri Medvedev of Russia, mentioned earlier, which was published two days before Russia marked the sixty-fifth anniversary of victory in World War II.

In one of the most damning assessments of the Soviet Union by a Russian leader, Medvedev said the Soviet state was a totalitarian regime that suppressed human rights. A Russian president, no less, spoke out against the crimes against humanity of both Stalin and the Soviet state. Medvedev said that "the Soviet Union was a very complex state and, frankly, the regime that emerged in the Soviet Union, *can only be described as totalitarian in nature.* Unfortunately, this was a regime that suppressed basic rights and freedoms, and not only those of its own people, some of whom, sadly, came home as victors after the war, only to be sent to labour camps, but also those of other peoples in the socialist countries, and this is something we cannot erase from history" (emphasis added).[33]

Medvedev even touched on Stalin's role in the war, a subject off-limits in the past. He said that "our people won the Great Patriotic War, not Stalin, not even the generals, as important as their role was. Yes, of course the role they played was quite significant but, all the same, it was the people who won the war as a result of enormous efforts and at the price of millions of lives." Medvedev observed that while some people believe that Stalin played a very important role, others do not think he did. But this is the wrong question, he said. The question is how Stalin is generally assessed as a figure. Medvedev said with regard to the official view of him, what current leaders think of him since the emergence of a new Russian nation, the verdict is clear: "Stalin committed a vast array of crimes against his own people. So despite the fact that he worked hard, despite the fact that under his leadership the country flourished in certain respects, what was done to our own people cannot be forgiven. That is the first thing."[34]

President Medvedev, who succeeded Prime Minister Vladimir Putin on May 7, 2008, said that after its World War II triumph, the

Soviet Union failed to allow its economy to develop. This failure was accompanied by deaths and everything connected with dictatorship. In the past, Medvedev and Putin have rarely criticized the Soviet system and instead focused on its achievements. In April 2010, as previously mentioned, Moscow published on the Internet documents proving that Soviet secret police massacred Polish officers at Katyn Forest in 1940, a crime the USSR long attempted to cover up by blaming it on the Nazis.

Russian political analyst Alexander Konovalov, director of the Institute for Strategic Evaluation, said that in his press interview Medvedev was moving gradually to change Russian public opinion on history. "These comments will contribute to re-establish historical truths," he said.[35] Many individuals wait for the time when American universities also will reestablish historical truths. Soviet crimes, terror, and repression are being exposed and acknowledged in Europe and in Russia, including the Kremlin. Perhaps this trend will eventually take hold in the American academic community. However, it may take several more generations for those in American universities to acknowledge the reality of Soviet crimes, or to acknowledge that Fascism was an ideology of the left, because of their scotomas; they live in cultural trances about this subject. A cultural trance occurs when members of a community fail to recognize that the cultural story of their community is subject to testing and change. Those individuals stuck in this cultural trance are in denial and suffer from cognitive dissonance, refusing to process facts that conflict with their deeply held beliefs and dogmas.

The question has been asked, how could so many of the intelligentsia have embraced Stalin as humanity's savior? It passes all understanding. John Haynes and Harvey Klehr, in a 2003 interview with historian Jamie Glazov, attempted to explain this intellectual distortion.[36] They echoed Courtois, claiming that the American intelligentsia seeks to "remold history to the service of the future. You will get few mea culpas from hard left academics because they feel no guilt. You think they should regret getting the facts of history wrong. They care not at all about the facts of history, only about the politics of the future. They feel they got the politics right and so no mea culpa is due." This view still prevails despite the acknowledgment of Stalin's crimes by Russia's leadership at various times and despite information now available even from Lenin's archives and included in Richard Pipes's book *The Unknown Lenin.*

The terror did not begin with Stalin. As Nicolas Berdyaev, the Russian religious and political philosopher, noted, Lenin was a despot. He fought for that "integral totalitarian view of life, which was necessary for the struggle and for the focusing of revolutionary energy." Lenin was antihumanist and antidemocratic.[37] Pipes's book contains documents from the Lenin archives that confirm this assessment and reveal the ruthlessness of Lenin in pursuit of his goals, including terrorizing and liquidating peasants, clergy, kulaks, "Whites," social democrats, and everyone else who was not a Bolshevik. For example, Document 94 bore Lenin's instructions to launch an offensive against the Orthodox Church (in other words, confiscating church valuables) by exploiting the famine and cannibalism occurring in the Ukraine. The desperate hunger, Lenin hoped, would provide the opportunity to break the power of the church and its hold on the peasant population. These documents and orders reflected Lenin's "utter disregard for human life."[37] And one might add the Kronstadt Rebellion to Lenin's acts of treachery and betrayal. Soviet military intelligence defector General Walter Krivitsky said, in suggesting that the evil of Communism went beyond Stalin: "The fascist character of Communism was inherent in it from the beginning. Kronstadt changed the fate of millions of Russians. It changed nothing about Communism."[39]

The political "left" today is still uncomfortable acknowledging Soviet crimes as well as Hiss's treason; it interferes with their worldview. Haynes and Klehr reminded their interviewer, Jamie Glazov, that the "left," in its defense of Stalin, distorts historical evidence. Haynes and Klehr drew needed attention to the problem of lack of objectivity in American universities. They observed "the shoddy history that is being done by many, not all but many, of an influential group of historian revisionists who study American Communism and attempt to 'normalize' the Soviet regime." Haynes and Klehr claimed that these academicians are in denial: "some of them minimized the number of victims of Stalinism and Leninism or denied that there was any mass terror." [These are crimes, as we have seen, that even the Russian leadership has recently acknowledged.] "Others deflected responsibility for terror away from Stalin and onto a bureaucratic process that spun out of control. And others apologized for the mass murders by claiming that they were necessary accompaniments to a process of modernization."[40] Such rationalizations of the Soviet regime by American academicians are disconnected from reality, historically false, and intellectually corrupt. Yet, incomprehensibly, they continue.

PART THREE

Accused and Convicted

XI

THE CASE

Hiss: Chambers Was Able to Carry Out Forgery by Typewriter

D URING THE CONGRESSIONAL hearings, the grand jury sessions, and the two perjury trials (1948–50), referred to collectively as "the case," Alger Hiss received support from two Supreme Court justices, former first lady Eleanor Roosevelt, top-level government officials, and leading lights in the worlds of academia and journalism. Influential journalists Walter Lippmann, James Reston, Joseph Alsop, and Marquis Childs of the *St. Louis Post-Dispatch,* as well as the *New Yorker* and the *New Republic,* were all Hiss supporters. The "enlightened," the "best people," and the "powerful" defended Hiss, such as Dean Acheson, John Foster Dulles, and Supreme Court justices Felix Frankfurter and Stanley Reed.[1] Acheson, Truman's secretary of state, insisted that he would not "turn his back on Alger Hiss."[2] These otherwise honorable and patriotic men had a sense of loyalty to someone of their own class that prevented them from viewing Hiss objectively. President Truman weighed in as well—he declared that the whole Hiss affair was a Republican-plotted "red herring."

Notably, several of Hiss's former employers refused to provide character witness: Jerome Frank (AAA), Francis Sayre (assistant secretary of state), former secretary of state James Byrnes, and

Stephen Raushenbush (Nye Committee).[3] The daily press was divided rather evenly, while the Hearst and Scripps-Howard syndicates were pro-prosecution.[4] The two protagonists were Whittaker Chambers, a former Communist operative who claimed among his friends a New Orleans prostitute named One-Eyed Annie; and Alger Hiss, the cool, well-bred Harvard Law School graduate and secretary to Oliver Wendell Holmes Jr.[5] Whittaker Chambers gave his first public testimony about some of his former Communist activities in the 1920s and 1930s during the August 3, 1948, hearing before the HUAC. This testimony set in motion a nasty and caustic national debate.

The case dominated the front pages for two years. Many books and hundreds of articles have been written about the political background and external issues and events that were occurring while the Hiss case unfolded. For example, who was manipulating the case for personal political advantage; what were the political agendas and ambitions of some individual members on the HUAC; how were the critics and supporters of the Truman administration and his policies using partisan politics during the presidential election year of 1948; who was behind the pre-McCarthy hyperbole that encouraged fear of Communist infiltration; how did the Elizabeth Bentley and Judith Coplon espionage hearings cause more alarm; what were the consequences of the Rosenbergs stealing U.S. atomic bomb information and providing it to the Soviet Union; what was the impact of the deteriorating situation with the Soviet Union; how did the Yalta "sellout" play into the story; who was responsible for Stalin's consolidation of power in eastern and central Europe; the Berlin Blockade; who lost Poland; who lost China. The list is long. While it is a given that these political events were swirling around the case and to various degrees affecting it, this chapter nonetheless will focus on the testimony and evidence presented during the HUAC hearings and inside the courtroom during the two trials.

The HUAC had its own detractors, accusing it of "witch-hunting."

Some Hiss defenders even felt that this congressional committee was usurping the function of a grand jury. In any event, the HUAC investigations proceeded. Chambers's revelations broke almost by chance: in 1948 he was called before the HUAC after investigators looking into Communist infiltration and/or espionage in the United States government kept coming across his name in the statements of other witnesses.

Chambers, who was questioned by Robert Stripling, an attorney who served as chief HUAC investigator, acknowledged his Communist Party affiliation and identified the Ware Group as an underground Communist apparatus of eight men, each of whom was a leader of a cell, including Lee Pressman, John Abt, Nathan Witt, Alger Hiss, Donald Hiss, Charles Kramer, Henry Collins, and Victor Perlo.[6] Chambers discussed his very close relationship with one of them, Alger Hiss. He said the purpose of the Communist cells at the time was "not primarily espionage" but rather to have these officials infiltrate the U.S. government and advance to high-level positions in order to influence U.S. policy. Chambers added, however, that "espionage was certainly one of its eventual objectives."[7] But Chambers made no reference to specific espionage activities having taken place. He testified that Alger Hiss had been a Communist, but said nothing about his past involvement in espionage.

Chambers told the committee about his meeting with Adolf Berle in 1939, when he identified the officials in the Ware Group as Communists at that time, but not about the espionage charges he suggested to Berle.[8] The FBI interviewed Chambers for the first time in May 1942. In 1943 the Bureau obtained the notes from Berle; he never turned them over to the FBI in 1939. When the FBI interviewed Chambers in 1946 and 1947, Chambers said he never had participated in a Soviet espionage ring and claimed to have "no documentary or other proof of espionage performed by underground Communists in Washington, D.C."[9] In his memoir, *Witness,* Chambers tried to explain the conflict that was within him—between telling everything to fight an evil (Communism) and protecting and shielding his former colleagues because of the compassion he felt for them.[10] Notably, because of his complicity in espionage activities, Chambers's silence on this issue was also protecting himself from possible charges of perjury and espionage.

"To fight Communism while sparing my former friends I had made a simple compromise," Chambers wrote. He informed the authorities of their Communist membership and their activities short of espionage. He suppressed that part of the story except for a few individuals whom he felt compelled to name because of the immediate danger they represented (for example, one was the head of an experimental steel laboratory). In trying to justify his omission and shift the blame, Chambers later asserted that the government had known for years about the Ware Group and its structure and membership; "the espionage implications were inescapable."[11] After all, as Chambers's biographer Sam Tanenhaus noted, the Communist Party existed for the specific purpose of overthrowing the government.[12] Chambers told the HUAC members he left the Communist Party in 1937, a date he later corrected as April 1938. At various times both sides needed to correct inaccurate memories of dates from ten years earlier.

This line of defense was reiterated by Chambers under further HUAC questioning. He said that while he was a member of the Communist Party he was unaware of any espionage. He acknowledged that he was aware his underground group "could always be diverted" to espionage and at some point "almost certainly would be." But he also said the purpose of the Ware Group was to influence policy and personnel placements in the U.S. government and "if deemed fit," it would be available for espionage if necessary.[13] Chambers continued to hedge and qualify and dance around this significant point throughout the hearings. In fact, Chambers had lied to the FBI when he told them he never participated in Soviet espionage.[14]

In a separate development, a federal grand jury for the Southern District of New York was looking into Soviet espionage. In March

1948, Alger Hiss appeared before it and denied he ever had been a Communist; this was five months before Chambers's HUAC testimony began. Chambers wrote in his memoir that when he began his HUAC testimony on August 3, he did not know that Hiss had denied being a Communist on five occasions: to the grand jury; to former secretary of state James Byrnes; to John Foster Dulles (his sponsor at Carnegie Endowment for International Peace); and to the FBI.[15] In addition, Stanley K. Hornbeck, Hiss's superior at the State Department in 1939, was told by Ambassador Bullitt that French premier Daladier warned him Hiss was a Communist agent. When confronted by Hornbeck, Hiss denied the allegation.[16]

Following Chambers's accusations on August 3, Hiss felt he had to answer the charges, although some friends wisely told him to ignore them. It is interesting to speculate: If Hiss had decided not to challenge Chambers, would everything have just faded away and ended? Probably. But Hiss volunteered to go before the committee, which he did on August 5 in a public hearing. Hiss categorically denied the allegation of being a Communist and member of the Ware Group; he also said he did not know anyone by the name of Whittaker Chambers (which was accurate—he and all the cell operatives knew Chambers by his underground name, "Karl"). He was shown pictures of Chambers but said he was not able to tell from them if he knew him; he needed to see Chambers in person. Hiss claimed he never heard of the name Chambers until two FBI agents interviewed him in 1947. Throughout the hearing Hiss kept qualifying his responses, such as by saying "as far as I know" he had never seen him. When asked again if he had ever seen Chambers he responded that the "name" meant nothing to him.[17] And so it went, Hiss continuously circumventing that question, probably realizing that such an admission would link him to espionage. It was Hiss's claim and insistence that he had no recollection of the man named Chambers that began the long series of dramatic hearings and trials.

The HUAC was disposed to drop the investigation after the Hiss appearance. However, Richard Nixon, congressman from California, interceded and convinced the committee to continue the probe, citing Hiss's reluctance to state categorically that he did not know Chambers. Nixon believed that the HUAC, even if it could not prove Hiss was a Communist, should be able to establish by corroborative testimony if they, Hiss and Chambers, knew each other and if Hiss or Chambers was lying. A three-man subcommittee was formed to question Chambers further, in executive (nonpublic) session on August 7, 1948. Chambers spoke about Hiss's personal life; the CPUSA dues he collected regularly from Hiss; Alger and Priscilla's nicknames for each other; the Hisses' vacation spot on the Eastern Shore of Maryland; Hiss's effort at being an amateur ornithologist—he went out mornings to watch birds along the Potomac—and his excitement in seeing a rare prothonotary warbler. And he related the story of Hiss as a boy selling bottled spring water from Druid Hill Park to his neighbors in Baltimore. Chambers presented many small, intimate details about Hiss that strongly suggested he knew him well.

In addition, Chambers told the committee that when Hiss bought a new car, he turned over his old Ford roadster to the open party to use for organization purposes. And he gave the transfer records to a service station whose owner was a Communist to dispose of the car. Chambers also testified that his contact, GRU colonel Bykov, gave him money to buy four Persian Bokara rugs to give to his assets as gifts when Chambers said that they would refuse money. Chambers asked his friend Meyer Schapiro in New York to purchase the rugs, without telling him the reason. Schapiro bought the Persian rugs; they were for George Silverman, Harry Dexter White, Alger Hiss, and Julian Wadleigh. The date of receipt of the rugs was December 1936. Then they were shipped to Washington and arrived sometime in January 1937. This proved that Hiss had known Chambers in 1937; Hiss had told the grand jury he had not.[18] Hiss maintained that he was associated with Chambers up until 1936, not after; therefore, he claimed, the Pumpkin Papers (dated in 1938) must have been typed by Chambers on his (Hiss's) typewriter through some subterfuge.[19]

Hiss was subpoenaed to testify in executive session on August 16. He was becoming indignant at this point, in that his credibility was being challenged by a "confessed Communist," and he accused the HUAC of leaking parts of the hearings to the press. It was during this session that he finally conceded, as he had testified previously, that there was a "certain familiarity" to Chambers's face and now in fact he could say he knew Chambers—but under another name, "George Crosley." He said "Crosley" was a poor struggling freelance reporter who wrote for the *American Magazine* and *Cosmopolitan*. Hiss remembered "George Crosley" coming into his office at the Munitions (Nye) Committee looking for material to publish articles in the *American Magazine*. Hiss admitted he had lunch several times with "Crosley" on the Hill when Crosley came to his office. He had a wife and child, and Hiss said he felt sorry for him so he let "Crosley" use his apartment for a short time until the lease ran out and he lent him money. Hiss also testified that while the "Crosleys" were waiting for their furniture to be delivered to Washington, the Hisses put the "Crosley" family up in their own home for a couple of nights. He also claimed that he gave "Crosley" his old car.[20]

It would seem unusual, to say the least, to do all this for someone Hiss said he met in passing. That he knew him enough to trust him with his apartment, the use of his furniture, and a stay in his home, besides giving him his automobile and making him a series of loans, suggested to the HUAC members that Chambers's version of their relationship was closer to the truth. The HUAC interrogators asked Hiss if he knew anyone who could corroborate that Chambers went by the name of George Crosley. Hiss replied that only those who worked with him at the Nye Committee, where "Crosley" used to show up, could have known him by that name. But the defense was never able to come up with one person who knew Chambers by the name Crosley. Hiss said they parted with bad feelings; "Crosley" never paid him the money he owed him—except for a few dollars and a rug. Hiss had at various times during the hearings described "Crosley" as "impecunious," a "sponger," "unproductive," and "almost repulsive in taste and appearance." [21]

The next day, August 17, 1948, the famous "confrontation scene" took place in Room 1400 of Manhattan's Commodore Hotel at Forty-Second Street and Lexington Avenue. Hiss and Chambers came face-to-face. What stood out from that first meeting of these two men was how Hiss peered at Chambers's teeth, listened to his accuser's low-pitched voice, and finally admitted recognizing the man—but only as a freelance writer named "George Crosley," whom Hiss had named the day before in executive session. He claimed he had briefly befriended this man in the 1930s. He observed that his teeth obviously were greatly improved and he must have had considerable dental work done since that time. Hiss repeated his previous denials of any Communist affiliation and added that he never knew Chambers by the name "Karl."

On August 25, both Hiss and Chambers went before the HUAC in an open session. Public interest was high and the *Washington Post* reported a huge overflow crowd. [22] During the session, both men repeated their stories. Hiss's explanation of how he disposed of his car at previous sessions was "refuted" by documentary facts, according to HUAC member Congressman Karl Mundt, Republican of South Dakota. At the end of the meeting, one HUAC member, F. Edward Herbert, a Democrat from Louisiana, said one of them was the "damnedest liar ever to appear on the American scene." [23]

Two days later, the HUAC issued an interim report summarizing the information to date. It concluded that the verifiable portions of Chambers's testimony had stood up strongly and his testimony was "forthright and emphatic"; the verifiable portions of Hiss's testimony had been badly shaken, and his testimony was "vague and evasive." This was particularly true with regard to the details of Chambers's use of Hiss's furnished home and Hiss's failure or

refusal to tell the committee the whole truth concerning the dispo-
sition of his 1929 Ford. The testimony about Hiss's Ford roadster
was the focus of the August 25 public hearing. Hiss claimed he
gave it or sold it to Chambers, when in fact he turned it over to
the Communist Party for use by a party organizer. The paperwork
for the car was transferred to William Rosen, a Communist Party
member. Chambers suggested in *Witness* that "Hiss's inability to
explain the documentary evidence of that automobile transaction
was the first to turn the tide against him."[24]

The committee also noted in its summary that Hiss not only
denied being a Communist, but also denied knowing any Communists. The committee found it difficult to believe that Hiss, who
admitted knowing Ware, Witt, Abt, Pressman, Collins, and Chambers, could have made this statement. Hiss denied that he knew any
of his colleagues were Communists. He was asked about Collins
and Pressman and Abt. When it was noted that it was an established public fact Harold Ware had been a Communist, *even then*
Hiss said, "It was not my practice then to ask people whom I met
casually whether they were Communists."[25] When they came before the HUAC in August 1948, Abt and Pressman denied charges,
which they referred to as a "red herring," and ignored the substance
of the testimony, and Nathan Witt, Collins, Perlo, and Kramer
took the Fifth Amendment—but not Hiss. He was credentialed,
composed, and accommodating.[26]

Three years later, in 1951, again under oath at the HUAC hearings, Lee Pressman testified that he, Witt, Abt, and Kramer in fact
had been Communists and members of the Ware Group. In time,
the number of subcells, managed by seven men, had an estimated
total of about seventy-five assets.[27] Then Moscow decided to separate out several for a parallel network more rigorously segregated
and subdivided. In 1948, Julian Wadleigh, a State Department official, testified before a grand jury and the HUAC, and was a key
witness in the Hiss prosecution. He did not actually know of Hiss's
role, but during the Hiss trial he corroborated the role Chambers

had played. Wadleigh said that he collaborated with Communists but never specifically became a party member. He admitted taking hundreds of classified documents for two years (1936–38) while working in the State Department and turning them over every week to Soviet intelligence (in other words, to Whittaker Chambers).[28]

Of all those accused by Chambers or Bentley of criminal Communist activities, Wadleigh was the first one to admit the accusations were correct. Given the highly charged political environment during the New Deal era in Washington, D.C., it is really difficult to believe that Hiss never knew any of his best friends or colleagues were Communists or that they even ever talked about Communism. Hiss testified he ended his relationship with Chambers in "late spring" of 1936 and had not seen him again until August 17, 1948, when they were brought together at the Hotel Commodore.[29]

The case was at a stalemate. Summarizing the hearings, the committee declared that Whittaker Chambers had been a forthright witness, while Hiss had been evasive. The transcripts reflect Chambers answering directly and Hiss responding with elusive, lawyerly, conditional answers. The *New York Times* reported that in discussing the events of a dozen years ago, Alger Hiss prefaced 198 statements with the phrase "to the best of my knowledge."[30] The records were turned over to the Department of Justice to determine which of the two might be prosecuted for perjury. Lacking further evidence, there was little likelihood that either could be indicted.

Again, it probably would have ended there, but Hiss felt compelled to discredit Chambers in order to preserve his "persona" and to maintain his adherence to Lenin's morality. During the hearings, Hiss had challenged Chambers to make the same accusations publicly outside the HUAC hearings where he had immunity; he threatened Chambers with a libel suit if he did go public. On August 27, Chambers appeared on the radio program *Meet the Press* (James B. Reston of the *New York Times* served as the moderator) and repeated his charge that Alger Hiss was a Communist "and may be now." This statement was not protected by congressional immunity. Chambers did not think Hiss would sue him for slander.[31] Chambers somehow thought Hiss would appreciate his silence on the espionage component of the case. But Alger Hiss did file a libel suit a month later, on September 27, 1948, in the U.S. District Court, Baltimore, Maryland, demanding $50,000 (on October 8 amended to $75,000) in damages.[32] His brother Donald, along with his partners at Covington & Burling, told Alger not to sue Chambers: it was not worth it.[33] As it turned out, they were correct. When Hiss attacked with a libel suit, Chambers finally introduced the charge of espionage, and to support his case, after ten years he retrieved the nearly forgotten classified government documents he kept hidden as his security. His nephew had stored the envelope with the documents and three tins of microfilm rolls inside an unused dumbwaiter shaft in his home in Brooklyn.[34]

At first the Hiss case seemed to involve only the word of a confessed ex-Communist agent accusing a government official who had been the trusted colleague of such individuals as former secretaries of state Cordell Hull and Edward Stettinius. Tanenhaus made the point that Chambers's reticence on some issues did not seem to concern the HUAC staff. He said Elizabeth Bentley "had reeled off thirty-two names, promiscuously lumping together her underground contacts with names she had picked up in casual conversation," whereas Chambers had been cautious and specific.[35] Then, gradually, and hesitatingly, as he revealed the extent of the conspiracy and his own involvement, Chambers produced the evidence that finally sent Hiss to jail for lying when he said that he had not given official documents to the Communist Party.

On August 30 the HUAC called Adolf A. Berle to the committee hearing room to shed light on the Hiss case. Although back in 1939 Berle said that he had passed the information he received at the meeting with Chambers and Isaac Don Levine to the White House, he did not give his four pages of notes titled "Underground

Espionage Agent" to the FBI. Weinstein noted that "only when the FBI requested his memo in 1943, having learned about it during an interview with Chambers the previous year, did Berle provide a copy to the Bureau." The FBI had this information two years before Hiss was sent to Yalta. The justification given to account for the Bureau's inaction was that in 1943 it was focused on the Nazi—not Soviet—threat. Moreover, Berle never filed the memo with the Department of State security office or military intelligence agencies.[36]

At the HUAC hearing, Berle had serious memory lapses— remembering Hiss as being cited at the 1939 meeting as a "sympathizer," not a Communist Party member. His own notes contradicted this statement! Berle's diary perhaps explained his "memory loss": it reflected his belief that Hiss may have been a liar but he wasn't a traitor. Berle wrote in his diary on September 3, 1948: "I am not prepared to think that he maintained these obligations after he got into a position of influence."[37] Another full-scale blind spot at work. Adolf Berle could not deal objectively with the evidence presented to him because of his predisposed beliefs about Alger Hiss (and Roosevelt).

Deposition proceedings for the libel suit began on November 4 in Baltimore. Hiss's legal team was led by his friend William Marbury. During much of the investigation before the libel suit the Hiss defense resorted to ad hominem attacks. The Hiss team implied that Chambers was mentally ill, had been institutionalized at one time, was an alcoholic, and a homosexual. Chambers denied all of these as smear tactics. In preparing for the libel suit, Hiss's attorney Marbury was concerned over Hiss's reluctance to discuss certain matters. For example, despite his enormous support from many government officials, some of those he had written for support (including Jerome Frank, Chester Davis, and James Byrnes, as well as Priscilla's former husband, Thayer Hobson) refused to provide character references.[38] No explanations were forthcoming.

It was at the pretrial deposition in Baltimore in November 1948 that Chambers finally realized he had to stop shielding Hiss from the charge of espionage. When Marbury pressed him for details on the work Hiss allegedly did once he had been separated into a parallel apparatus during the Ware Group days, Chambers was vague. But then Chambers admitted for the first time to having read—but not obtained—State Department documents that Hiss brought home from time to time. Marbury asked Chambers to produce any documentation he may have had to support his case. Chambers finally decided to retrieve the documents he had safeguarded.

Chambers traveled to Brooklyn to get the documentary evidence from his nephew, Nathan Levine. He opened the package when he returned to his farm in Westminster, Maryland, not remembering what material he had saved ten years earlier as a safety net. He found four small sheets of paper, handwritten notes of Alger Hiss; sixty-five typewritten documents, which summarized or copied completely seventy State Department cables and one War Department report; four sheets of yellow paper bearing the handwriting of Harry Dexter White; two short strips of developed film; three cans containing rolls of undeveloped film; and one small piece of paper. Since most of the material Hiss gave him was from early 1938, before Chambers defected, the existence of this evidence showed that Hiss lied about not seeing Chambers after mid-1936 and about his involvement in espionage.[39] The hard evidence of authentic State Department documents was the decisive turning point in the case.

On November 17, 1948, Chambers produced the documents at the deposition, and they were turned over to the Justice Department. Hiss denied he had provided any material to Chambers and wondered who had stolen these documents from his office at the State Department and given them to Chambers. Chambers held back the microfilm. On December 1, Nixon and Stripling visited Chambers at his Maryland farm. When pressed by his two visitors, Chambers told them he had more evidence.[40]

Nixon had Stripling seek a subpoena for the material, which was served the next day. On December 2, Chambers led the HUAC investigators to the pumpkin patch on his Maryland farm where he had hidden in a carved-out pumpkin two developed rolls of microfilm and three cans of undeveloped microfilm. Chambers surrendered the microfilm only when he became convinced that a committee member suspected him of withholding evidence. The famous designation "Pumpkin Papers" came to refer to all the hard evidence Chambers had sequestered, whereas it was actually only the microfilm that was hidden in a carved-out pumpkin. He also gave the HUAC investigators photostat copies of the State Department documents hidden in the dumbwaiter that he had turned over to Justice. The Justice Department, which had two weeks to study the classified State Department documents given to them by Chambers during the Baltimore deposition, did nothing with them and announced nothing.[41]

The whole dynamic and significance of the case changed dramatically with the presence now of hard evidence pointing to espionage. Clearly the documentary evidence of stolen classified State Department material subsumed the "he said, he said" aspect of the case of who was lying. All the other issues became secondary. Yet Truman continued to call the charge a "red herring" and the Justice Department was preparing to indict Chambers—not Hiss—in New York for perjury. Nixon pointed out that Truman's position did no service to the national interest of the United States. On December 10, 1948, Chambers resigned as editor of *Time* magazine. Hiss submitted his resignation as president of the Carnegie Endowment for International Peace on December 13, 1948, according to one account. The board of trustees voted not to accept it and instead granted him a three-month leave of absence.[42] However, Hiss wrote, "I did not resign from the Presidency of the Endowment. Under its by-laws, presidents are elected annually for a term of twelve months. My term expired May 5th and I notified the Board that I would not be a candidate for re-election."[43]

As Nixon and Truman argued the political dimensions of the controversy, the case went to the New York grand jury that examined the evidence and heard testimonies from, among others,

Chambers (not until October 1948), Hiss, Priscilla (accused of typing many of the documents—all but one was typed on the same Woodstock typewriter that belonged to the Hisses), Donald Hiss, Hede Massing, Henry Collins, Julian Wadleigh, George Silverman, and Nixon on December 13.[44] During his testimony, Nixon was asked why he did not turn the microfilm over to the FBI; he answered that the Justice Department had issued instructions to the FBI not to cooperate with the HUAC.[45]

At the end of 1948, Weinstein noted, two newspapers that had been sympathetic to Hiss were now raising questions. In a December 9, 1948, editorial, "Let's Have the Facts," the *Washington Post* denounced the investigation as a "four-ring circus" and criticized the Truman administration's handling of the case, citing Hiss's slander suit, the HUAC investigation, the Justice Department's grand jury inquiry, and a special investigation at the State Department. The *Atlanta Constitution* on December 11, 1948, charged the Justice Department with "dereliction of duty in its failure to follow up leads" on the espionage cases.[46]

Chambers's decision to come forward with the documents, as he told Nixon and Robert Stripling, was due to his belief that Hiss was determined to destroy him and his wife. He was especially upset by Marbury's aggressive questioning of Esther on November 16 and 17 and the smear tactics used against him. So his revealing the documents was a form of retaliation.[47] Another, and probably the determining reason was that without this evidence, Chambers thought that the Baltimore jury would accept Hiss's story, and if Chambers lost the libel suit he might then be indicted for perjury by the Justice Department. During his grand jury testimony on October 14, Chambers was asked if he was aware of any one person guilty of espionage against the United States. Chambers answered, "I do not believe I do know such a name."[48] Because of this statement and Chambers's earlier claim that no espionage had been committed, there was concern that Chambers would be charged with perjury by the grand jury.

On the last day of its tenure, December 15, 1948, the grand jury indicted Alger Hiss on two counts of perjury: that he lied to the grand jury in denying that he had turned over documents to Whittaker Chambers in early 1938 and that he had lied in denying he had met with Chambers at this time. Hiss pled not guilty at the arraignment hearing on both counts of the indictment; bail was set at five thousand dollars.[49] During his testimony, according to later accounts by jurors, Hiss provoked laughter when he said: "Until the day I die, I shall wonder how Whittaker Chambers got into my house to use my typewriter."[50]

The first Hiss trial opened in New York at Foley Square on May 31, 1949, with Judge Samuel H. Kaufman presiding. The Hiss defense strategy was to put Chambers on trial; he was questioned about his background, attacked with unsavory character smears, and had his public record compared to Hiss's. For his part, U.S. Attorney Thomas Murphy emphasized the "incontrovertible" evidence represented by the State Department documents and microfilm. Prosecution lawyers correlated the stolen materials with the original cables and reports in the State Department's files and authenticated them. The State Department confirmed the authenticity of the documents.[51] A personal assault was the only real defense for Hiss and his supporters.

Chambers observed in *Witness* that Hiss's testimony showed endless evasiveness, equivocations, dodges, discrepancies, contradictions, twists, and turns. Hiss was indignant (especially over the Ford car) and at times insolent and arrogant. Yet oddly, at the same time, he was composed and calm, never yielding an inch in his denials. Hiss matched wits with the lead prosecutor, Thomas Murphy, and in the end, his story was unshaken. Knowing he had the establishment behind him, his lawyers used the strategy of innocence by association with distinguished names. But according to Chambers, Hiss's most effective tactic to rally support against the charges was to suggest those charges were an attempt "to discredit recent great achievements of this country in which I [Hiss] was privileged to participate."[52] Discrediting Hiss was discrediting Yalta and the UN.

Judge Kaufman refused to allow Murphy to call two government witnesses. One was Hede Massing, who had previously testified to the HUAC that she met Hiss in the home of former State Department official Noel Field and that Hiss was trying to recruit him for underground work until he found out that Field already was a Soviet asset in Massing's network. The second witness was William Rosen, who had signed the Ford title transfer.[53] Critics denounced Judge Kaufman, citing that his rulings on admissible evidence usually favored the defense.

One major highlight of the first trial was the Woodstock typewriter and whether or not the Hisses still owned it at the time the documents were typed in their home. The defense attempted to show that the Hisses no longer had the typewriter at the time the stolen documents were typed on it. FBI laboratory analysis identified the State Department documents as having been typed on the Woodstock owned by the Hisses during the 1930s. The typewriter was the critical link between the documents and Hiss.

Other highlights were that two Supreme Court justices, Frankfurter and Reed, led Hiss's reputational defense and praised his character. Prosecutor Murphy documented Priscilla's registered membership in the Socialist Party in 1932, which she denied. Hiss denied Priscilla had ever typed anything and claimed that they had given the typewriter to their maid. He denied ever meeting Colonel Bykov, and said Chambers never visited him in 1937–38 at his Thirtieth Street or Volta Place residences. He also denied lending Chambers four hundred dollars in 1937 to buy a car; the loan took place a few days after Priscilla showed a withdrawal of that amount from her checking account, which she claimed she was using to buy furniture, before she actually moved into her new residence.

Hiss's attorney Lloyd Paul Stryker rested his case by emphasizing that someone could have taken Hiss's handwritten notes from his trash can and suggesting that Julian Wadleigh could have been that person. Stryker summed up by calling Chambers a liar with an "abnormal" background and Hiss "a pillar of righteousness." He denounced the HUAC for lending credence to Chambers's story and accused the committee and Chambers of using the case to affect the 1948 presidential election. Another significant point was Murphy's question about motive. He asked why would this drifter "George Crosley" want to frame Hiss? The question of motive was never answered satisfactorily.

Priscilla Hiss testified at both trials. Her testimony centered on two key prosecution contentions: that she had typed, on a family-owned Woodstock typewriter, copies of the secret documents for transmission to Chambers in 1937 and early 1938, and that she had seen Chambers after January 1, 1937. She firmly denied both contentions. During the time of the trials Priscilla by many accounts was in a state of panic; she was always worried about money because the case would incur huge legal fees; she feared she would lose her teaching job and that they would have to pull their son, Tony, out of private school. And she hated the publicity.

Since the Hisses had meager funds, their friends, many of whom were lawyers, helped with legal costs, either donating money to a defense fund, or volunteering research, or providing free services, as in the case of Hiss's brother Donald, who received substantial unpaid legal help from his law firm, Covington, Burling, Rublee, Acheson, & Shorb. Also, the firm of Cleary, Gottlieb, Friendly & Cox (Hugh Cox was Donald Hiss's lawyer) "paid a good portion of Alger Hiss's investigative expenses."[54]

Other support came from family and friends. The Hiss family lived in Greenwich Village on Eighth Street and the trials, which Alger and Priscilla both attended, were at the Federal Court Building at Foley Square. Friends made sure Tony, seven years old during the first trial, and who was attending Dalton School in midtown, got to school every day and was picked up. And the Hiss family was invited to many dinners on Sundays by supporters.[55]

In the summer, Priscilla continued to vacation with Tony in

Peacham, Vermont, as the family had done for years. During the Peacham vacations there were many summer letters from Priscilla to Alger; his letters and postcards included very affectionate responses to Tony, who by 1950 was old enough to respond.[56] Moreover, letters of support poured in from all quarters, from friends of both Alger and Priscilla. They were all rallying around Alger over "the very ugly business going on" and suggested the anti-Hiss people were "out for blood" trying to swing the election to the Republicans. One letter from a friend, dated August 5, 1948, claimed "we love you even if you are a communist."[57] Letters of support continued to flow throughout 1949–50.

After six weeks, the trial ended. The jury of ten men and two women deliberated for six hours and ten minutes but could not reach a verdict. At 9:01 P.M. on Friday, July 8, a hung jury was announced. The deadlocked jury voted 8 to 4 to convict.[58] Attorney General Clark said that the case would be retried as soon as possible. The second trial began in the courtroom of Judge Henry Goddard on November 17, 1949, with a jury of eight women and four men (seven housewives, three businessmen, and two professionals).[59]

During the second trial, Thomas Murphy continued to lead the prosecution team. Murphy shifted focus away from Chambers's credibility, stressing the evidence instead. Hiss replaced Stryker with Claude B. Cross. Stryker, "widely considered the ablest criminal lawyer in the country," and recommended by Frankfurter, had said he could get another hung jury but Hiss wanted vindication.[60] So he changed lawyers. Cross was a corporation lawyer from Boston. Cross put emphasis on the possibility of Wadleigh's having taken the documents from Hiss's office. Wadleigh denied typing summaries or copies of State Department documents and denied giving any typed summaries or copies to Chambers or anyone else.[61]

The second trial made juridical history. It was the first time psychiatric testimony ever had been used in a federal court to impeach the credibility of a witness. The defense had called psychiatrist Dr.

Carl Binger to observe Chambers during the first trial, but he had not been allowed to testify. At the second trial, Judge Goddard, over strong prosecution objections, allowed Dr. Binger's testimony. Murphy objected that there had been no proof that the witness had received any treatment by a psychiatrist or physician, only a dentist for his teeth.[62] A psychologist, Dr. Henry Murray, was also called to testify. Both doctors claimed that Chambers was suffering from a "psychopathic personality." In closing statements, Murphy said the psychiatric testimony was a case of "unconscious bias."[63]

Goddard, again unlike Kaufman, allowed Hede Massing to take the stand. She told the Noel Field story. It was the first time Massing had given public testimony. She was the former wife of Gerhart Eisler, a Soviet "illegal" operative that fled the United States to Germany. Massing said she started "working" for the CPUSA in 1933. She positively identified Hiss and said she saw him only one time, in 1935 at the home of Noel Field, a member of Massing's apparatus. Hiss tried to recruit Field but Massing said he was hers. Hede Massing was thus a second witness to testify about Hiss's involvement with the Communist movement, corroborating Chambers's story of having met Hiss as an underground Communist.[64]

Also at the second trial, Murphy introduced new evidence—the notes Berle had made following his meeting with Chambers (with Isaac Don Levine in attendance) on September 2, 1939. After the meeting, Berle typed his notes in a memo titled "Underground Espionage Agent" and this memo became a government exhibit at Hiss's second trial. Hiss revamped his strategy for the second trial: to supplement the destruction of Chambers's credibility with a frontal attack on the evidence.

On Friday, January 20, 1950, at 3:10 P.M., the jury of eight women and four men retired to begin deliberations. The second trial was twice as long as the first trial and had double the testimony. The next day, on January 21 at 2:48 P.M., Hiss was pronounced guilty of two counts of lying to the grand jury: the first lie being that he had not seen Chambers after January 1, 1937, and the second that he had not given Chambers any stolen documents. Because of a three-year statute of limitations on espionage, Hiss's conviction was on two counts of perjury, but the technical charge of perjury was perceived as an allegation of espionage. In his last remarks to the bench before sentencing, Hiss predicted that "in the future the full facts of how Whittaker Chambers was able to carry out forgery by typewriter will be disclosed."[65]

The *Herald Tribune* front-page story describing Hiss's reaction to his conviction on two counts of perjury said Hiss accepted the verdict "with the same stoic calm" he had shown throughout the ordeal.[66] Judge Goddard sentenced Hiss to five years in prison and released him on ten thousand dollars bail pending appeal. Immediately Hiss and his legal team prepared to appeal the decision. Heading the new defense team was Chester Lane, a Harvard Law School classmate. On December 7, 1950, the Court of Appeals for the Second District rejected Hiss's appeal. In March the U.S. Supreme Court denied to hear the Hiss case. Hiss began serving his prison term on March 22, 1951.

In his memoir, published forty years after the second trial, Hiss blamed his conviction on the political environment and hostility toward Roosevelt, stating that the New Deal was on trial by a corrupted judicial system and jury. Hiss claimed that "despite public hysteria" and "prosecutorial misconduct" he felt the jurors would give him a fair hearing, focusing on the charges. Hiss said he was "stunned with the guilty verdict." He stated, "I couldn't believe that such a blatant miscarriage of justice was possible. Prejudices, bias, and lies had vanquished those of *us* who had taken the rule of law so seriously that all *our* procedures had been circumspect, honorable, and aboveboard" (emphasis added). For Alger Hiss, using the first-person plural in these remarks, it was not about individual guilt but rather "the rightness of *our* cause" (emphasis added).[67] He said he did not take the Fifth Amendment when he testified before a grand jury because of "the mistaken belief that *our* federal judicial system was proof against public prejudice and was free of prosecutorial chicanery. I was certainly naïve in believing that jurors would be insulated from the phobias of the Cold War in 1949 and 1950" (emphasis added). Hiss believed that the entire jury of public opinion (all of those from whom his jury had been selected) had been tampered with. The jury was prejudiced.[68] In short, Hiss went beyond his accusers and condemned the entire American legal and political system.

An interesting perspective on the case was given by Leslie A. Fiedler, a literary critic who during his college years in the 1930s had joined the Young Communist League and later was a proponent of the ideas of Trotsky. Fiedler wrote that had Hiss not lied, the case might have attained dignity. Fiedler asked, "Why did he lie, and lying, lose the whole point of the case in a maze of irrelevant data: the signature on the transfer of ownership of a car, the date a typewriter was repaired . . . ?" Fiedler went on to criticize not only Hiss, but also William Remington (accused by Elizabeth Bentley) and the Rosenbergs, all of whom acted like "common criminals" pleading innocent on advice of counsel rather than, as political idealists and "believers in a new society," welcoming the trials as an opportunity to "declare to the world the high principles of their actions" and their "loyalty to the eventual triumph of socialism." They might have appeared more as martyrs than as petty thieves, Fiedler declared.[69]

The first phase of the case was influenced by Nixon's tough stance when he convinced the HUAC to allow the Hiss case to go forward. In the second phase of the case, Thomas F. Murphy made it possible to win by keeping a laser focus on the evidence. Hiss received all the sympathy from the press and powerful pro-Hiss people. They never discussed Chambers and the impact of the trials on him; he lost his career and a $21,000 a year salary[70] as senior editor of *Time* magazine; and he suffered indignities, gossip, defamations, and pain to his family. Philip Rahv, in the *Partisan Review*, wrote in 1952 that when faced with "the disorder and evil of history," the pro-Hiss faction "fought to save Hiss in order to safeguard its own illusions."[71] Chambers was condemned as a turncoat by Communists and their fellow travelers for accusing Alger Hiss, and, since Hiss had been at Roosevelt's side during Yalta, for helping loose the "paranoia" that created the Cold War.[72]

For his part, Chambers's last word on the Hiss case was printed in 1959 by *National Review,* for which he worked briefly as an editor. Alger Hiss, declared Chambers, had not paid his penalty "except in the shallowest legalistic sense. There is only one possible payment, as I see it, in his case. It is to speak the truth. Hiss's defiance perpetuates and keeps a fracture in the community as a whole."[73] And that defiance continued until Hiss died.

In his memoir, Whittaker Chambers wrote in his typical poetic prose: "In accusing Hiss of Communism, I had attacked an architect of the UN, and the partisans of peace fell upon me like combat troops. I had attacked an intellectual and a liberal. A whole generation felt itself on trial. . . . From their roosts in the great cities, and certain collegiate eyries, the left-winged intellectuals of almost every feather (and that was most of the vocal intellectuals in the country) swooped and hovered in flocks like fluttered sea fowl . . . and gave vent to hoarse cries and defilements. I had also accused a 'certified gentleman' and the 'conspiracy of gentlemen' closed its retaliatory ranks against me."[74]

XII.

LEWISBURG PRISON

Hiss: Three Years at Lewisburg Is a Good Corrective
to Three Years at Harvard

O N MARCH 22, 1951, Alger Hiss turned himself over
to federal marshals at the Foley Square courthouse in
New York to begin his five-year prison sentence. His
appeal from his January 1950 conviction on two counts of perjury
had been unanimously denied by a three-judge panel of the U.S.
Court of Appeals for the Second Circuit on December 7, 1950. On
March 12, 1951, the Supreme Court of the United States had denied his petition for certiorari (review of the lower court's decision),
thereby upholding his conviction.

Hiss stayed for about a week at a detention center on West
Street in New York City before being sent by bus to Lewisburg,
a maximum-security federal facility in Pennsylvania. He used this
opportunity to learn about the conditions and customs of prison
life. Hiss and his attorneys met with Austin McCormick, former
assistant director of the Federal Bureau of Prisons during the New
Deal. Hiss wrote in his memoir that McCormick at the time was
helping convicts get jobs and readjust to civilian life and McCormick even did voluntary service of several prison terms to learn
what it was like to be in prison. McCormick provided Hiss with

many useful insights and details on prison life and what he could expect in the pattern of daily life.[1]

By law Hiss could be released in forty-four months for good behavior, which he was, on November 27, 1954. Hiss had been "the beneficiary of nine first-rate attorneys' services, hundreds of thousands of dollars in past and present contributions to legal expenses, two dozen eminent character witnesses [including a former First Lady, secretaries of state, two Supreme Court justices, among others], and countless additional well-known supporters in government and in the press."[2] He had everything going for him except the facts.

Alger Hiss once again displayed his remarkable powers of self-control—living in a prison environment and yet able to adapt successfully. His insistence on his innocence and push for vindication probably enabled him to cope with his calamitous downfall. At Lewisburg he was an inmate among criminals, while a few years earlier he was sitting with the U.S. president and other world leaders determining the fate of the postwar world. Outwardly this difference did not seem to affect him. Compared to his life before as a privileged official, he proved he could endure, even prosper while in prison, preserving his "persona," planning his goal to vindicate himself, and convincing others of his innocence. He projected serenity and suppressed anger.[3] Hiss remained polite and aloof, but cooperative and helpful to others. He assumed the role of a diligent and an uncomplaining prison worker.[4] However, years later, Hiss shared his views of what it really was like in jail, as he told his biographer John Chabot Smith in the 1970s. Hiss said that "jail is a terrible place"; his surroundings at Lewisburg were "grim" and "oppressive."[5] Privacy was nonexistent but at the same time there existed an "isolation that seemed designed to make each man feel alone and helpless." Yet Hiss went about developing a prison "persona"—he was framed and a victim but also an average inmate who blended in and helped others.

Hiss taught a few inmates to read, discussed personal problems with some, helped others prepare letters, and even gave free legal advice at times. His son wrote that Hiss's sweetness and acts of kindness made strangers feel welcomed and at ease, as if he appreciated their company and cared about them, such as Leo, whom he had helped to learn to read. He never made special requests.[6] He worked in the prison warehouse as a stock clerk; for a time he worked in the library. Murray Kempton wrote in 1978, based on comments from a couple of Hiss's inmates, that in prison Hiss was kind, helpful, and a "comrade you could ask to hide your contraband and know he would never either use it himself or hand it over to the guard." Kempton found a "curious moral purity" in Hiss's position not to "fink," as though it were a protest against the system that had incarcerated him.[7] Hiss managed to maintain his dignity under the duress of life in a federal penitentiary.

Timothy Hobson, Hiss's stepson, said in an interview on August 16, 1974, that prison served as a turning point in Hiss's life, strengthening his self-assessment and his ego, and reducing an "obsessive altruism."[8] (The one thing that Alger Hiss did not seem to be in need of was a strengthening of his ego.) Tim believed that "jail is where Alger became a human being." Tim felt Alger was a "severely repressed and morally rigid person." Prison changed this, Tim said. "He could never have left Pros before prison nor could he have sustained a relationship of the sort he has with Isabel before then."[9] (Isabel Johnson lived with Hiss for years; Priscilla reportedly refused to give Alger a divorce. Isabel became Hiss's second wife when Priscilla died.) Hiss's son, Tony, had similar feelings about the effect prison experience had on his father. Alger left prison with a deeper understanding of how to reach out to people, Tony said, and this understanding was summed up in a remark his father made to him years later: "three years at Lewisburg is a good corrective to three years at Harvard."[10]

Hiss's relationships with other prisoners, especially those in organized crime, were very good. He said the convicts he found most companionable were the "racket guys," or the "regular guys," as they called themselves. They were mostly Italian-Americans from New York.[11] They were affectionate family men, loyal, and personable. Two of his best friends were in organized crime. Hiss even struck up a friendship with Frank Costello, who had asked Hiss for legal advice.[12] Hiss noted that the racket guys were the "healthiest inmates in prison" because "they had absolutely no sense of guilt"; he also perceived them as "the most stable group in prison," with "wonderful family relationships."[13]

Tony Hiss wrote that Al (which is how he often referred to his father) was generally well liked and respected by inmates, civilian employees, and guards alike.[14] Al's closest friends were all Italians, he said. One, named Vinnie, gave Hiss a new name, "Alberto," because he said "Alger" was not a name. Alger seemed to follow Vinnie's philosophy: "what was important was whether you could do your time like a man and keep your self-respect or just behave like a punk and forget your own humanity."[15] Hiss's friendships with Mafia inmates may have protected him against any assaults. Tony maintained that the one person no one could stand was David Greenglass, who was an inmate. He was Ethel Rosenberg's brother; it was his testimony that helped convict her and she was subsequently executed. Tony said his father despised Greenglass for testifying against his sister.[16]

Hiss had access to newspapers and the *New Yorker* and *New Statesman*. He also had access to the library and its limited selections. He and another inmate were successful in acquiring for the prison a library of recorded classical music. In his second year, *Witness* had been released and was serialized in the *Saturday Evening Post*. Hiss began reading the installments as soon as they appeared. In a February 7, 1952, letter to Priscilla, Hiss evaluated *Witness* by drawing a contrast between the "liberating affirmation" he was seeking to achieve in prison and the "self-imprisoned despair" that "doomed" Chambers.[17]

On entering Lewisburg, Hiss was required to present a list to the prison administration of seven people he intended to write to each week. He was allowed to write a total of three letters a week to those people and he was restricted to receiving a total of seven letters a week. His list included Priscilla, Tony, Timothy Hobson, Minnie Hiss (his eighty-three-year-old mother), Donald Hiss, his sister Anna Hiss, and one of his lawyers, Helen Buttenweiser. Priscilla sent about four letters a week (many containing postcards of Hiss's favorite paintings); his mother wrote once a week. Almost all of his letters went to Priscilla and Tony.[18] Hiss, the inveterate letter writer, sent them hundreds of letters during his prison stay.

His letters to Pros were cheery and indicated that he was making the best of his ordeal. He wrote about teaching an inmate to read and write. There were no hints of bitterness or despair.[19] One letter, written April 2, 1951, was particularly poignant. In it he wrote, "Today, Tony started back to school. I get up at quarter of seven, make my bed, get dressed, and finish breakfast before eight—just the way Tony does. So we'll all be doing the same things at the same time each school morning."[20] Another moving letter to Tony mentioned how much fun he, Alger, had in the little game he played each day with his son. When Tony got home from school, he would ring the lobby doorbell four times (the family ring) and Alger would rush downstairs to see if he could get to the second-floor landing before Tony could get up to it. Tony, who still lives in the same apartment, said he played this little daily game with his own son years later.[21]

Alger wrote letters to Tony, who was ten years old, to encourage him because of the emotional impact his imprisonment was having on his son. He felt his absence was taking place at a critical time in his son's life. The letters were cheery, supportive, and filled with doodles. They contained made-up stories about the "Sugar Lump Boy" and riddles, and drawings and many rebuses.[22] Hiss's 1957 biography, *In the Court of Public Opinion*, written after he was released from prison, had been criticized as legalistic, wooden, and detached. For Tony the letters his father wrote from prison reflected the inner man—his father's real autobiography—showing his affection, concern, and attentiveness for Priscilla and him. Tony believed that the hundreds of letters Hiss sent home from prison were really "the book he never wrote."[23] In effect, they were the true measure of Alger's "face one."[24] For his part, Alger rejoiced in his letter writing.

Alger knew that prison visits were troubling for Tony. The prolonged absence of his father and the stigma of the case were an emotional burden on him. In late 1952, Priscilla got a job and Tony was coming home from Dalton School to an empty apartment each day. He became a New York "latchkey" kid. By early 1953, Tony suffered a series of accidents and there was concern about thoughts of suicide. He was then taken to a psychiatrist twice a week.[25]

Visits were allowed only for a prisoner's immediate family and, by federal regulations, visiting time was for a maximum of two hours a month. Priscilla, who lived in New York, had been a faithful visitor, taking the eight-hour trip each month. At times she came to the prison for an hour Saturday, and then spent the second hour there on Sunday, after staying overnight at the Lewisburg Inn. The trip from New York was long; by train to Scranton, Pennsylvania, then another train to West Milton, and then a bus to Lewisburg. She took a cab from the bus station to and from the prison for a ninety-cent charge each way. Priscilla ate at a local restaurant on Market Street. She had the reputation in town of a pleasant, friendly woman, and a modest tipper. She never disclosed her identity to anyone.[26] Tony accompanied her on some of these visits.

Alger Hiss was released from Lewisburg at about noon on November 27, 1954, after forty-four months in prison, and about two weeks after his fiftieth birthday. He was not released ahead of schedule; he earned time off for good behavior. He had been a model prisoner and a popular one. He drove back to New York with his lawyer Chester Lane, Priscilla, and thirteen-year-old Tony. He said he looked forward to time with family and friends. "I dreamed of going to museums and galleries; to concerts and plays, and simply walking freely about the street."[27] His period of "conditional release" was sixteen months, during which he reported to a parole officer and could leave New York and its environs only with the officer's permission, even to visit his mother in Baltimore.

Outside the prison more than seventy newsmen surrounded Hiss, who made his first public statement on being released: "I am very glad to use this chance—the first I have had in nearly four years—to reassert my complete innocence of the charges that were brought against me by Whittaker Chambers. . . . I have had to wait in silence while in my absence, a myth has been developed. I hope that the return of the mere man will help to dispel the myth. I shall renew my efforts to dispel the deception that has been foisted on the American people." He said he hoped to "allay" the "fear and hysteria of those times." Then, with his family and his lawyer, Alger Hiss drove off in a red convertible.[28]

XIII

CRUSADE FOR VINDICATION, 1954–96

*Hiss: The Juries, the Judges, and the Court System
Were Politicized and Corrupt*

ALGER HISS WAS released from prison in November 1954 and spent the rest of his life—he died in 1996 at age ninety-two—launching a crusade to vindicate himself. For forty-two years Hiss waged an unsuccessful struggle to exonerate his name. As the decades passed and new information became available from Soviet archives, Hiss's guilt was being confirmed. Whittaker Chambers commented on the outlook for Hiss following his release from Lewisburg. On his Maryland farm, Chambers, thinner than he was before his two major heart attacks in the previous two years, observed: "Alger Hiss will be passing from the ordeal of prison to the ordeal of daily living, which may well prove more trying. Hiss is approaching the most difficult moment of his life." The next day, a reporter repeated this comment to Hiss as he arrived at his home. Hiss responded tersely: "Was that his hope or a statement?"[1]

In New York City, Hiss moved back into his Greenwich Village apartment at 22 East Eighth Street, the place the Hisses rented when Alger first moved from Washington, D.C., to work for the Carnegie Endowment in 1947, and where Priscilla and Tony lived while he was in prison. While on parole, he reported his activities to a parole officer. Hiss was confined to New York's Southern District; he could not travel beyond fifty miles from New York.[2]

Being disbarred, Hiss was no longer able to practice law. The Hiss family's big worry now was money; their savings (along with money from friends and family) were depleted for legal fees. Hiss thought about teaching but was blacklisted at prep schools and colleges that deferred to the concerns of trustees and contributors. He continued to search for employment, but refusals came in from other areas as well, such as minor executive jobs in publishing and business. He had great difficulty in finding work.

While still in prison, Hiss had secured publishers' advances from Alfred Knopf in the United States and John Calder in England for ten thousand dollars for his upcoming book. And they had Priscilla's salary at a Doubleday Doran bookstore where she had taken a job while Hiss was in Lewisburg; her take-home pay was thirty-seven dollars a week.[3] Priscilla's wages were supplemented by money from her brother and the Hiss family. Tony's school tuition then and through college was paid for through scholarships. The rent for their apartment was modest. Nonetheless, their financial situation remained strained; their income enabled them to live simply. But they still went to the Philharmonic at Carnegie Hall, to chamber music concerts, to galleries and museums that were free, or an occasional play on or off-Broadway.

After his parole period ended, in the mid-1950s, Hiss began to receive invitations to lecture on foreign policy and the Cold War on college campuses. The first one was at Princeton University in the spring of 1956 on the "Meaning of Geneva." Hiss accepted an invitation from the Whig-Clio Society of Princeton University to speak on the likely effects of the Eisenhower-Khrushchev summit meeting. His reception was inhospitable, he claimed. Hiss also had written an article on Yalta that appeared in the *Pocket Book*

Magazine in September 1955.[4] His book, *In the Court of Public Opinion,* appeared in 1957 to mixed reviews and poor sales.

Now Hiss really needed to find a job. Hiss tried to learn typing and shorthand skills but failed miserably. Despite increasing marital problems with Priscilla and tight finances, Hiss said he remained self-confident. Then Peter Kihss of the *New York Times* interviewed Hiss and reported he was seeking a job. Andre Smith, president of Feathercombs, a company that made rhinestone-decorated barrettes, offered Hiss a job at six thousand a year, which was later raised to eleven thousand. He worked at Feathercombs for two years on the administrative staff. When sales started to drop drastically, Hiss had to leave and find another job. Feathercombs eventually went under.[5] Hiss collected unemployment most of 1959 and part of 1960. However, he was not completely destitute. His mother, Minnie, died in 1958, and according to her will she left Alger $15,000 and his $9,500 IOU debt.[6]

Domestic troubles had begun about a year after Hiss's return. Priscilla had never been able to cope with the trauma of the Hiss trials. She had been a grade school English teacher at New York's Dalton School (where son Tony was a student) during the Hiss case; the publicity from the case led the school to replace her.[7] Her job at Doubleday was an administrative one with an office in the basement. Priscilla did not want to be involved in Hiss's crusade for vindication. According to Tony, Pros wanted them to run away and change their name; however, for sixteen months Alger had to report to a parole officer once a week.

After Hiss completed his parole requirement, Priscilla still wanted to start a new life under a new name in a different part of the country. She never overcame the psychological and emotional damage the case and indictment had done to her. Tony Hiss felt that Alger was composed throughout while Pros was filled with anxieties "and each deeply resented the other's behavior."[8] Alger wrote that his wife did the best she could during the strains of the trials; she wasn't paranoid (he said he found out later the FBI was tapping their phone); he said he actually was at fault for his assurances that everything would be okay because they were in the best of hands: the courts.[9]

Alger had other plans; he was determined to devote his energy and life to proving his innocence. However, Hiss wrote that when he came home, Priscilla wanted to flee the scene. "She suggested we change our names and try to get posts as teachers at some remote experimental school impervious to public opinion."[10] Hiss said his goals and needs were the opposite; he felt that the lies should be confronted and faced down. He wrote about the travesty of the HUAC hearings and the trials.[11] For Priscilla, who was a very private person, it was reliving the nightmare. Hiss said, "I dedicated the book (i.e., *In the Court of Public Opinion*) to her, but it gave her no pleasure." Moreover, "Our disagreement as to our future goals became irreconcilable and spread. We disagreed about Tony's education, about summer vacation plans, even about what friends to see."[12] The friction only increased and Hiss finally left.

According to Hiss, Priscilla asked him to leave in the fall of 1958. But Hiss insisted on staying until Tony came home from Putney School for the Christmas holidays.[13] He wanted to tell his son in person about the marital breakup. Hiss then moved out of the family apartment. They tried reconciliation several times but it did not work. He spent the next several years in rented rooms and at friends' apartments. Hiss met another woman, Isabel Johnson, whom he lived with for years after he left Priscilla; Alger married Isabel when Priscilla died in 1984.

Isabel Johnson, a model, writer, and editor, was born Isabel Dowden in Montclair, New Jersey, on July 11, 1908, the only child of Elsie (Ruckelshaus) and Dawson Dowden. She graduated from Montclair High School in 1926 and went to Syracuse University, where she met Malcolm Perry Johnson, a student at St. Lawrence University whom she married in 1931. A well-known model in Paris and New York, she was photographed by Louise Dahl-Wolfe, Edward Steichen, and Alfred Stieglitz, among others, and modeled for illustrator René Bouché. Isabel was the health and beauty editor for *Glamour* magazine (1943–45) and the *New York Times* (1945–46), and worked for the National Association for Mental Health (1951–56) and the American Cancer Society (1956–58), where she was education director of the Los Angeles County branch. Johnson was subsequently married to a merchant marine and then to Lester Cole, author of screenplays and one of the Hollywood Ten blacklisted during the McCarthy era. In 1984 she married her fourth husband and longtime friend Alger Hiss. Isabel died in Manhattan at the age of ninety-one on May 3, 2000.[14]

The *New York Times* reported on February 17, 1959, that Hiss and his wife, Priscilla, had parted after thirty years of marriage; no information was given as to cause. When the Hisses separated, Alger moved out and eventually took an apartment at 391 West Street, also in Greenwich Village. Priscilla remained in the same apartment for more than two decades, until she died. Tony Hiss and his own family live in the very apartment to this day.

Priscilla had difficulty keeping a job after Hiss's indictment. During this time period, she held various jobs. In 1955 she was employed by the Doubleday store; she also worked for Pantheon Books, and as an editor at several other publishing houses in New York City, including the Golden Press and the children's book division of the Western Publishing Company. She got a job in 1960 as a clerical assistant to the director of the E. Weyhe Art Gallery at 794 Lexington Avenue, and in 1961 she went to work for the John Day Company, a publisher with offices at 210 Madison Avenue.[15] Her memory of those years was that "she was carrying the flag for the family." She told Tony to be cheerful outside the house or in front of company. She didn't buy clothes or spend much on food, but paid for Tony to have piano lessons and kept her subscription to the New York Philharmonic. Tony wrote: "I was angry at Al for leaving me . . . and I felt that Prossy was somehow stronger than Al, because she was still there and he wasn't."[16]

Finally, in 1960 Hiss was hired as a salesman for a stationery and printing company, Davison-Bluth, which was later taken over by S. Novick and Son.[17] He claimed, "I went to work with a will. My many friends sent me to see friends or business acquaintances of theirs. Entrée was easy. I sensed that the business executives who received me genially were looking forward to saying at dinner parties: Guess who wants to sell me rubber bands and paper clips."[18] He began this position with a draw of fifty dollars a week against his monthly commissions.

Before long, Hiss had achieved some success as a salesman. His experience, he maintained, as a storehouse clerk at Lewisburg enabled him to cope with the great number of standard stationery items. Hiss held this job, which he claimed to enjoy, longer than any other in his life, until he retired in the late 1970s. The way Alger Hiss was able to adapt both to prison and his life after as a salesman was truly remarkable. He seemed to handle with great equanimity the disgrace of his fall, from being center stage with world leaders at Yalta and the founding of the United Nations, to being a convict and then stationery salesman.

Because Alger had sent Tony to the Putney School in Vermont after Hiss was released from prison, his son missed much of the marital fighting during these several years. In January 1959, Alger walked out on Prossy the day Tony returned to Putney for winter term his senior year. Money was always a problem. Tony said he was told he was on full scholarship but years later he found out that his father's friends actually paid his tuition.[19] Throughout Alger's post-prison life, his close circle of really devoted friends frequently provided financial assistance to him. In addition to the inheritance from his mother's death, he received royalties from his book. Tony had good grades until his parents separated, after which he didn't study much. Alger wanted Tony to go to the University of California at Berkeley, but Tony went to Harvard, where he majored in English history and literature and received a bachelor's degree in 1963. He then had a job writing for "The Talk of the Town" section of the *New Yorker*.[20]

Tony moved back with Prossy; he said she was in a "bad way."
He saw his father every week or two for lunch; Tony admitted
that he always was late and argumentative with his father, and was
rude to his friends. Tony was jealous of Alger not being at Eighth
Street.[21] His half-brother, Tim Hobson, wrote Alger a letter from
San Francisco, where he was a medical intern, telling him to give
Prossy whatever she wanted because it was necessary to support her
anxieties and not confront them.[22]

Tony finally moved out and got his own apartment on West Tenth
Street. At this point, Tony said he felt his life started to change and
he was much happier. He went to work and made lots of friends; he
improved his relationship with Alger and they became much closer;
he finally started to get to know his dad, he said. He wanted to learn
to tend bar, and did so at a place on West Seventy-Second Street.
Alger didn't say much about this, and Tony wondered what he was
thinking. "Al can still play it close to the chest when he feels like
it."[23] Over the years Tony was a strong advocate for his father's innocence, as was Hiss's stepson, Timothy. Tim, almost seventy when
Alger died, was a retired surgeon living on the west coast. He had
been married and had four children and seven grandchildren. Timothy separated amicably from his wife after thirty-five years of marriage and "has now found happiness in a stable gay relationship."[24]

In later years, Priscilla became involved in local Democratic
politics, serving with Community Board 2 in Greenwich Village,
the Village Independent Democrats (from which Mayor Ed Koch
emerged), and the Democratic County Committee of New York
County. Toward the end of her life, Priscilla Hiss was appointed
to Manhattan's Community Planning Board No. 2 by Borough
President Percy Sutton. She died at eighty-one years old in October 1984 in St. Vincent's Hospital of complications resulting from
a stroke she had suffered four years previously. Priscilla had lived in
Greenwich Village since 1947 and at the Village Nursing Home
since 1982. A memorial service was held at the Episcopal Church
of the Ascension, on Fifth Avenue.[25]

During her lifetime, including the twenty-five years after she and Alger separated, Priscilla Hiss maintained that Alger was innocent despite his 1950 conviction for lying to conceal Communist espionage. Throughout the ordeal, her loyalty to Hiss never wavered.[26] Priscilla had an enormous influence and impact on the first half of his life. It is thus surprising that in his memoir, Hiss did not mention Priscilla until late in the book, when he discussed the perjury trials. Hiss wrote that Priscilla was "deeply wounded by the trauma of the trials and the resulting invasion of her privacy."[27]

When their marital difficulties came to a head and Priscilla asked him to leave, Hiss wrote, "I was astounded to discover the break she proposed was a relief." Several attempts at reconciliation failed: "the wounds were too deep."[28] Hiss felt his determined effort to achieve vindication "was profoundly distasteful to Priscilla."[29] Nonetheless, to marginalize Priscilla in his memoir, written years later, when she had been such an intricate part of his life, may reflect some level of enduring bitterness toward Priscilla or that his effort at vindication eclipsed even his relationship with his wife. However, it's worth noting that even Isabel was barely mentioned: "It was at this time that I came to know the talented and beautiful Isabel, who is now my wife."[30] The one person Alger seemed to be unequivocally devoted to his whole life was his son, Tony.

In the fall of 1967, Hiss gave four lectures on the Depression and the New Deal at the New School for Social Research. Hiss felt his lectures were well attended during the 1960s because the civil rights movement and opposition to the Vietnam War had created a political atmosphere similar to the 1930s. The New School invited him back to conduct seminars on the New Deal. He spoke at Brandeis and Columbia in 1968, and gave many lectures in England in 1972. He expanded his list of topics to include the Yalta Conference, the United Nations, Far Eastern policy, Justice Holmes, and the McCarthy era.[31]

There was a lull in the crusade to redeem himself until 1974 and Watergate. Then Hiss's campaign for vindication profited from

Richard Nixon's disgrace. During the Watergate episode, the anti-Nixon mood of the country caused a renewed interest in the Hiss case and Nixon's role in it. As the momentum picked up, Hiss received many invitations to speak at universities and public forums. In addition to his lectures, Hiss said he felt obliged to help students and researchers writing on the case. He gave interviews and provided files to Dr. Meyer Zeligs and John Chabot Smith, both of whom wrote biographies on Hiss. The most significant example, however, was Allen Weinstein. Hiss gave many interviews and full access to his files to Weinstein, who initially thought that Hiss was innocent. However, at the end of his monumental book, *Perjury*, based on exhaustive evidence from FBI files and hundreds of interviews, Weinstein claimed Hiss was guilty, which Zeligs and Smith had not.[32] Historian Arthur Schlesinger Jr. wrote that *Perjury* was "the most objective and convincing" account of the case to date.[33]

In March 1972, the so-called Hiss Act was ruled unconstitutional and Hiss's government pension was restored. Another victory, Hiss felt, occurred in August 1975 when he was readmitted to the Massachusetts bar by decision of the state supreme court. In July 1978, based in part on information Hiss received from FBI files under the Freedom of Information Act, he filed a petition for a writ of error coram nobis. According to Hiss, these FBI files showed that the government had withheld evidence damaging to the prosecution and helpful to his defense. They also showed, he claimed, the government's tampering with witnesses and infiltration of his legal staff.[34] It was denied in 1982. The appeal was denied in February 1983 and on October 1983 a writ of certiorari was rejected by the U.S. Supreme Court. Three times over the years, the Court had refused to hear Hiss's case. Hiss invoked every appeal process the U.S. federal system had to offer, but to no avail. At age seventy-nine, Alger Hiss had exhausted all legal remedies.

After a half century, Hiss had lost every single case he took to the U.S. court system. All his appeals were rejected, despite his defense by some of the U.S.'s best legal talent. Yet even late in life, in his outrage he continued to blame the system. The pillars of justice, he said, are "undermined when appellate judges—all 'honorable men'—are so inflamed by their prejudices that they brush aside the government's concealment of exculpatory evidence, evidence that had it been timely disclosed, would have resulted in a different verdict."[35] Because the U.S. legal system continued to find him guilty, Hiss denounced all aspects of it as fraudulent.

Over the decades, Hiss had managed to keep stirring the embers of doubt about his guilt. Some observers thought he probably knew Chambers more than he said; others believed he may have been a Communist, but not involved in espionage; and still others maintained that even if he was involved in espionage, it was at a time when the USSR was an ally and the information he gave to Moscow was harmless. Hiss took advantage of that position by avoiding the issue of individual guilt and during the trial speaking in the first person plural: "*We* were convinced of the rightness of *our* cause and that *we* would prevail" (emphasis added). Hiss deflected his own culpability and put a "cause" on trial.[36]

At the late age of eighty-eight, Hiss made one last attempt at redemption. John Lowenthal was one of Hiss's most outspoken defenders. His 1980 film, *The Trials of Alger Hiss*, was a summary of Hiss's campaign to restore his innocence. After the dissolution of the Soviet Union in 1991 and the opening of some Soviet archives by Boris Yeltsin, together Hiss and Lowenthal devised a plan to request Moscow to search its intelligence files for any evidence against Hiss. In August 1992, Hiss wrote a letter to several Russian officials asking for evidence confirming that he was "never a paid, contracted agent of the Soviet Union."[37] His careful use of the qualification "paid, contracted" would have ensured a negative answer.

Lowenthal went to Moscow in September 1992 as Hiss's representative and met with Dmitri Volkogonov, who for years served as an official historian. After a few weeks, Volkogonov gave a letter to Lowenthal saying that he had found no evidence that Hiss was either a recruited agent or a paid contract agent. Volkogonov also said there was no evidence that Chambers was an agent, only a party member. On October 29, 1992, Lowenthal released the letter and held a press conference with Hiss. The media (the *New York Times, Washington Post,* and the TV networks) ran wild with the story of Hiss's innocence. However, Soviet scholars such as Richard Pipes at Harvard, Alexander Dallin at Stanford, and Robert Tucker at Princeton cautioned that Volkogonov may have overstated his findings.[38]

And this precisely turned out to be the case. Volkogonov's research, he admitted, was cursory—only two days! And he had looked only at materials from party archives that included KGB reports to the party. In any event, both Alger Hiss and Whittaker Chambers worked not for the KGB but for the GRU, whose files to this day have never been opened. All of Volkogonov's public statements on this matter would have to have been cleared by Russian intelligence and security officials, or perhaps even scripted in conjunction with them. Later, in a letter published in the Moscow *Nezavisimaya Gazeta* on November 24, 1992, Volkogonov essentially retracted his initial statements; he said his categorical comments were an accommodation to Hiss and Lowenthal. He maintained that Hiss had said to him "he wanted to die peacefully" and Lowenthal had "pushed me hard to say things of which I was not fully convinced." In December 1992, in an interview with Moscow's *New York Times* correspondent Serge Schmemann, Volkogonov repeated that he had been pressured by Lowenthal in his initial communication. He reiterated that military intelligence files were not searched and also noted that many documents have been destroyed.[39] The U.S. media's coverage of Volkogonov's retraction ranged from minimal to none.

Notably, some Hiss defenders seemed to ignore the legal dimension of the story. As recently as 1996, former senator and presidential candidate George McGovern wrote, "I've always believed that Hiss was a victim of the 'red scare' and of Nixon's political rapacity.

It is a national outrage that this essentially decent and patriotic American went to prison as a consequence of the demagoguery of Nixon and the ignominious House Committee on Un-American Activities."[40] In a letter written in September 1996, McGovern suggested he would "speak to President Clinton about a possible pardon for Mr. Hiss after the election."[41] McGovern seemingly dismissed the fact that, Nixon and the HUAC aside, after a grand jury indictment, two trials, and all the appeals Hiss had made over the years, including to the Supreme Court, it was the United States legal system that found Alger Hiss guilty.

The Hiss controversy was thrust into the national news again in 1996, when President Clinton had nominated Anthony Lake to be director of central intelligence. Lake's grandfather had been a clergyman in the Church of England prior to coming to the United States and Lake's father was a New Deal Democrat. Lake attended the prestigious Middlesex boarding school in Concord, Massachusetts, and then Harvard College, where he was a member of the exclusive Fly Club, whose membership has also included Franklin Roosevelt and Senator Jay Rockefeller.

Lake started his career in the State Department as a Foreign Service officer; during the Nixon years he worked as an assistant to Henry Kissinger. In 1992 he was one of presidential candidate Bill Clinton's chief foreign policy advisors. Following the election, Lake served as national security advisor (1993–97). In 1996 Clinton nominated Lake to the CIA leadership position. The nomination failed, in part because Lake, when asked on NBC's *Meet the Press* in November of that year whether Hiss was a spy, answered, "I don't think it's conclusive."[42] After coming under attack in Congress about his foreign policies, Lake asked his nomination be withdrawn. Lake's comment is an example of how the elite eastern establishment remained loyal to Hiss, and was unwilling to accept the facts and reality. And the Hiss story remains radioactive. Hiss supporters were aghast in 2004 when President George W. Bush nominated Allen Weinstein to be archivist of the United States.

Weinstein's book *Perjury* had made a major impact with its portrayal of Hiss as guilty of spying.[43]

In his eighties, Hiss's eyesight began to deteriorate because of macular degeneration. His many friends took turns reading to him in New York and, in the summers, at his East Hampton home on Long Island. He died in New York on November 15, 1996, four days after his ninety-second birthday. He was survived by his wife, Isabel; his son, Tony, and Tony's wife, Lois Metzger, and their son, Jacob; and Priscilla's son, Timothy Hobson.[44] Condolences poured in, recounting how Alger was a "lovely man" and great friend. In a memorial service held at St. George's Episcopal Church in New York in December 1996, Hiss was eulogized as a man of civility and sophistication who had spent the second half of his life seeking vindication.[45]

Though Hiss lost every court appeal he initiated, his crusade for vindication to some extent was successful. His government pension was restored in 1972, retroactive to November 1966; he was reinstated to the Massachusetts bar in 1975; adoring audiences at university campuses came to hear him speak; a chair in his honor at Bard College was created; and a following of loyalists proclaimed his innocence until and after he died.

In his 1950 book, *Men Without Faces,* Louis Budenz, who had been managing editor of the *Daily Worker* from 1940 until his break with the party in 1945, offered some ideological perspective that seems to explain Hiss's persistent defiance. Writing about his Communist education, Budenz said that the party represented discipline; its comrades had to be "steeled to meet any emergency." Budenz wrote that there is a "peculiar Communist morality," according to Lenin, one that is derived from the interests of the class struggle of the proletariat. "That morality calls for the employment of illegitimate and illegal methods when required, for the concealment of facts." Budenz went on to state that this "Communist morality" had been pointed up recently by the Hiss-Chambers trial. The Communist is not a pathological liar, he wrote. The Communist will lie and spread falsehoods and "on the witness stand, he will resort to perjury, if necessary, to protect the interests of his Party. But this is done under Party orders and for Party purposes, and is regarded as a cardinal feature of Communist morality."[46] Communist ideology and "Communist morality" thus apparently enabled Hiss to present a persona of righteousness for a half century in defiance of the facts and the abundant evidence of his treason.

PART FOUR

The Evidence

XIV.

TESTIMONIES

*Hiss: As Long as I Live I Will Never Understand How
Chambers Stole Those Documents from My Office*

B EYOND THE DRAMA of the Hiss case, which captured
the nation's attention from 1948 to 1950, and beyond the
partisan politics surrounding Truman, Nixon, and Mc-
Carthy, there is a large, compelling body of evidence—testimonial,
documentary, and archival—pointing to Alger Hiss's guilt as a
Soviet asset involved in espionage against the United States. The
evidence is discussed in this and the next two chapters. This chapter
focuses on the testimonies of a variety of people who over a period
of years maintained that Hiss was a Communist involved in Soviet
underground activities. While some of what appears here has been
referred to earlier in this narrative, it is important to present the
data in aggregate here to stress the totality of the testimonies. The
Venona program and archival material also will be examined.

Alexander Barmine

One of the first of the testimonies came from a former chargé
d'affaires at the Soviet Embassy in Athens, Alexander Gregory-
Graff Barmine, who had defected in 1937. Barmine was interviewed

by the FBI in New York City on December 14, 1948. He claimed
that in 1938, shortly after his defection, he visited Walter Krivitsky,
a GRU general who also had just defected. (Stalin's purges of his
own intelligence operatives led to many defections during this period.) Krivitsky's last post before he defected to the West was as "illegal" *rezident* in Holland. Barmine claimed that he was suspicious
of Krivitsky; he feared Krivitsky may have been sent by Moscow
to force him to go back to the Soviet Union. Barmine said he told
Krivitsky of his misgivings during his visit to him in Paris, and that
in order to establish Krivitsky's reliability as a defector, Barmine
asked Krivitsky to name some individuals who were working for
the GRU in the United States. Krivitsky named about ten persons,
including Alger Hiss and Harry Dexter White. During Barmine's
interview by the FBI in 1948, he was asked about Alger Hiss; he
said that "he had heard Alger Hiss referred to as being an agent of
Soviet Military Intelligence."[1] During the same interview, Barmine
also said that while he was attached to the Trade Commission in
Moscow, he saw the GRU chief, General Jan Berzin, every other
day. Barmine claimed Berzin told him during one such visit that
the Soviets had some Americans working for them in China. He
named Owen Lattimore and Joseph Barnes. It is highly improbable
that the chief of the GRU would divulge the names of its agents to
a non-GRU diplomat. Therefore one would assume that the diplomat, Barmine, was also a GRU officer.

Yet the background on Alexander Barmine is somewhat unclear.
In his autobiography he stated that he had attended the Minsk
Infantry Officers' School and as a *koursanti* (student officer) fought
during the Russian Civil War and the 1920 Polish campaign.
He then was accepted to study at the newly constituted General
Staff College for senior officers. Barmine wrote that he studied at
the school's faculty for Oriental languages, which was conducted
jointly by both the War College and the Foreign Office.[2] In his
book, he never claimed that he was a military intelligence officer
of the Red Army (in other words, in the GRU), but wrote that he

ALGER HISS   223

went on to become a diplomat. However, British author Gordon Brook-Shepherd, in his book *The Storm Petrels,* stated that a few days after Ignace Reiss (also a GRU operative) defected in Paris, "Alexander Barmine, a senior employee of the GRU who was masquerading as a diplomat at the Soviet Embassy in Athens," also decided to defect. Owen Lock also maintained that Barmine was "experienced in the GRU and in the Ministry of Foreign Affairs."[3] After Barmine defected he went to the United States, became a U.S. citizen, and served with the U.S. Army and OSS during World War II.[4] The question arises: Why, if he was a GRU officer, would Barmine not have included this fact in his memoir? On the other hand, if he was not a GRU officer, why would he have asked GRU general Krivitsky, in order to test his bona fides, to name GRU agents in the United States? How would Barmine have known if the individuals Krivitsky identified were indeed GRU sources if he was not in the GRU himself?

U.S. Ambassador William Bullitt

The next testimony describing Hiss as a Soviet agent came from the former U.S. ambassador to France, William C. Bullitt. In September 1939, Bullitt said he had been told by French premier Edouard Daladier that Alger Hiss was a Communist. Bullitt later told President Roosevelt, who reportedly brushed it off.[5] Bullitt said he also relayed this information to Hiss's superior at the State Department, Stanley K. Hornbeck.[6] Bullitt warned Hornbeck that before his departure from France the French premier stated that "two brothers named Hiss," both in the State Department, were "Soviet agents." Daladier, according to Bullitt, attributed his information to French counterintelligence sources.[7] Hornbeck confronted Hiss, who denied the allegation.[8] Bullitt repeated this information to the FBI in October 1949 and in testimony before the Senate Internal Security Subcommittee in April 1952.[9] A February 4, 1949, FBI memo reported that the coincidence of Daladier's remarks to

Bullitt and former GRU officer Walter Krivitsky's earlier interrogation by French counterintelligence (which would not have typically come across Hiss's name in their duties) suggested that Krivitsky probably was the source for Daladier.[10]

Igor Gouzenko

Lieutenant Igor Gouzenko (1919–82) was born in the village of Rogachevo, not far from Moscow. He joined the military and trained as a cipher clerk for the GRU. In 1943 he was stationed in Ottawa, Canada, with the office of the Soviet military attaché. On September 5, 1945, Gouzenko defected and handed over to Canadian authorities detailed data about Soviet intelligence operations he had access to for two years. He turned over more than a hundred top-secret military intelligence documents that proved the existence of a large Soviet espionage network in both Canada and the United States. Gouzenko lived outside the Soviet compound in the military attaché house, a major transgression of standard operational procedures for cipher clerks, thus facilitating his defection. The list of agents "given up" by Gouzenko after his defection included a number of well-known people both in Canada and internationally, in the United States and Great Britain. These included members of the Canadian Parliament and nuclear scientists. One of those arrested by the Canadians was Alan Nunn May, a British scientist working in Canada on part of the British-American atomic bomb project.[11] According to an FBI memorandum in September 1945, Gouzenko, when questioned by the FBI and Canadian security officials, stated that he "had been informed by Lieutenant Kulakov in the office of the Soviet military attaché that the Soviets had an agent in the United States in May 1945 who was an assistant to the then Secretary of State," Edward R. Stettinius.[12] While Stettinius had a few assistants, Alger Hiss was one who held this post at that time.

Elizabeth Bentley

At almost the same time, on November 7, 1945, Elizabeth Bentley, another Soviet defector but unconnected to Gouzenko, provided the FBI with a similar allegation. She later testified on July 31, 1948, before the HUAC, publicly accusing Harry Dexter White and Lauchlin Currie of being Soviet agents. Bentley, a Soviet underground courier, testified that one member of the Perlo Group (the network that she ran), Harold Glasser, earlier had been part of a separate Soviet network headed by Alger Hiss. Bentley testified that when Glasser returned from a European assignment, he asked to go back with the Perlo Group. She then said she found out who was "running" Glasser; she had been told about Hiss by Charles Kramer, a Hiss associate in the Agricultural Adjustment Administration and a person identified as a member of the Ware Group by both Lee Pressman and Nathaniel Weyl.[13] Kramer said that a man named Hiss who worked as an advisor in the State Department had taken Harold Glasser of the Treasury Department away from Victor Perlo's group and turned him over to direct control by the Soviet representatives in the United States. Bentley recalled his name as "Eugene" Hiss.[14]

Whittaker Chambers

The identification of Hiss as a Soviet spy by Whittaker Chambers was the central and most definitive of all the testimonies. It was the most critical testimony because it went beyond the verbal; he produced documentary evidence (the Pumpkin Papers) that probably was the single most important piece of evidence against Hiss at his trials. In addition, other documentary evidence such as the title for the car that Hiss had given to the Communist Party; the paid receipts for the four Bokhara rugs given to four Soviet assets, including Hiss; as well as the typewriter used to type the stolen classified material, all corroborated Chambers's testimony rather than Hiss's continuous and all-encompassing denials.

At first Chambers identified Hiss as a member of the Communist Party; testimony of his espionage activities came later. On November 27, 1945, the FBI disseminated a secret memo to the State Department, the attorney general, and the Truman White House, reporting Chambers's identification of Hiss as a secret member of the Communist underground apparatus in contact with the Ware Group.[15] Whittaker Chambers's comprehensive memoir, *Witness,* detailed his close relationship with Hiss. After initially denying he knew Chambers, Hiss finally and reluctantly backpedaled and confessed he knew him, but only in passing and by another name, George Crosley. It is not possible to read *Witness* and the transcripts of the HUAC hearings, as well as the testimonies of the two trials, and not conclude that the two men knew each other and had a close personal relationship. An enormous body of literature has been written on all these events. The next few paragraphs will cover the highlights of Chambers's testimony providing evidence against Alger Hiss.

Chambers's close relationship with Hiss is reflected in his memoir, where he remembered many intimate details and stories from Alger Hiss's life. He was familiar with the interior of Hiss's various homes. During Chambers's testimony, when he was providing such details of Hiss's life to establish he knew him, he recounted the story of Hiss as a young boy selling spring water from Druid Hill Park in Baltimore. This type of small detail, one of many, lent enormous credibility to Chambers's testimony that he knew Hiss; how could he possibly be aware of this particular from Hiss's childhood unless Hiss shared this boyhood memory with him? Chambers was aware of nicknames of the Hisses and he knew that Hiss was an enthusiastic bird watcher. Chambers testified that when the Hisses moved to 2905 P Street NW in Washington, D.C., from an apartment at 2831 Twenty-Eighth Street, there were a few weeks left on the lease and Hiss offered the place to Chambers and his family to stay there until the lease expired.[16] In addition, the Chambers family stayed with the Hiss family in their home on P Street for a few nights on another occasion.[17] Hiss met Chambers on various occasions for lunch when he worked on the Hill in the Senate Office Building for the Nye Commission, and at least one time gave Chambers a ride to New York from Washington.[18]

Hiss admitted that he lent Chambers money and claimed he threw in his old Ford car along with the sublease for the apartment. Hiss said that except for a few dollars and a rug, Chambers never paid him the money he owed from rent or had borrowed. The 1929 Ford that Hiss insisted he gave to Chambers was actually given to a member of the Communist Party, William Rosen, for his use as a party organizer. Congressional investigators produced motor vehicle records with Hiss's signature to show the car was turned over to an official of the Communist Party.[19] Hiss never adequately explained why he had done so much for some casual passerby he called George Crosley. A list of things (car, apartment, rug, loans) suggests that the relationship was much more than "casual" as Hiss tried to portray in his testimony. On every salient point Chambers's version was verified.

Chambers claimed that just before Christmas 1936, Soviet colonel Boris Bykov, head of Soviet military intelligence in the United States, had given him eight hundred dollars to buy four Bokhara rugs from Soviet Uzbekistan for his network: Alger Hiss, Harry Dexter White, George Silverman, and Julian Wadleigh. According to Whittaker Chambers, Bykov meant the gifts to be in recognition of their services to the Soviet Union. Hiss would later claim that Chambers had given him his rug in 1935 in partial payment for rent. Chambers's version was corroborated by Columbia University art historian Meyer Schapiro, who confirmed that he arranged the purchase (and produced the canceled check dated December 23, 1936); by the Massachusetts Importing Company of Manhattan, which confirmed selling Schapiro the four rugs (and produced the bill of sale); by White's widow and Silverman, who acknowledged that they had received their rugs sometime between late 1936 and the fall of 1938; and by Wadleigh, who confessed to having been a member of Chambers's apparatus and delivering classified government documents to him, who confirmed that he had received his rug for New Year's 1937, and who admitted that he understood the rug to be a gift from the Soviets. The time it would have taken to ship the rugs to Washington, D.C., established that Hiss had known Chambers in 1937, which he had denied to the grand jury.[20]

In November 1937, Whittaker Chambers bought a car, using four hundred dollars he said Alger Hiss had lent him. Hiss denied the loan. The prosecution was able to produce a bill of sale that showed Chambers purchased a car for $486.75 from Schmitt Motor Company, a Maryland car dealer, on November 23, 1937. Hiss denied making the loan, yet records showed that the Hisses withdrew four hundred dollars in cash from their savings on November 19, four days before Chambers bought the car. At first the Hisses claimed that they had used the money to buy furniture for a new house, but they had not signed a lease at the time and could not produce receipts for any purchases, nor explain why they had used cash from savings rather than the checking and charge accounts they otherwise used for such purchases.[21] In addition, documentation strongly indicated that Hiss was not truthful in his testimony that he lost all contact with Chambers in 1936. Hiss stated that Chambers had never visited him during 1937–38 on Thirtieth Street or subsequently at his residence 3415 Volta Place in Georgetown.

And, of course, there is the infamous typewriter. The story surrounding the old Woodstock typewriter owned by the Hisses, originally given to Priscilla by her father and used to type the stolen State Department classified material, could fill a book. It was an important part of the prosecution's case to tie Hiss to the stolen State Department documents (the Pumpkin Papers) Chambers had hidden. The defense strategy rested on an attempt to show that the Hisses had not possessed the Woodstock at the time the stolen documents were typed. Eventually the typewriter was tracked down; the Hisses had given it to one of their maids, Claudia

Catlett. Catlett (and her two sons) provided much contradictory testimony, for example, on Chambers's name (but she did recognize him); on when she received the typewriter; and on what condition it was in. When asked during his grand jury testimony how the typewriter was disposed of, Hiss testified that he had no idea what happened to it.[22]

The recovered typewriter was compared with items previously typed on it by the Hisses and with the typed material from the Pumpkin Papers documents. For example, the headmaster of the private school attended by Timothy Hobson turned over pages from his file typed by his mother, Priscilla Hiss. These papers as well as other family correspondence matched the typeface on the documents that Chambers had produced. An FBI documents expert who had performed these tests testified that they were typed on the same typewriter.[23] Hiss denied he or his wife typed any documents for Chambers. The Hiss defense then charged there were two typewriters. As Chambers's biographer Sam Tanenhaus pointed out, "the government's case against Hiss had never rested on the authenticity of the recovered Woodstock, but on the similarity of the typeface on the two sets of documents, evidence not linked to any particular typewriter." And second, it rested on the fact that "Chambers had also been in possession of handwritten notes whose authorship Hiss acknowledged."[24]

Because of the controversy over the Woodstock, during his closing arguments for the prosecution Thomas Murphy asked the jury to forget the typewriter and whether the documents were typed on it—and focus on the four pages turned over to Chambers of material that was handwritten by Hiss. Alger Hiss never had an explanation for this material. Hiss and his defenders tried to come up with alternate scenarios, unsuccessfully, on how Chambers could have sneaked into Hiss's office in the State Department to steal the documents. Or how someone else could have taken them from Hiss's office and given them to Chambers. In his closing arguments at the second trial, Murphy pointed to a serious flaw in

Hiss's testimony: he never offered any credible motive of why some passerby "stranger" named "George Crosley" would want to frame him.[25]

Hiss claimed that he had never met Colonel Bykov, Chambers's GRU control officer. In fact, Chambers described the meeting he arranged between Bykov and Hiss in Brooklyn in a movie theater in early 1937.[26] Bykov took this occasion to tell Hiss, among other things, that Moscow needed all materials related to Japan and Germany and their preparations for making war against the USSR. Allen Weinstein wrote that although Chambers was the only source for this conversation, "Julian Wadleigh described receiving a similar pep talk from Bykov."[27]

After breaking with the party in 1938 and after the 1939 signing of the Nazi-Soviet Pact, Chambers met with Assistant Secretary of State Adolf A. Berle Jr. on September 2, 1939. Chambers provided Berle with the names of about twenty members of the Soviet underground, including Alger Hiss. Chambers noted in *Witness* that at no time during the meeting was the word *espionage* used, yet Berle seemed to understand what Chambers was really talking about: Berle titled his notes of the meeting "Underground Espionage Agent."[28]

The term "Pumpkin Papers" erroneously referred to both the set of documents stored with Chambers's nephew and the microfilm he later hid in a carved-out pumpkin at his farm. The documents were never placed in a pumpkin—only the microfilm. The documents, hidden in 1938 and turned over to the Justice Department in November 1948, included four sheets of paper in Hiss's own handwriting with summaries of State Department information, and sixty-five typewritten pages copied from classified State Department material that had passed through Hiss's office in early 1938.[29] The three cylinders of microfilm reels of State Department material from 1938 with Hiss's initials on them were hidden for ten years in the dumbwaiter with the documents; however, when Chambers turned over the documents in 1948, he held back on the microfilm reels and hid them in a carved-out pumpkin on his farm. He finally turned them over to the HUAC investigators as well on December 2, when served with a subpoena.[30] The microfilm yielded a three-foot pile of photocopies of highly confidential military and State Department cables. One was from Ambassador William Bullitt, in Paris, and another had been handed to the German ambassador by Undersecretary of State Sumner Welles. They were dated during the years 1937 and 1938.[31]

Harry Dexter White, assistant secretary of the Treasury, was not a member of the Communist Party, according to Chambers, but a Soviet sympathizer who willingly assisted Soviet intelligence. He provided Chambers with classified information either in the form of oral briefings or written summaries. One such summary by White, four letter-sized pages handwritten by him, was with the material secreted by Chambers.[32] These documents, which Chambers decided to keep for his "safety net" (in other words, protection for him and his family against a possible assassination attempt by Soviet intelligence because of his defection), represented only a small amount of the material Chambers received from Hiss. Chambers testified that he went to Hiss's home regularly once every ten days or two weeks to receive government documents from Hiss not only in early 1938 but throughout 1937.

The coincidence of the Gouzenko-Bentley-Chambers revelations of extensive spying within the U.S. government for the Soviet Union, by some high-level officials in the State Department (Alger Hiss), Treasury (Harry Dexter White), OSS (Duncan Lee), and even the White House (Lauchlin Currie) dovetailed to such an extent that it would have been irrational to continue denying the extent of espionage and infiltration into the U.S. government by Soviet intelligence. The mood in the U.S. government then shifted against the Soviet Union, and many politicians, even Truman, motivated in part by their own political survival, no longer unthinkingly and reflexively denied any charge of Soviet espionage within the U.S. government as Cold War hysteria.

Hede Massing

Hede Massing, an Austrian-born KGB intelligence operative, had been married to Gerhart Eisler, the Comintern representative in the United States. Her second husband was a publisher of Communist literature, Julian Gumpertz. During the 1930s, she and her third husband, Paul Massing, were members of a KGB apparatus and operated under the direction of a Soviet "illegal" officer based in New York. Hede originally was recruited by GRU officer Ignace Poretsky and subsequently shifted to the KGB, where she was both a courier and an agent recruiter. She was prevented by Judge Kaufman from testifying at the first Hiss trial, but testified in the second trial for the government.[33] At that time, she was the only person to corroborate Chambers's story of having met Hiss as a member of the Communist underground.[34]

Hede Massing said that Noel Field, a State Department official, had told her he was being pressured by his friend Alger Hiss to join his underground apparatus. For her part, Massing had been cultivating Field for a long time for her own network and therefore wanted to meet this Hiss person. In the fall of 1935 she met him at a dinner arranged by Noel Field in his home. Hiss and Massing accused each other of trying to get Field away from the other; they laughed about who would win. Then one of them stated it didn't matter since they both "were working for the same boss." Massing wrote she was severely reprimanded by her Soviet contact for becoming involved with a person in another network, which was a serious breach of tradecraft. Hiss denied knowing Hede Massing.[35]

Chambers claimed that Hiss had told him about the Massing/Field/Hiss dinner meeting and that Chambers reported this to J. Peters, his Soviet contact in the CPUSA. Chambers said it was Peters who ruled that Field should stay with Massing. Both Chambers and Massing, independently, told the same story about the Hiss/Field/Massing dinner meeting. (The meeting was also confirmed by Noel Field in Hungarian archival material discovered by historian Maria Schmidt, discussed in chapter 16.) This time Hiss had been linked with the Soviet underground by someone other than Whittaker Chambers.[36]

Oleg Gordievsky

Colonel Oleg Gordievsky had been appointed KGB *rezident* in London shortly before his defection in 1985. Gordievsky, a KGB officer for twenty-three years, at the same time had been secretly working for British intelligence as a penetration agent inside the KGB since 1974. He claimed that by 1940 Alger Hiss was among a handful of the Soviets' most important agents, who were run individually and not through spy networks.[37]

According to Gordievsky, Hiss's wartime controller was Iskhak Abdulovich Akhmerov (aka William Greinke), the leading KGB "illegal" in the United States.[38] In a lecture that Gordievsky had attended by Akhmerov (when he was in his sixties) to a KGB audience, Akhmerov identified Alger Hiss as a Soviet agent during World War II. Gordievsky thus confirmed that Hiss continued his operations into the mid-1940s.[39] The Venona decryptions support Gordievsky's claim that Hiss was still active during the war. The Venona decrypt No. 1822, dated March 30, 1945, citing "Ales" (that is, Hiss), claimed he worked for the "neighbors" (that is, the GRU). (See chapter 15 for a discussion of this cable.) Moreover, the March 1945 Venona message said a group of GRU agents received awards in Moscow; and an April 1945 memo from KGB archival material (discussed also in chapter 16) said "Ales" and his group were awarded Soviet medals. Although Gordievsky said Hiss was being run by a KGB "illegal" during the war, there is no evidence that Hiss was ever turned over to the KGB; rather the evidence suggests that Hiss probably remained a GRU agent. GRU networks, which had the lead for foreign intelligence collection and operations in the 1920s and 1930s, were in chaos after the purges by Stalin and subsequent defections. As a result, many GRU operations were shut down. By the 1940s, the KGB stepped in and took over some GRU operations, and ever since it has had priority for the mission of foreign political and economic intelligence collection and operations.

Nathaniel Weyl

Nathaniel Weyl, a Communist Party member and a member of the Ware Group, stated in 1952 that Alger Hiss was a member of the Communist Party and the Ware Group. He said Hiss attended Ware Group meetings regularly; he was seldom absent from the meetings. "We all paid dues. I saw Hiss pay dues at the meetings," said Weyl. Hiss was "pleasant, but also aloof and withdrawn. . . . He was a devoted Communist. . . . Every member of the Ware Group was a Communist member . . . No outsider or even fellow traveler was ever admitted." Weyl never met Whittaker Chambers at the time, since he left the Ware Group several weeks before Chambers arrived to take it over in mid-1934, which is why Chambers did not name Weyl to Berle. Weyl was the first person to confirm Chambers's testimony about the existence of the Ware Group, without attributing espionage activities to it. Weyl had provided this information to the FBI in 1950. He then came forward publicly in February 1952, testifying before the U.S. Senate Internal Security Subcommittee (McCarran Committee) that early in 1934 he had been a Communist and a member of a Communist cell, the Ware Group, with Hiss for approximately nine months. Weyl denied ever being involved in espionage activities.[40]

Julian Wadleigh, Vincent Reno, Felix Inslerman, Lee Pressman, John Abt, Nathan Witt, Charles Kramer, Mrs. Katherine Perlo, Laurence Duggan

A large part of the Hiss case revolved around the single question of who was telling the truth, Whittaker Chambers or Alger Hiss.

Although the following testimonies do not directly implicate Hiss, they do corroborate Chambers's testimony—not Hiss's—and for that reason they are part of the evidentiary database in determining who was telling the truth. Julian Wadleigh, a State Department official, denied Chambers's story at first, but then confirmed Chambers's testimony by confessing that he had turned over more than four hundred documents to Chambers for Soviet intelligence between 1936 and 1938. During the second Hiss trial, Wadleigh admitted he knowingly committed espionage in violation of the law.[41]

After originally denying Chambers's story, Vincent Reno, a mathematician at the U.S. Army's Aberdeen Proving Grounds, also confessed—both to the FBI and to a grand jury in December 1948—that he had turned over classified government documents to Chambers's network.[42] And Felix Inslerman testified that he had been sent to the Soviet Union for training in photography and then returned to the United States, where he worked for the GRU. Inslerman specifically worked in Baltimore for Chambers's network as a photographer of stolen government documents; his testimony corroborated Chambers's story. In addition, a former GRU agent, William Edward Crane, also admitted to the FBI that he photographed documents from the Treasury Department and State Department for Chambers in Baltimore.[43] A third photographer that Chambers had identified, David Carpenter, showed up in the Gorsky Memo (see chapter 16).[44]

In addition, Lee Pressman admitted that he, John Abt, Nathan Witt, and Charles Kramer were in fact members of the Communist Party, as Chambers had stated. The existence of the Perlo Group was confirmed not only by Chambers and Bentley, but also by Mrs. Perlo. Katherine Wills Perlo, the estranged wife of Victor Perlo, sent an anonymous letter to the White House and the FBI in 1944 naming some members of the group, such as John Abt, Henry Collins, Charles Kramer, Nathan Witt, and George Silverman—but not Hiss, since he was not a member of the Perlo Group. Nonetheless, she confirmed many of the same people Chambers had identified, thereby corroborating his testimony.[45] Chambers had told Berle that Henry Collins was a Communist; he was also listed in the Gorsky Memo. Collins denied being a party member. However, Laurence Duggan told the FBI on December 10, 1948, that Collins, whom he had known since 1934, had approached him in June 1938 to assist him in furnishing information to the Soviet Union. Duggan said he turned down Collins's request.[46]

Louis Budenz

In the wake of the Nazi-Soviet Pact, the editorial staff of the *Daily Worker*, a newspaper published in New York by the CPUSA, tried to decide how to handle the turn of events. There was discussion over what party line to use. Many Communists viewed the pact between Stalin and Hitler as a betrayal and broke with the party. Should the paper continue to be anti-Nazi? The managing editor of the *Daily Worker*, Louis Budenz, who joined the Communist Party in 1935, suggested that Alger Hiss was a "good comrade" who would be helpful in trying to sort out what the paper's position ought to be on the pact.[47] In any event, Budenz soon got his answer from Moscow. On August 31, Soviet foreign minister Molotov said when submitting the pact to the Supreme Soviet that it would constitute "a new turn in the development of Europe." Fascism, Molotov said, was after all, a matter of "taste." Budenz wrote in his autobiography that "the entire anti-fascist campaign was to be dropped, forgotten, and all its literature burned and buried." The new alliance with Nazi Germany now was opposed to any aid to England.[48] Subsequently Budenz asserted that high party leaders had discussed Hiss as a secret Communist Party member, but he offered no proof.[49] Budenz defected in 1945 and told his story to the FBI.[50]

All of these corroborating testimonies came from Soviet defectors or former Communists, with two exceptions. One was from a U.S. ambassador who probably received his information from a defector, and the other was from the wife of a former Communist. It is more than notable that over the years Hiss (and his defenders) focused like a laser on Chambers, as though he were Hiss's sole accuser. These testimonies clearly demonstrate, however, that there were others, including some of Hiss's former colleagues in the Ware Group, who acknowledged Hiss's Communist connection. Moreover, Hiss had little if anything to say about the confessions of his former close friends and colleagues as Communist Party members, some of whom were involved in espionage activities. He essentially ignored their revelations as a way to distance himself from their admissions.

Above left: Mrs. Mary Lavinia Hughes Hiss (1867–1958), Baltimore, Maryland. Alger Hiss's mother, who was preoccupied with her status in the Baltimore civic community, urged her five children to strive for professional and social prominence. None succeeded more than Alger. Courtesy of Tamiment Library, NYU; Hiss Family Papers. *Above right:* Following his graduation from Harvard Law School in 1929, Alger Hiss and his brother, Donald, vacationed during the summer in Giverny, France. In his memoir, Alger described the artistic history and landscape of the area, and the joy he had experienced. A copy of his passport obtained for the trip. Courtesy of Tamiment Library, NYU; Hiss Family Papers. *Below:* Alger Hiss as legal counsel to the Special Committee on Investigation of the Munitions Industry and U.S. Involvement in World War I. 1934. Senator Gerald Nye (R-N.D.), on Hiss's right, headed the committee, which received wide support for its disclosures on inordinate war profits and the destabilizing effects of arms traffic in peacetime, according to Hiss. Bettmann/Corbis

Soviet foreign minister Vyacheslav Molotov (along with German foreign minister Joachim von Ribbentrop) signed the Nazi-Soviet Non-Aggression Pact as Stalin looked on, August 23, 1939. One immediate result of this pact was the partition of Poland by Germany and the USSR into spheres of influence and the subsequent mass execution of thousands of Polish military officers by the Soviets in the Katyn Forest. CORBIS

The Katyn massacre of 1940. The discovery of the bodies of Polish officers in mass graves in 1943 precipitated the severance of diplomatic relations between the Soviet Union and the Polish government-in-exile in London. Moscow accused the Germans of the atrocities. In 1990, Mikhail Gorbachev acknowledged Soviet culpability in the tragedy. In 1992, Boris Yeltsin fully admitted Stalin's Politburo had sole responsibility for the 1940 massacre at Katyn Forest and its cover-up.
WOJTEK LASKI/GETTY IMAGES

Warsaw Uprising, Poland. German soldiers fighting against the Polish Home Army, the Polish resistance movement, in August 1944. By October the Germans crushed the rebellion, while the Soviet military, which had pledged support, sat on the sidelines in the Warsaw suburbs. The Germans killed approximately 200,000 military and civilians. The Soviets entered Warsaw in January 1945, when the uprising had ended, shortly before the Yalta Conference commenced. Schremmer/Galerie Bilderwelt/Hulton Archive/Getty Images

Yalta Conference, February 1945. Plenary session of the Conference at Livadia Palace, USSR. On the left are Molotov and Stalin. U.S. secretary of state Edward Stettinius is to the right of President Roosevelt. Alger Hiss is sitting behind them. Prime Minister Churchill and British foreign secretary Anthony Eden are on the right, in the forefront. In his role as advisor to Stettinius, Hiss attended both plenary sessions as well as the foreign ministers' meetings. Bettmann/Corbis

Left: Yalta Conference, February 1945. Alger Hiss is standing to the left of Secretary of State Stettinius. During the Conference, Hiss played a major role in substantive issues, working on key questions, including Poland's new boundaries, the plans for the founding of the UN, Kuomintang-Communist cooperation in the war effort against Japan, and the trusteeship for French Indochina. COURTESY OF NATIONAL ARCHIVES #111-SC 260468

Right, top: Opening of the Conference of San Francisco, April 25, 1945, charged to write the charter of the United Nations. Seated from left to right: State Department diplomat Alger Hiss; California governor Earl Warren; Secretary of State Edward Stettinius; and San Francisco mayor Roger D. Lapham. Hiss was the secretary-general of the conference. KEYSTONE-FRANCE/ GAMMA-KEYSTONE VIA GETTY IMAGES.

Right, bottom: Secretary of State Stettinius, Chairman of the Steering Committee of the UN Conference in San Francisco, calls the May 8, 1945, meeting to order. Left to right at the head table: Sir Alexander Cadogan, British Undersecretary of Foreign Affairs; V. K. Wellington Koo of China; Dr. Guillermo Belt of Cuba; Stettinius; Secretary-General Alger Hiss; and Vyacheslav Molotov of the Soviet Union. COURTESY OF THE NATIONAL ARCHIVES #208-LU-46P40180 COPYRIGHT ASSOCIATE PRESS

Big Four honor Hiss. Representatives of the Big Four at the UN conference in San Francisco present signed statements to Alger Hiss (and to all those whose efforts helped make the conference a success) on June 25, 1945. Left to right: Lord Halifax, V. K. Wellington Koo, Stettinius, Hiss, and Andrei Gromyko, the Soviet Union's ambassador to Washington. Hiss was considered one of the chief architects of the United Nations. COURTESY OF NATIONAL ARCHIVES #208-LU-46-Q-10. COPYRIGHT ACME NEWS PHOTOS

Whittaker Chambers, senior editor at *Time* magazine, and confessed former Communist, testifies before the House Un-American Activities Committee, where he named Alger Hiss as being a Communist Party member. August 1948. BETTMANN/CORBIS

Alger Hiss examining photographs of Whittaker Chambers while testifying before the House Un-American Activities Committee. Hiss insisted that he could not recognize Chambers, but said that he resembled a man he knew by another name—George Crosley. BETTMANN/CORBIS

Louis Budenz, a former Communist and editor of the *Daily Worker,* talking in August 1948 with Elizabeth Bentley, a KGB underground courier and a self-confessed Soviet spy, after a session of the Congressional Committee during which he related many details of the wartime activities of Soviet spy networks in the United States. Bentley had claimed that a member of her network said he used to work for Hiss's network. Budenz, in his memoir, attributed Hiss's life of denial to "Communist morality"—a Communist's will to lie and commit perjury, if necessary, to protect the interests of the party. It is done under party orders, Budenz claimed. BETTMANN/CORBIS

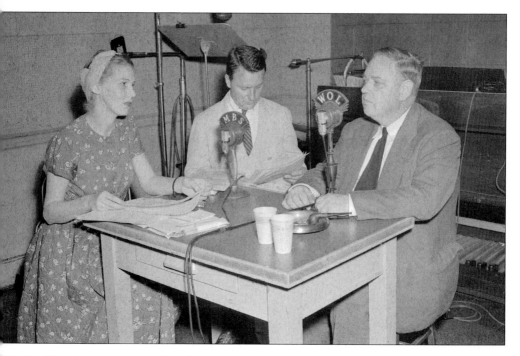

Whittaker Chambers as a guest on the radio program *Meet the Press* at Station WOL in Washington, D.C. Left to right: Martha Rountree, moderator; James Reston of the *New York Times;* and Chambers. During the interview, Chambers stated, and while not under immunity protection of the House Un-American Activities Committee, that Hiss was a Communist. Following this broadcast, in September 1948, Hiss sued Chambers for libel. BETTMANN/CORBIS

Alger Hiss takes an oath during the hearings before the House Un-American Activities Committee. He denied Whittaker Chambers's accusation that he was a Communist. BETTMANN/CORBIS

Left: Donald Hiss (identified as a Communist Party member by Chambers and in KGB archives), and brother, Alger Hiss, walking into Federal Court in New York on December 8, 1948. A federal grand jury was trying to discover who had stolen State Department secrets before World War II. Donald Hiss was called as a surprise witness. BETTMANN/CORBIS; *Right:* Alger Hiss and his wife, Priscilla, during his first perjury trial in 1949, which ended in a hung jury. Priscilla was a central figure in Hiss's life until after he was released from prison in November 1954. Hiss wanted to focus his life on vindication, while Priscilla wanted them to leave New York, change their names, and go to a place where they were not known. They subsequently separated in late 1958. BETTMANN/CORBIS

XV.

VENONA PROGRAM

1945 KGB Cable: "Ales" Worked
for the GRU Continuously Since 1935

T HE VENONA PROJECT was handled with extreme secrecy for more than forty years. Code-breakers at the U.S. Army's Signal Intelligence Service at Arlington Hall, in northern Virginia, analyzed encrypted high-level Soviet diplomatic intelligence messages intercepted during and immediately after World War II by American, British, and Australian listening posts. This message traffic, which was both coded and enciphered with a "one-time pad" system, was analyzed and stored. A serious mistake on the part of the Soviets—someone reused pages of some of the one-time pads—made some of the traffic vulnerable to cryptanalysis.[1] The project to decipher this material began in 1943, under the orders of the deputy chief of the Special Branch of the Army's Military Intelligence Service, Colonel Carter W. Clarke.

A June 1939 presidential directive had given responsibility for counterintelligence to the FBI, the War Department's Military Intelligence (the G-2), and the Office of Naval Intelligence. The three organizations together made up what was known as the Interdepartmental Intelligence Conference (IIC). The Army's G-2, headquartered at Arlington Hall, took the lead in the Venona project.

Meredith Gardner, the most prominent Venona analyst, kept the British liaison informed of developments and from 1948 on there was U.S.-British signals intelligence cooperation on this program. The control term for the translated messages was originally "Gardner Material," then the formal term was "Bride," and during the 1950s it was "Drug." Finally, in 1961, "Venona" was invented as the arbitrary code word for the program to restrict access.[2]

The body of Venona documents included more than 2,900 Soviet encrypted cables transmitted between 1940 and 1948, out of hundreds of thousands sent. Those decoded were random, and vulnerable to deciphering, but at times only partly decrypted. Translated messages corroborated many charges made by Elizabeth Bentley and Whittaker Chambers.[3] Only a few of the decrypted Venona messages were from the GRU, hence there was little on Hiss. The decrypted cables provided insights into mostly KGB operations during the time in which duplicate one-time pads were used. Significantly, Venona revealed the existence of Soviet espionage operations at the Los Alamos National Laboratory. Various spies were identified by National Security Agency (NSA) analysts in the cable traffic, such as Klaus Fuchs, Julius Rosenberg, and British spy Donald Maclean.[4]

The messages showed that the United States was targeted as early as 1942 in major espionage campaigns; among those Soviet assets identified by NSA analysts were the Rosenbergs, Alger Hiss, Harry Dexter White, Lauchlin Currie, and Maurice Halperin, a section chief in the OSS. Identifying individuals was complicated, and sometimes disputed, as was the case with Alger Hiss, since the same person sometimes had different code names and the same code name could be reused for different people.[5] John Earl Haynes and historian Harvey Klehr claimed that the Venona transcripts identified about 349 Americans involved covertly with Soviet intelligence. Fewer than half of these have been matched to real-name identities, and nearly two hundred remain hidden behind cover names to this day.[6]

By the mid-1950s, after the conviction of Alger Hiss for the perjury-related-to-espionage indictment and the Rosenbergs' execution for atomic spying, the mood in the United States gradually had shifted from a pro-Russian attitude for a World War II ally to greater acceptance of the fact that U.S. government officials who were Russian intelligence assets had betrayed their country. The Venona messages confirmed this concern; however, very few people knew this fact. The messages were not released to the public at the time, and in fact would not be for another four decades.

The secrecy surrounding Venona was decided on by the U.S. Army code-breakers, along with officials from the FBI and CIA (which wasn't actively brought into the program until 1952) who were aware of Venona. In fact, it is not clear if even President Truman had been read into the program.[7] Keeping Venona a secret enabled Truman to launch his uninformed "red herring" campaign. The "Ales" cable (which involved Hiss), according to former CIA official John Ehrman, should have been made public years earlier; it would have prevented much of the Hiss controversy that had ensued.[8] While Moscow was aware of the Venona program by the late 1940s as a result of its British asset, Kim Philby,[9] and American asset, William Weisband, a Soviet agent in the Army Security Agency,[10] the American people were denied access to Venona based on a "need-to-know" rationale, which was irrelevant since Moscow knew about the program.

Finally, during the 1990s, Senator Patrick Moynihan was instrumental in having the Venona material declassified. He argued successfully that secrecy was no longer necessary since the program no longer had any operational value after more than forty years. The view within the intelligence community (in both the NSA and the CIA) toward declassification also had changed. Haynes and Klehr revealed that James Angleton, the former head of CIA counterintelligence, told colleagues in 1987 that the Venona messages should be declassified. "Open the messages up, he had argued, and historians and journalists with different perspectives from those of professional security officers would probably be able to attach real names to the cover names of Soviet intelligence sources that the combined efforts of the FBI, the CIA, and the NSA had been unable to identify."[11]

Venona decrypt No. 1822, dated March 30, 1945, and sent from the KGB *rezidentura* (station) in Washington, D.C., to Moscow, refers to an American agent who worked for Soviet intelligence, code-named "Ales." Alger Hiss's name was not spelled out, but NSA analysts concluded that the cable was discussing Hiss and that he was probably "Ales." The cable, translated by expert NSA intelligence and language analysts, stated that as a result of a conversation with "A" (Iskhak Akhmerov, the KGB "illegal" *rezident* in the United States) and "Ales," it turned out:

1. "Ales" had been continuously working with the "neighbors" (this was the KGB term for its sister organization, the GRU, military intelligence) since 1935.

2. "Ales" had been director of a small group of probationers of the "neighbors" (GRU spy-recruits), for the most part consisting of his relatives.

3. Moscow wanted more information on military issues and less on diplomatic and political subjects of interest to the "Bank" (the State Department).

4. In recent years, "Ales" had been working with "Pol" (Maxim Lieber[12]) who also met at times with other members of the group.

5. "Ales" told Akhmerov that he and his group had recently been awarded Soviet medals.

6. After the Yalta Conference, back in Moscow, a prominent Soviet official ("Ales" implied it was Andrei Vyshinsky,

Soviet deputy foreign minister at the time) got in touch with him and at the request of the military neighbors (GRU) he conveyed to them their thanks.

The message was sent by "Vadim," cover name for Gorsky, the KGB *rezident* in Washington in March 1945.[13]

In parsing this cable it appears that the most likely candidate for "Ales" must be and probably is Alger Hiss.

1. The GRU ran Hiss since 1935.

2. Hiss's relatives—his wife, Priscilla, who had typed Hiss's State Department notes for delivery to Chambers, and brother Donald—both were identified by Chambers as members of the Communist Party and Donald also by Gorsky in the Vassiliev KGB notebooks.

3. Hiss worked for the State Department, and shortly after this cable was sent, he made a deliberate attempt to expand his access to military intelligence by suggesting an internal reorganization of his office, whereby a special military representative would be selected and would have access to classified military intelligence. Although the reorganization did not occur, in 1946 Hiss actually was able to obtain top-secret reports on atomic energy, which was outside his area of responsibility.

4. There is no corroboration of whom Hiss's control officer was after Chambers defected. "Pol" (likely Maxim Lieber, a former member in Chambers's 1930s apparatus) probably took over after Chambers's defection.[14] As noted in the previous chapter, Gordievsky claimed KGB "illegal" Akhmerov ran Hiss.

5. Following the Yalta Conference, most of the U.S. delegation, including Roosevelt, left for the United States via Iran. Hiss, who had attended the Yalta Conference, was one of only eight of the U.S. delegation that accompanied Secretary of State Stettinius to Moscow.

6. An item in May 5, 2006, *Krasnaya Zvezda* (*Red Star*), the official newspaper of the Russian Ministry of Defense, confirmed that in Moscow five members of a Soviet military intelligence apparatus in Washington, D.C., received Soviet decorations in February 1945.[15] Presumably one of the recipients was "Ales."

The late U.S. Air Force historian Eduard Mark matched the clues in decrypt 1822 with the profiles of all eight individuals in the Stettinius party that flew to Moscow. After exhaustive research and examination, Mark came to the conclusion that "Ales" was Alger Hiss: he argued that "there was no other plausible candidate in the small universe of suspects."[16] Of the small field of candidates, it was clear to Mark that only Hiss met all the criteria to be "Ales." Hiss defenders Kai Bird, a U.S. writer, and Svetlana Chervonnaya, a former Soviet propagandist, also discounted seven members and by process of elimination claimed it was another member of the delegation—Wilder Foote, another one of Stettinius's assistants.[17] One problem with the Foote theory is that the cable stated that "Ales" worked "continuously" for the GRU since 1935. Foote was a newspaper publisher living in Vermont from 1931 to 1941. There is no record of a GRU presence in Vermont at that time. Also, Foote had no relatives working at the State Department. And he did not live or work in Washington, D.C., during the 1930s.[18] He moved there in November 1941.

Other Venona messages provide only small pieces of reference to Hiss/"Ales." An FBI memo reports that Hiss is named openly in a September 28, 1943, GRU cable (#1579) noting that a KGB report about the State Department mentioned Hiss. The remainder of the cable was undeciphered.[19] The Venona project deciphered a KGB message about a meeting between a KGB officer and a GRU source with the cover name "Ales."

According to another Venona transcript, dated March 3, 1945, the KGB chief of foreign intelligence, General Lieutenant Pavel Fitin, assigned Akhmerov to procure information on U.S. plans for the upcoming UN charter conference. Normally a KGB officer would not contact an agent of the GRU. However, this breach may have been necessary since Alger Hiss, a GRU agent, was responsible for planning the United Nations conference in San Francisco and thus would have the best access, since he would receive sensitive intelligence on all the proceedings.[20]

A partially decoded Venona cable to Fitin (code-named "Viktor") dated September 28, 1943, sent to Moscow by the controller of military intelligence for the KGB (code-named "Moliere"), who was undercover as Soviet vice consul in New York, "Pavel B. Mikhailov," identified the real names and code names of several agents in the United States, and said the GRU (the "neighbors") had reported that "[unrecovered group] from the State Department by the name of Hiss."[21]

In its unanimous final report in 1997, the bipartisan Moynihan Commission on Government Secrecy agreed that "Ales" "could only be Alger Hiss."[22] NSA analysts have also gone on record that "Ales" was Alger Hiss. Eduard Mark wrote a detailed, exhaustive account of this cable and why "Ales" was not Wilder Foote. Mark concluded that the evidence showed that "only one possible candidate can be given the dubious distinction of being "'Ales.'" And that person was Alger Hiss.[23]

John R. Schindler, professor of strategy at the Naval War College and himself a former NSA intelligence analyst, agreed, calling the evidence "compelling." He maintained that "the identification of 'Ales' as Alger Hiss, made by the U.S. Government more than a half-century ago, seems 'exceptionally solid' based on the evidence now available; message 1822 is only one piece of that evidence, yet a compelling one."[24] John Ehrman of the CIA's Directorate of Intelligence concurred: "It is clear that Hiss alone remains the best candidate to be Ales."[25] The code name "Ales," concluded Mark Kramer, director of the Project for Cold War Studies at Harvard University, "seems to fit only Hiss."[26]

XVI.

ARCHIVAL MATERIAL

A. Hungarian Archives

Noel Field: I Gave a Great Deal of Documents to the Soviets

I N ADDITION TO personal testimonies and the Venona cables, two major pieces of archival material that surfaced after the Cold War conclusively point to Alger Hiss as a spy. Before examining the Hiss material from the Soviet KGB archives, a review will be given of Hungarian archival documents concerning Noel Field, a former State Department official and friend of Alger Hiss, that became available from Hungarian historian Maria Schmidt. In February 1992, while researching the files of the Hungarian Secret Police, Schmidt found a stack of restricted files of the Interior Ministry in Budapest. They were the original transcripts of Noel Field's interrogation by the Hungarian security service in 1954. (Field had been arrested and falsely accused of being an American spy during Stalin's campaign to purge various Eastern European Communist leaders.) She was surprised to find information on Alger Hiss. Now there emerged another (unwitting) witness for the prosecution: Noel Field. Schmidt showed that the transcripts of Field's statements to Hungarian security corroborated both Hede Massing's and Whittaker Chambers's testimony by describing how Alger Hiss tried to recruit Field for his own spy ring.[1] These several sources all told the same story about the attempted recruitment of Field.

Noel Haviland Field was born on January 23, 1904, in London. His father, an American physician, moved soon afterward to Switzerland, where he became director of an international zoological institute in Zurich. His mother, who was British, moved to the United States in 1921, after her husband died. Noel took university classes in Switzerland, where he met his future wife, Herta Vieser, a German. He then moved back to the United States and finished his studies at Harvard College. Field joined the State Department in 1926 and was assigned to the Western Europe Department. He had worked with Hiss at State in the 1930s. During this time he became convinced of the "correctness of Communism."[2] In 1935, Paul and Hede Massing recruited Noel Field into the service of Soviet intelligence (KGB) and Hede was his regular liaison contact.

Noel, although a committed Communist, initially was reluctant to provide documents to Massing and thus commit espionage. To resolve this conflict, Field resigned from the State Department and took a job in the League of Nations secretariat in Geneva in the spring of 1936. In his mind, according to his biographer Flora Lewis, as an international civil servant Field was not betraying any particular country by working also as an agent for Soviet intelligence. In Geneva, he felt, again according to Flora Lewis, "the issue of loyalty would be blurred."[3] The Massings introduced him to his new Soviet contacts in Europe, Walter Krivitsky and Ignace Reiss.[4] After their defections, Field was left with no connection to the party. The Massings returned to the United States from Moscow in June 1938, when they also broke with the party.[5] In the eyes of the KGB (and especially Stalin as well), Field was associated with four traitors, which by itself was enough to make him suspect. Field's Communist activities (which he was rather open about to various people) cost him his job at the League of Nations. Hiss tried to help him—he recommended Field for a job as an assistant to the newly appointed governor in the Philippines, but it fell through. There was opposition to Field in certain circles within the State Department because of his Communist commitment.[6]

After he left the League of Nations in 1940, Noel Field obtained a post directing war refugee relief for the Unitarian Service Committee. He was known to use this post to give preferential treatment to Communists. Moreover, these exiled Communists maintained underground organizations that attempted to keep their party organizations viable and to prepare for their return home, when the war ended, with a functioning apparatus. Under the cover of his refugee relief work, Field traveled in neutral countries and in Vichy, France, to service and help maintain the courier networks set up by exiled Communist groups (Hungarian, Czech, Polish, and German). He did not perform this work at the direction of Moscow. In 1943, Soviet intelligence renewed contact with Field, by then director of the Unitarian Service Committee. Since the KGB did not approve of secret underground agents mixing with open Communist political activities, he was instructed to break all contact with open Communist Party networks. He hesitated to agree, and the KGB broke off with him.[7]

In 1942–43, Field also played an intermediary role between the underground Communist groups he was helping and the United States' OSS. Aware of Field's close ties to the underground Communist groups, Allen Dulles, head of OSS operations in Central Europe, who was operating out of Switzerland, asked Field to put him in contact with these groups to suggest cooperation on some project. These groups had links back to their countries that were under Nazi occupation. Dulles wanted information from these occupied areas to assist the Allied war effort. In return, the exiled Communist groups would receive material aid. Unable to get Moscow's response, the political leaders accepted the offer. At the end of the war, Field lost his job at the Unitarian Service Committee.[8] Stalin later used Field's role in the OSS affair to accuse Field falsely of being an American spy.

In a KGB disinformation campaign, Moscow spread the false story that as a liaison officer, Field was working for the West in order to undermine Communist parties in Eastern Europe. In fact,

Field was being used by the Soviets to implicate some Eastern European leaders (such as Poland's Gomulka, Hungary's Rajk, and Germany's Paul Merker and Franz Dahlem).[9] Stalin's KGB tagged Field as the "puppet-master of the vast anti-Communist conspiracy during the Czech purge."[10] Moscow used Noel Field as the mastermind of an imaginary conspiracy to target the leadership in Prague. The Poles, who had arrested and imprisoned Hermann Field, Noel's brother, accused Hermann of being the ringleader of the Polish section of the plot, in their move against Gomulka.

After he was arrested and imprisoned in 1949, Field was questioned by Hungarian authorities, who falsely accused him of being a spy for the United States. Field told his Hungarian interrogators that he made friends with Alger Hiss, and through their gatherings, they discovered that they were both Communists. In fact, three couples, the Hisses, the Fields, and the Duggans, became very good friends, especially the Fields and Duggans.[11] Laurence Duggan, who had worked for the State Department in the Latin American division, also had been recruited by Hede Massing in the 1930s. At the time of the Hiss trials, the FBI met with Duggan, who had been mentioned by Chambers; while Duggan provided some names, he did not name his good friends Hiss and Field. A few weeks later, on December 20, 1948, he was found dead. He either jumped or fell from the Fifth Avenue high-rise office building where he worked in New York City.[12]

Field confessed to Hungarian security that Hiss also was working for the Soviet Union. Both reported to J. Peters. Field found out Hiss was working for Soviet intelligence in the fall of 1935, when Hiss approached him to recruit him for espionage for the Soviet Union. He informed Hiss that he was already doing such work for another network (Massing's).[13] Field said in his interrogation by the Hungarians, "I then committed the unforgiveable indiscretion of telling him that he had come too late." Field's testimony to Hungarian security included the story of the Hiss/Massing/Field dinner meeting told by both Hede Massing and Whittaker Chambers.

Moreover, this incident is also recorded in the Vassiliev notebooks containing KGB archival material. In one of three messages in the "Yellow" notebook involving Hiss and Field, Hiss is identified in clear text by his real name. In her April 1936 report to the KGB, Massing wrote, "Roughly a week before his [Field's] departure from Washington, he was approached by Alger Hiss. A. [Hiss] informed him that he is a Communist, that he has ties to an organization working for the Sov. Union; and that he is aware that 'Ernst' [Noel Field] has ties as well; however he fears that they are not robust enough and that his knowledge is probably being misused."[14]

The various versions of the story of Hiss's attempt to recruit Field into Soviet intelligence—versions given independently by Chambers and Massing during the Hiss trials, Massing's communication to KGB headquarters in Moscow found in KGB archives, Field's interrogation report in the Hungarian archival documents, and Czech archival material—all corroborate each other. These independent, separate sources of data, separated by people, time, and geography, all support the accuracy of the story of Hiss's attempt to recruit Noel Field. Hede Massing met Alger Hiss at the Fields' apartment at a dinner party. Massing was introduced to Hiss by Field; Massing, a KGB operative, complained to Hiss that he was trying to tempt Field into his own organization, the GRU. They were not too upset over the rivalry because they both were working for Soviet intelligence.[15] However, Massing's handler told her in no uncertain terms to forget Hiss; don't ever talk to Noel about him; never mention his name. Keep away from him and forget him.[16] And Massing in turn reproached Field, saying contact with another undercover network did great damage and was bad tradecraft.

Field also told Hungarian interrogators in September 1954 that in the summer of 1939 he was back in the United States from Europe on a visit. He made a one- or two-day detour to meet Hiss in Washington. He felt endangered because Krivitsky, his former control officer, had defected and was in Washington, D.C., and might expose him.[17] Field felt that one of the few people he could confide in on this matter was Alger Hiss, who knew about him; Hiss could inform him if he was in danger because of the traitor (Krivitsky) who had defected to the West. They agreed that if Hiss came to know anything, he would send Field a warning message under a cover name.[18]

By 1948, Field feared being called back to the United States by the HUAC to testify during the Hiss case; he thought that he might harm his friend, Alger Hiss, as well as implicate himself and possibly be convicted of espionage. After World War II, Field was unable to get work with the underground. So he fled from Switzerland to Eastern Europe on May 5, 1949, and then disappeared. He had gone to Prague where he was arrested by Soviet and Hungarian state security authorities.[19] He was transported to Hungary, imprisoned in Budapest, and became a target in one of Stalin's show trials.[20] Field was interrogated by Hungarians under Soviet supervision and direction. Maria Schmidt said the Russians knew everything he was confessing—or could check it—"It would have endangered Field's rehabilitation if he lied about easily verifiable facts. He would not have risked his release."

Field's wife, Herta, went looking for him and she too disappeared in Prague, in August 1949. She was arrested by the Czechs and then turned over to the Hungarian authorities. She also was subjected to severe interrogation and imprisoned. His brother Hermann tried to locate Noel and was arrested by the Polish Communist police; he was interrogated, confessed, and was secretly imprisoned for five years. Field's adopted daughter, Erika, was arrested in East Berlin, convicted by a Soviet military court, and sent to Vorkuta prison camp.[21]

Documents in the Hungarian security services' archives show that Noel Field was arrested on May 11 by Czechoslovak security police acting under the direct supervision of General Fyodor Byelkin of the KGB and the deputy head of the Hungarian state security.[22] Field was then taken to Hungary, investigated/tortured/forced to confess, then imprisoned. He was never publicly tried.

The KGB was orchestrating the case all along. They extracted a confession that he worked for U.S. intelligence and recruited scores of Hungarians, Czechs, Poles, and East Germans into the service of U.S. intelligence. Years later, during his rehabilitation, Field was re-interrogated and denied all these confessions, in 1953 after Stalin's death.[23] He always insisted on his complete loyalty to the Communist cause.[24] Field was a Communist believer, according to Schmidt, despite the murders in Spain, Stalin's domestic terror, and the Hitler-Stalin pact. None of the Soviet atrocities disconcerted Field. This was happening in the service of a "lofty cause." He never wavered, even after the Communists imprisoned and tortured him and his wife and brother. He simply said it was all a mistake.[25] This is yet another vivid example of Leninist morality held by committed Communists—that the end justifies any means.

Field was released from prison on November 17, 1954, as part of the de-Stalinization program. His wife, brother, and adopted daughter also were released in the following months. The Eastern European countries involved in his case admitted it was all a mistake and that Field had been a loyal Communist. It was all an unfortunate error that had been corrected. And Field's Communist loyalties were not shaken.[26] Three months after his release, in February 1955, Field denied he ever spied and denied he had any knowledge of Alger Hiss's work for Soviet intelligence. In July 1957, Field wrote a letter to Hiss offering to declare publicly that he, Hiss, was neither a Communist nor a spy. The letter was later made public by Hiss's defenders as evidence that Chambers and Massing had lied about the Field-Hiss recruitment story.[27]

However, in the archives of the Ministry of Internal Affairs in Hungary, there is a draft dated February 1953, written two years before the revised version of the letter that was mailed. The letter contradicted Field's testimony to the Hungarian rehabilitation interrogators. Hiss's supporters then said, disregard the testimony, it was coerced. According to Schmidt, Hungarian Communist security police had no motive to torture Field into naming Hiss as a fellow Soviet intelligence source. Nor would it make sense, according to Schmidt, for Field to make fraudulent statements about Hiss and himself to convince Communist authorities of his loyalties. Hungarian police could have easily checked this with Moscow. If he was lying, it could have damaged his chance of rehabilitation and release. He had no reason to lie.[28]

But the public letter coincided with the propaganda campaign of the Hungarian regime at the time. In 1956, former Hungarian prime minister Imre Nagy and freedom fighters revolted against the Soviet regime and announced Hungary's withdrawal from the Warsaw Pact. Moscow viewed these reformers as "counterrevolutionaries." The Soviets invaded in October 1956 and crushed the rebellion. Nagy was subsequently arrested and executed. Field sided with the hard-liners. In 1961, he published an essay in the United States in which he celebrated his long loyalty to Communism. Noel and his wife never returned to the United States. On December 24, 1954, he asked the Hungarian government for and received political asylum. The Fields were given "an elegantly furnished" villa, a compensation payment of one hundred thousand forints, and a monthly pension of ten thousand forints. Noel Field died in Budapest in September 1970.[29]

During Noel Field's 1954 rehabilitation process, he made the following admission to Hungarian state security: "From 1927 I started to live an illegal life separate from my official life. At first, I was concerned the tasks I was assigned were 'espionage,' but overcame this inhibition and eventually took on espionage for the Soviet intelligence service." Some things he passed, for example, were a report by Ambassador Bullitt (to Moscow) and the report on the preparation of the Fleet Conference in London in 1935–36.[30] He passed material to Hede and Paul Massing, his liaison with Soviet intelligence. When Hungarian security interrogated Field's wife, Herta, she said she was aware of Noel's work but did not participate in it. When asked to assess his work she revealed that "it is my firm belief that Paul Massing was thoroughly informed by Noel on what was going on in the State Department and behind the scenes of the conference on disarmament." She went on to claim that she was not aware of any particular documents given to Paul but she had asked Noel, following Chambers's revelations of the Pumpkin Papers, "While Alger Hiss presented all those documents to Whittaker Chambers, you did not give so many to Paul, did you?" Noel responded: "I gave a great deal to him."[31]

A similar story unfolded in Czechoslovakia. During the doomed 1968 uprising known as the Prague Spring, Czech historian Karel Kaplan assisted the reform Dubček government in an investigation of the 1952 execution of Rudolf Slánský, general secretary of the Communist Party, on the false charges of cooperating with U.S. intelligence. Stalinist prosecutors cited Noel Field's activities as evidence of the charges. After Kaplan fled to the West he told author Allen Weinstein that he had examined both Czech and Hungarian files and they corroborated Massing's testimony. In his report, Kaplan confirmed Massing had recruited Field as a KGB source in the mid-1930s. In 2000 a Czech human rights activist, Karel Skrabek, obtained a copy of the Czech security police reinvestigation of Field in 1955. It said that "Hiss worked for the USSR as a spy . . . and Hiss tried to convince Field to work with him."[32]

B. KGB Archives

KGB Archives: Alger Hiss Told Noel Field That He Was a Communist and That He Had Ties to an Organization Working for the Soviet Union

In 1993, after the collapse of the Soviet Union, Random House's Crown Books division reached an agreement with the Russian SVR (Foreign Intelligence Service and successor to the First Main Directorate of the KGB) Association of Retired Intelligence Officers (former KGB officers) that would allow some access to KGB archives by approved American writers, who would collaborate with a Russian counterpart in producing a book. Crown offered a substantial payment to the SVR's retirement pension fund in return for this access to KGB archives.[33] Four books resulted before Moscow ended the deal and the archives were again shut down. One of the books was *The Haunted Wood: Soviet Espionage in America—The Stalin Era.* The SVR had given Alexander Vassiliev, a former KGB official, permission to examine the KGB archives as editor and translator for a book on Soviet espionage with Allen Weinstein. Between 1994 and 1996, Vassiliev, a press officer with the Russian intelligence service, was given full access to KGB files. He transcribed thousands of documents into a series of notebooks, which he subsequently was able to get out of Russia. Vassiliev donated them to the U.S. Library of Congress.

The book deal allowing archival access to Americans became controversial in parts of the Russian government. By 1996, Vassiliev had received death threats and fled to England, leaving his notebooks with a friend. Hence *The Haunted Wood* was written by Weinstein on the basis of Vassiliev's summarized chapters as sanitized by the SVR. The information, albeit important, was limited. Vassiliev then retrieved the original notebooks that were sent to him in 2001. Based on this extensive archival material, scholars John Earl Haynes and Harvey Klehr produced *Spies: The Rise and Fall of the KGB in America*, which provides the most comprehensive and complete accounting to date of KGB espionage activities inside the United States government in the 1930s and 1940s, including infiltration of the OSS and the Anglo-American atomic project.[34] The Alger Hiss story, which was a GRU operation, was only one chapter in Haynes and Klehr's history of massive KGB operations against the United States.[35]

The Vassiliev Notebooks (Vassiliev's transcribed KGB archive notes) contain a small but still surprising number of references to the GRU source, Alger Hiss, in view of the fact that these documents are from the KGB archives, not GRU. Some of the documents used Hiss's cover names ("Jurist" or "Leonard" or "Ales");

other times his name is referenced in clear text. After exhaustive research of the notebooks, Haynes and Klehr stated that the Vassiliev documents "unequivocally identify Hiss as a long-term espionage source" of the GRU and that the material "fully corroborates" the testimony of Chambers and Massing and Field, and others.[36] Although the material supports this conclusion, some members of the Hiss cult, impervious to evidence, nonetheless rose up and argued against the validity of this KGB archival material. Their arguments and at times irrational theories to discredit the documentary evidence have been recorded thoroughly in the body of Hiss literature, both in books, journals, and online in H-DIPLO discussions.[37] They will not be recounted here. Suffice it to invoke Vassiliev: "Alger Hiss is a religion, and there is no point in arguing with people about their religious beliefs."[38]

Some of the Hiss material in the notebooks is discussed below. One of the most significant documents is the so-called Gorsky Memo. Anatoly Gorsky was head of the KGB *rezidentura* in Washington in 1944 and 1945. When J. Edgar Hoover informed Sir William Stephenson, head of British intelligence in the West, of Elizabeth Bentley's defection, Kim Philby, head of British counterespionage against the USSR as well as a Soviet spy himself, alerted Soviet intelligence. All operations connected with Bentley immediately stood down because they were compromised. In 1948, the KGB's summary damage assessment noted that "intelligence work in the USA was completely deactivated in November/December 1945 and did not resume until September 1947."[39] In December 1948, Gorsky authored an internal KGB damage assessment that listed forty-three Soviet sources likely to be compromised by Bentley after her defection. The list included, among others, Alger Hiss, Donald Hiss, Harry Dexter White, Henry Collins, Henry Julian Wadleigh (his correct full name), and Lee Pressman.[40]

In a section of the memo titled "Failures in the U.S.A. (1938–1948)," Gorsky noted a list of names and code names of American agents and sources apparently attached to a memorandum itself headed "A. Gorsky's report to Savchenko S.R. December 19, 1948." The list was divided into five groups of agents who had been compromised by defectors from Soviet espionage. The first was "Karl's Group." "Karl" is identified as Whittaker Chambers. Of the twenty-one names listed in "Karl's group," who are all identified by code name and *real name*, Chambers discussed fifteen in his testimony and his autobiography, *Witness*. And, without providing names, he mentioned three minor participants whose jobs match the positions of three others on Gorsky's list.[41] The complete list of "Karl's Group" in the Gorsky memo includes:

1. "Karl"—Whittaker Chambers, former editor in chief of "Time" magazine. Traitor.

2. "Jerome"—Barna Bukov (Altman), our former cadre employee. Currently in the USSR.

3. "Leonard"—Alger Hiss, former employee of the State Dept.

4. "Junior"—Donald Hiss, former employee of the Dept. of the Interior

5. 104th—Henry A. Wadleigh—former employee of the State Dept.

6. 118th—F. V. Reno—former employee of the Aberdeen Proving Ground

7. 105th—Henry Collins, former employee of Dept. of Agriculture, at pres., director of the American-Russian Institute in NY

8. 114th—William W. Pigman, former employee of the Bureau of Standards

9. "Storm"—Joseph Peters (aka Isadore Boorstein), former member, Central Committee, CPUSA

10. "Vig"—Lee Pressman, former legal adviser of the Congress of Industrial Organizations

11. 116th—Harry Azizov, former employee of a steel-smelting company in Chicago

12. 101st—Peter MacLean, journalist and photo reporter, not used since '37

13. 103rd—David Carpenter, newspaper employee

14. 107th—Felix Inslerman, place of employment unknown

15. 113th—Harry Rosenthal, employee of an insurance company in Philadelphia

16. 115th—Lester Hutm, former employee of the Frankford Arsenal

17. "Ernst"—Noel Field, former employee of the State Dept.

18. "Rupert"—V. V. Sveshnikov, former employee of the War Dept.

19. "Richard"—Harry White, former assistant to Sec. of the Treasury Morgenthau, died in '48

20. "Aileron"—G. Silverman, former chief of the Planning and Statistics Division of the AAF

21. "Ruble"—Harold Glasser, former director of the Monetary Division of the Dept. of the Treasury (Dept. of Justice?)[42]

In addition, three individuals Bentley identified as working with her networks during World War II are listed by Gorsky as working in the mid-1930s for "Karl's Group" (in other words, Whittaker Chambers). These were Harry Dexter White, George Silverman, and Harold Glasser. She told the FBI that one member of her network, Glasser, had for a time worked for a network she knew little about except that it was run by a man named "Hiss" at the State Department. Glasser, as described by himself in a December 1944 handwritten autobiography for Moscow, was born in Chicago in 1905, the son of Lithuanian immigrants, and studied economics at the University of Chicago. He joined the Communist Party in 1933 and the Treasury Department in 1936. With the assistance of Harry Dexter White, he rose to be assistant to the director of monetary research in January 1942.[43] Both Alger and Donald Hiss, working for the State Department, were also listed under Karl's Group.

Gorsky's memo was written before the Hiss trials. By the time of the report, Wadleigh had already confessed, in his 1948 grand jury testimony, to being part of Chambers's group, testimony repeated at Hiss's trials. Haynes and Klehr have indicated that because the code name for Hiss given in the deciphered 1945 KGB cables (the Venona decryptions) was "Ales," and because earlier KGB memos discussed in *The Haunted Wood* referred to Hiss as "Lawyer,"[44] and Gorsky referred to him as "Leonard," "several defenders of Hiss astoundingly found the Gorsky memo exculpatory." But the KGB frequently changed cover names. "That Hiss has a new one in this memo does not prove his innocence; his mere inclusion is yet additional proof that Chambers was telling the truth and that Hiss was a Soviet source."[45]

An April 26, 1936, letter to Moscow from Boris Bazarov ("Nord"), an officer of the KGB's "illegal" *rezidentura,* provided a summary of the damage done by Noel Field's actions. "The outcome is that '17' [Field] and Hiss have, in effect, been completely deprived of their cover before '19' [Duggan]. . . . It seems that apart from us, the persistent Hiss [the reference is to his attempt to recruit Field] will continue his initiative in that direction." In this KGB document, Hiss is identified by his real name. A Moscow Center annotation on the letter showed Hiss's cover name as "A. Hiss—Jurist" and noted that Hiss was an attorney in Washington.[46]

In a report to the KGB that accompanied Bazarov's April 26 letter, Hede Massing told how Field mentioned to her that he had been approached by Alger Hiss before he left for Europe. The document identified Hiss by name in clear text: "Roughly a week before his departure from Washington, he [Field] was approached by Alger Hiss. A. [Alger Hiss] *informed him that he was a Communist, that he had ties to an organization working for the Sov. Union;* and that he is aware that 'Ernst' [i.e., Field] has ties as well; however he fears that they are not robust enough and that his knowledge is being misused."[47] Here Hiss is identified by name in clear text as a Soviet agent. Hiss is also explicitly identified in another message, which claims "Hiss is very ideologically progressive" and again "he will figure out Hiss is a member of our family."[48]

A November 1936 cover note from Bazarov indicated the KGB's awareness of Hiss as a GRU agent. Bazarov sent Moscow a copy of the just-released State Department directory. The cover note said, "You will not find the neighbors' 'Jurist' in the photograph directory because he has worked there only since September."[49] Hiss had started work for the State Department in September 1936.

By the fall of 1944, the KGB took over complete control of the Perlo network from Elizabeth Bentley. As part of his revetting, the KGB asked Perlo ("Raid") to provide a list of Soviet intelligence assets who were not in his own apparatus. The list, in English, was in KGB files that Vassiliev copied into his notebooks. The list, dated March 15, 1945, included fourteen names; among them were Alger Hiss, Donald Hiss, Gregory Silvermaster, George Silverman, and Henry Collins. With this list, Perlo was the fourth Soviet asset (after Whittaker Chambers, Hede Massing, and Noel Field) who identified Hiss as a Soviet agent.[50] Several others identified him only as a Communist.

According to Allen Weinstein, a KGB cable from April 1945 stated that Glasser ("Ruble") slipped Gorsky a warning note (Gorsky had acknowledged that "Ruble" was still the KGB's only link to "Ales"). The note said that "an FBI agent informed Stettinius that one of their agents had seen a batch of [State Department] documents that were delivered in a suitcase to New York to be photographed. Afterwards, they were returned to Washington within 24 hours." These documents included a political report and important cipher communications. Based on the nature of the documents, only three people had access to them. One of these people was "Ales." The FBI agent said that in the next seventy-two hours they would conclusively identify who had been responsible for leaking these documents. According to Stettinius, the FBI agent had told him that operations of this sort involving documents have been going on for eighteen months now, and that "hundreds upon hundreds" of documents had been removed as a result. Stettinius asked the FBI agent whether these documents ended up at "PM" [a left-wing journal], to which the latter replied: "No, much further left than that." Toward the end of his conversation with "Ales" on this subject, Stettinius told him: "I hope it isn't you."[51] The incident referred to was the *Amerasia* case, where hundreds of stolen State Department and OSS documents were found at the office of *Amerasia*, a journal published by a Communist.[52]

A March 3, 1945, cable signed by General Lieutenant Pavel Fitin, director of KGB foreign intelligence operations, contained an urgent order for "illegal" chief, Akhmerov ("Albert"), to work with Nathan Silvermaster ("Robert") to obtain any and all information on the UN conference being held in San Francisco the following month. Akhmerov, KGB liaison with Silvermaster, arranged to get information on the U.S. negotiating strategy from Harry Dexter White, who was a delegate to the conference. However, Gorsky must have realized that a better source would be Alger Hiss.[53]

A follow-up cable from Gorsky on March 5 said that "Ales" had gone to Mexico City from Moscow (after the Yalta Conference) "and hasn't returned yet." The group, including Stettinius, Matthews, Foote, and Hiss, went to Mexico City for the Chapultepec Conference starting February 21. Hiss left early and returned to Washington, D.C., to prepare for the UN conference. Matthews also did, since he was a European specialist not needed for a Latin American meeting. Only Stettinius and Foote stayed until the conference ended on March 8. Hiss's defenders used the fact that Gorsky thought "Ales" was still in Mexico City as proof that Foote was "Ales."

To suggest that because Gorsky must have known that Hiss had returned early was evidence of Foote's being "Ales," against the weight of all the other biographical, archival, and Venona data suggesting otherwise, is very thin gruel indeed. The rest of the cable described the relationship between "Ruble" (Treasury Department official Harold Glasser) and "Ales" and it pointed only to Hiss. Gorsky said that "Ruble" and "Ales" used to work in "Karl's" (Chambers's) group, which was affiliated with the GRU. Wilder Foote never had any links to Chambers; nor was he working or living in Washington, D.C., in 1936–38 when Chambers's group was operating in Washington.[54] If "Ales" worked in Karl's GRU-affiliated group, than "Ales" was Hiss.

The remainder of the KGB cable of March 5 said "Ruble" gave "Ales" an "exceptionally good political reference as a member of the Comparty."[55] Glasser told the FBI he had known Hiss since 1938 and had a close personal relationship with Donald Hiss. There is no evidence of such a relationship with Foote. In January 1945, at the request of the KGB, Glasser drew up a list of his close contacts; thirty-one persons were listed. Alger Hiss and his brother Donald

Hiss were on the list but not Wilder Foote.[56] Cables from March 3 and 5 were the background that resulted in the March 30 cable, number 1822, which was deciphered by the Venona project (see chapter 15).

General Fitin sent a memo in April 1945 to Vsevolod Merkulov, KGB chief, to review the work Glasser ("Ruble") had done for the KGB. The memo stated that according to information from Gorsky, a group of agents of the GRU, to which Glasser had previously belonged, had recently received awards for their work. "Ruble" learned this from his friend and leader of the group, "Ales." Fitin wrote that since "Ruble" missed out on an award, and given his productive work over the past eight years, he recommended "Ruble" receive the Order of the Red Star. As Haynes and Klehr observed, this passage confirms the March 30 cable that "Ales" and his group were awarded Soviet medals, but adds that Glasser had been working with the "Ales" group, further confirmation that "Ales" was Hiss.[57]

By 1948, various Soviet defectors—Massing, Bentley, Chambers, Gouzenko—had compromised many Soviet intelligence officers and their U.S. agents and assets. The GRU and KGB went into damage control mode and operations stood down. In an effort to minimize the damage, especially from the notorious Hiss case, Moscow suggested an active measures campaign.[58] In December 27, 1948, a cipher telegram indicated that a KGB disinformation campaign against "Karl" (Whittaker Chambers) be advanced:

> It would be highly desirable to oppose the Americans' anti-Soviet and anti-espionage campaigns with effective measures of some kind on our part. In connection with this, the station asks that you consider the following proposal . . . "find" a file on "Karl" in the German archives revealing that he is a German agent, that he worked as a spy for the Gestapo in the U.S. and, on a mission from them, had infiltrated the American Comparty [Communist Party]. If we print this in our newspapers and publish a few "documents" that

can be prepared at home, it would have a major effect. This report would be seized upon not only by foreign Comparties, but also by the progressive press in all countries, and, as a result, the position of the Committee on the investigation of Unamerican Activities, the Grand Jury, and other agencies would be seriously undermined. We could also claim that "Karl" was known to the Committee, the Grand Jury, and oth. American agencies as a Gestapo agent, but that because the leaders of these institutions were vehement opponents of the USSR, the Comparty, and the progressive movement in general, they had represented the matter as if "Karl" and others had been spying for the USSR rather than Germany.[59]

Moscow rejected the plan. Its response to this initiative was a report addressed to the chairman of the KI (KGB) and signed by P. Fedotov and K. Kukin, dated December 1948:

The station's proposal to manufacture and publish documents in our newspapers about the fact that the traitor Chambers is a German agent, conducted espionage work in the USA on assignment from the Gestapo, and on German instructions, infiltrated the CPUSA—cannot be accepted. The publication of such "documents" would undoubtedly have a very negative effect on our former agents who were betrayed by Chambers (A. Hiss, D. Hiss, Wadleigh, Pigman, Reno) [these real names were used] and oth., because, knowing that they had worked for us, but having "turned" into German agents, these people could, for example, choose to cooperate with the authorities, give them candid testimonies, etc. Moreover, the transformation of these individuals from alleged Sov. intelligence agents into established agents for a country that had been at war with the USA would certainly not help them from a purely legal standpoint.[60]

By the late 1940s, Soviet intelligence networks in the United States were in disarray. The Gorsky Memo in 1948, discussed earlier, attempted to capture the damage that was done from all the defections.[61] In the December 1948 memo above, both Alger Hiss's and Chambers's names are used in plain text. In addition, Gorsky's report identified Hiss by his real name (while also citing his new cover name, "Leonard") as a Soviet agent betrayed by Chambers.

Finally, a March 16, 1950, document in Vassiliev's notebook contained a plan to restart Moscow's intelligence presence in the United States; it included a summary of the 1940s setbacks from defections and purges. The document noted that the trial of the GRU agent "Leonard," a division chief at the State Department and a member of "Karl's group," had "ended in his conviction at the beginning of 1950."[62] Alger Hiss, a State Department official and member of Chambers's espionage apparatus, was put on trial and then convicted in January 1950. It doesn't get any clearer than that. Hiss was a Soviet asset of the GRU.

EPILOGUE

THE NOTEBOOKS OF Alexander Vassiliev show conclusively, along with all the other documentary and testimonial evidence, that Alger Hiss was an agent of Soviet military intelligence. Whittaker Chambers told the truth; Hiss did not. Alger Hiss never broke. He had no reservations about deceiving his family, friends, and supporters during his entire life. Hiss lied to them for almost a half century. He most likely was able to do this because from his perspective, he was following Communist morality as defined by Lenin. He developed a persona of sterling character and became an establishment figure with many high-level officials supporting him. After prison, he developed another persona, that of innocent victim of the 1950s Red Scare and Cold War hysteria.

Hiss's son, Tony, wrote: "It would sadden me to learn that Alger was once a spy and had committed the crimes he was tried for—although I have never, in fact, doubted his innocence . . . but it is at least abstractly conceivable that the man who opened himself up to me could have been someone who had stolen government papers in his safekeeping." Tony goes on to say, however, there is no way he can integrate the father he got to know (Face One) with the spy Chambers talked about (Face Three).[1]

Tony further reflected on his father: "Had Chambers' charges been true, had the third Alger been the real Alger, then Alger's story would today carry an abiding balm and comfort—the knowledge that it now had ended, for better or for worse, and could be laid to rest with his ashes."[2] And, he continued, if Alger were guilty then the story would have had recognizable pain—"the tragedy of a man of great promise who turns away from high purposes has been one of the towering themes of Western literature for the last twenty-five centuries."[3] These musings by Alger Hiss's son seem to suggest, if not a realization of the weight of evidence against Hiss, at least a resignation and possible wish that it could all finally be put to rest, even if the final verdict may have been "guilty."

Alger Hiss fastened upon an illusory ideology claiming to answer all questions, promising utopia, but in reality concealing tyranny. In the process he betrayed his country. Dedicated by oath and office to serving his country, he became a secret agent of the adversary, the Soviet intelligence apparatus. He had closed his mind, blind to the inhumanity of Communism, and adopted Lenin's notion that the choice of revolution is ultimate and irrevocable, an act of passion as well as intellect. Hiss worked hard to appear urbane and sophisticated and behind this persona was his single-minded devotion to Communism, leading to a lifetime of defiance and denying any wrongdoing.

Hiss has become emblematic of the ideological divide that continues to this day in the United States. The Hiss case has become the touchstone for many progressive intellectuals. And that is one of the best explanations for the fact that despite the existence of overwhelming evidence against Hiss, there are still those today who cannot bring themselves to assimilate that evidence and acknowledge that Alger Hiss was a Soviet asset and guilty of espionage. They focus on Hiss's message, not his actions. Hiss's advocacy of collectivism and the need for government control over society and his support for international policies ahead of national security interests still resonate today. Many current political elites continue to champion strong, overreaching government control—that is to say, socialism—despite the bankruptcy of socialist solutions in the former Soviet Union and the washout of a socialist agenda so visible today in Europe. And they also advocate internationalism—despite ongoing foreign policy failures from succumbing to antidemocratic rulers in the Middle East and Asia in the name of global peace.

Vladimir Bukovsky, a former Soviet dissident living at present in the United Kingdom, spent twelve years in Soviet prisons, labor camps, and forced-treatment psychiatric hospitals used by the Soviet government to hold political prisoners. Bukovsky drew a comparison between the former USSR and the European Union (EU), where, he claimed, a few dozen bureaucrats in Brussels who are not accountable to the people decide their fate; where nationalism is suppressed in an attempt to establish a socialist European state; and where an intellectual gulag exists, in that people are ostracized in the name of political correctness for expressing their independent views. Bukovsky summed up his comments with a warning to the EU: "I have lived in your future and it didn't work."[4]

NOTES

Prologue

1. Ron Chernow, *Alexander Hamilton*, p. 320.
2. George F. Will, speech delivered at the Biennial Dinner for the Cato Institute's Milton Friedman Prize for Advancing Liberty, May 13, 2010.
3. Patrick Swan, ed., *Alger Hiss, Whittaker Chambers, and the Schism in the American Soul*, p. 204.
4. Christopher Hitchens, as quoted in ibid., p. xxii.
5. Louis E. Tice, "Overcoming Blind Spots," in *Smart Talk for Achieving Your Potential* (Seattle, WA: Pacific Institute Publishing, revised version 2005), pp. 85–87; Louis E. Tice, "How Your Mind Works," in *Personal Coaching for Results* (Nashville, TN: Thomas Nelson Publishers, 1997, copyright held by The Pacific Institute, Inc.), p. 17. See also David C. Korten, "Breaking the Cultural Trance," Living Economies Forum (online). Korten observes: "Every human community has a cultural story field comprised of the shared stories that define the community's shared values, understanding, and expectations." The term *cultural trance*, according to Korten, refers to a situation in which members of a community fail to recognize that the stories that comprise the cultural story field of their community are theories and therefore subject to continuous testing and change. The persons who have developed the capacity to step back and recognize the cultural story field as a collection of shared stories subject to choice live in a state of cultural awareness. The persons who have not yet developed this capacity live in a cultural trance, which limits their creative expression and leaves them subject to manipulation by propagandists.
6. Tony Hiss, *The View from Alger's Window*, p. 43.
7. New York University, Tamiment Library, Robert F. Wagner Labor Archives: Collection of Alger Hiss Family Papers (1892–2007), TAM 134, Boxes 1–3. See especially Box 1, Folders 1–23. Box 1 has folders from 1913 through 1945, but no folders for years 1936 and 1937—the years

when Whittaker Chambers was "running" Hiss. The folders go from #15 1935 to #16 1938. Did this avid, lifelong letter writer not write any letters in 1936 and 1937?

8. Whittaker Chambers, *Witness,* p. 373.
9. Tony Hiss, *The View from Alger's Window,* p. 47.
10. Ibid., p. 182.

1. Growing Up in Baltimore

1. Murray Kempton, *Part of Our Time: Some Ruins and Monuments of the Thirties,* pp. 16–19.
2. G. Edward White, *Alger Hiss's Looking-Glass Wars,* p. 4.
3. John Chabot Smith, *Alger Hiss: The True Story,* p. 32.
4. Ibid.
5. Hiss Family Papers (1892–2007); TAM 134, Box 7, Folder 19, "Maryland Women," p. 171.
6. Ibid.
7. Allen Weinstein, *Perjury,* p. 73.
8. Ibid.
9. Smith, *Alger Hiss,* p. 33.
10. Ibid., pp. 33, 36.
11. Ibid., p. 40.
12. Ibid., p. 34.
13. Tony Hiss, *Laughing Last,* pp. 6–7.
14. Ibid., p. 7.
15. Alger Hiss, *Recollections of a Life,* p. 2.
16. Ibid.
17. White, *Alger Hiss's Looking-Glass Wars,* p. 9.
18. Weinstein, *Perjury,* p. 74.
19. White, *Alger Hiss's Looking-Glass Wars,* p. 5.
20. Alger Hiss, *Recollections of a Life,* p. 58.
21. Smith, *Alger Hiss,* p. 52.
22. Hiss Family Papers: TAM 134, Box 1, Folder 11.
23. Ibid.
24. *The Handbook of Texas Online,* s.v. "Anna Hiss."
25. Smith, *Alger Hiss,* p. 65.
26. White, *Alger Hiss's Looking-Glass Wars,* p. 5.
27. Smith, *Alger Hiss,* p. 40; White, *Alger Hiss's Looking-Glass Wars,* pp. 5–6.
28. Smith, *Alger Hiss* p. 64.
29. Weinstein, *Perjury,* p. 76.

30. Alger Hiss, *Recollections of a Life*, p. 2.
31. Ibid., p. 1.
32. Ibid., pp. 3–5.
33. Tony Hiss, *Laughing Last*, p. 18.
34. Smith, *Alger Hiss*, p. 38.
35. Ibid., p. 43.
36. Ibid., p. 47.
37. Ibid., p. 50.
38. Weinstein, *Perjury*, p. 599, fn. 18.

11. Hopkins and Harvard Law

1. Alger Hiss, *Recollections of a Life*, p. 27.
2. Ibid., pp. 55–56.
3. On April 15, 1920, a paymaster and his guard were carrying a factory payroll of $15,776 through the main street of South Braintree, Massachusetts, a small industrial town south of Boston. Two men standing by a fence pulled out guns and fired on them; they grabbed the cash boxes and jumped into a waiting automobile. The bandit gang, numbering four or five in all, sped away, eluding their pursuers. At first this brutal murder and robbery aroused only local interest. Three weeks later, on the evening of May 5, 1920, two Italians, Nicola Sacco and Bartolomeo Vanzetti, although originally not under suspicion, were carrying guns at the time of their arrest and when questioned by the authorities they lied. As a result they were held and eventually indicted for the South Braintree crimes. The case, in which many condemned the men as anarchists and revolutionaries, became one of the most notorious and controversial American political trials.
4. Kempton, *Part of Our Time*, p. 18.
5. Smith, *Alger Hiss*, p. 50.
6. Ibid., p. 50.
7. Ibid., p. 51.
8. Ibid., p. 52.
9. Ibid.
10. Ibid.
11. Alger Hiss, *Recollections of a Life*, p. 58.
12. Chambers, *Witness*, p. 360.
13. David Cort, "Of Guilt and Resurrection," *Nation*. March 20, 1967, in Swan, ed., *Alger Hiss, Whittaker Chambers, and the Schism in the American Soul*, p. 135, citing Dr. Meyer Zeligs.

14. Ivan Chen (J.D. candidate, Harvard Law School, 2008), "Alger Hiss 1926–1929," http://works.bepress.com/cgi/viewcontent.cgi?article=1000&context=ivan_chen, p. 39.

15. Ibid., p. 4.

16. Ibid., p. 40.

17. Chen, "Alger Hiss 1926–1929."

18. Ibid., p. 7.

19. Ibid., pp. 9–12.

20. Ibid., p. 17.

21. Ibid., pp. 19–20.

22. Ibid., p. 26.

23. Ibid., pp. 27–28.

24. Ibid., p. 29.

25. Weinstein, *Perjury,* p. 75.

26. Chen, "Alger Hiss 1926–1929," pp. 30–32.

27. Alger Hiss, *Recollections of a Life,* pp. 12–14.

28. White, *Alger Hiss's Looking-Glass Wars,* p. 12.

29. Alger Hiss, *Recollections of a Life,* pp. 10–11.

30. Chen, "Alger Hiss 1926–1929," p. 42.

31. Alger Hiss, *Recollections of a Life,* p. 11.

32. Chen, "Alger Hiss 1926–1929," p. 42.

33. Smith, *Alger Hiss: The True Story,* p. 58.

34. Alger Hiss, *Recollections of a Life,* p. 16.

35. Ibid., pp. 16–17.

36. Chen, "Alger Hiss 1926–1929," pp. 45–47.

37. Ibid., p. 49.

38. Kempton, *Part of Our Time,* pp. 20–21.

III. PRISCILLA HISS

1. Tony Hiss, *Laughing Last,* p. 45.

2. Smith, *Alger Hiss,* pp. 66–67.

3. Aaron Finestone, "Priscilla Hiss," http://www.microbrewjournalism.com/page8/page8.html.

4. Smith, *Alger Hiss,* p. 54.

5. Ibid., p. 55.

6. Ibid., p. 56.

7. Tony Hiss, *Laughing Last,* p. 49.

8. FBI Report 65-56402-3683, pp. 942–43; FBI Report NYC 1/21/49 74-1333-1477, pp. 62–64.

9. Weinstein, *Perjury,* p. 79; White, *Alger Hiss's Looking-Glass Wars,* p. 14.

10. Weinstein, *Perjury,* p. 79; Smith, *Alger Hiss,* pp. 66–67.

11. Smith, *Alger Hiss,* p. 66.

12. Weinstein, *Perjury,* p. 79.

13. Smith, *Alger Hiss,* pp. 68–69.

14. FBI File: NY 65-15867, Background Memo on Pricilla Hiss, p. 3.

15. White, *Alger Hiss's Looking-Glass Wars,* p. 27.

16. Weinstein, *Perjury,* p. 81.

17. Tony Hiss, *Laughing Last,* p. 64.

18. Weinstein, *Perjury,* p. 96.

19. White, *Alger Hiss's Looking-Glass Wars,* p. 27.

20. Tony Hiss, *The View from Alger's Window,* p. 28.

21. Chambers, *Witness,* p. 569.

22. Hiss Family Papers, TAM 134, Box 1, Folders 1–8.

23. Ibid., Box 1, Folder 10.

24. Weinstein, *Perjury,* p. 97.

25. Hiss Family Papers, TAM 314, Box 1, Folder 12.

26. Weinstein, *Perjury,* pp. 457, 485.

27. Ibid., pp. 97–99, 457; FBI File: NY 65-15867.

28. Weinstein, *Perjury,* pp. 98–99.

29. Kempton, *Part of Our Time,* p. 24.

30. Alger Hiss, *Recollections of a Life,* p. 57.

31. Smith, *Alger Hiss: The True Story,* p. 73.

32. Chambers, *Witness,* p. 335; United States House of Representatives, Committee on Un-American Activities, Washington, D.C., August 28, 1950. Reprinted as Exhibit No. 1402, U.S. Congress, Senate, 82nd Cong., Committee on the Judiciary, *Hearings to Investigate the Administration of the Internal Security Act and Other Internal Security Laws,* Second Session on the Institute of Pacific Relations (Washington, DC: U.S. Government Printing Office, 1952), p. 5503.

33. Weinstein, *Perjury,* pp. 40–41, fn.

34. FBI File: 100-345686-4, "Memorandum from Mr. Tamm to the Director, re: Soviet Espionage in the U.S." p. 5, September 5, 1946.

35. Bryn Mawr Archives: Priscilla Hiss; Weinstein, *Perjury,* p. 110.

36. Smith, *Alger Hiss: The True Story,* p. 75.

37. Ibid., p. 77.

38. FBI File: P. Hiss, FBI Memo NY 65-15867.

39. Ibid.

40. FBI File: P. Hiss, FBI Memo April 23, 1953, p. 13, 100-376016-3; FBI Memo: NY 165-15867.

41. FBI: Memorandum 100-376016; NY 65-15867 April 26, 1971.

42. FBI File: P. Hiss, NY 65-15867, July 18, 1955; 5-Bureau (100-376016) RM; 3—New York 65-15867.

43. Smith, *Alger Hiss: The True Story*, p. 70.

44. Ibid.

45. Tony Hiss, *The View From Alger's Window*, p. 220.

46. Chambers, *Witness*, p. 374.

47. Smith, *Alger Hiss: The True Story*, p. 76.

48. Tony Hiss, *Laughing Last*, p. 73.

49. Ibid.

IV. SUPREME COURT CLERK AND ATTORNEY-AT-LAW

1. Weinstein, *Perjury*, p. 78.

2. Alger Hiss, *Recollections of a Life*, p. 31.

3. Ibid., p 32.

4. Ibid., p. 34.

5. Ibid., p. 33.

6. Ibid., p. 35; Chen, "Alger Hiss 1926–1929," p. 54.

7. White, *Alger Hiss's Looking-Glass Wars*, p. 17.

8. Alger Hiss, *Recollections of a Life*, p. 35.

9. Ibid., p. 37.

10. Ibid., p. 47.

11. Ibid., p. 51.

12. Tony Hiss, *Laughing Last*, p. 55.

13. Smith, *Alger Hiss: The True Story*, p. 71.

14. Ibid., p. 59.

15. Alger Hiss, *Recollections of a Life*, p. 62.

16. Smith, *Alger Hiss: The True Story*, p. 16.

17. Kempton, *Part of Our Time*, p. 23.

18. White, *Alger Hiss's Looking-Glass Wars*, p. 28.

19. Smith, *Alger Hiss: The True Story*, p. 15.

20. Ibid., p. 18.

21. Alger Hiss, *Recollections of a Life*, p. 61.

22. Weinstein, *Perjury*, pp. 97–98.

23. Ibid., p. 133.

24. Ibid.

25. Chambers, *Witness*, pp. 342–46.

26. Ibid., p. 349.

27. The Soviet Union's organization responsible for foreign intelligence went through a variety of name changes over the years (CHEKA, GPU, OGPU, GUGB, NKVD, NKGB, MGB, KI, and KGB). *KGB* is used in this book to refer to all periods of time and name changes since it is the most familiar to the reader. Today, the SVR, successor to the KGB's First Chief Directorate, is responsible for Russia's foreign intelligence.

28. Louis Budenz, *Men Without Faces: The Communist Conspiracy in the USA,* p. 281.

29. Weinstein, *Perjury,* p. 134.

30. Illegals were officers in the Soviet intelligence services who generally traveled and operated under false documentation, usually posing as a citizen of a Western country, and thus had no official connection with the Soviet Union; as such they had no diplomatic immunity. By contrast, a legal officer of the KGB (and GRU) served abroad under official cover of an embassy, consulate, trade mission, or other organization formally tied to the Soviet Union.

31. See William E. Duff, *A Time for Spies: Theodore Stephonavich Mally and the Era of the Great Illegals.*

32. Christopher Andrew and Oleg Gordievsky, *KGB: The Inside Story,* p. 184.

33. "Arthur Wynn, Member of the CP of England," *Times* (London), May 13, 2009.

34. John Earl Haynes and Harvey Klehr, *Venona: Decoding Soviet Espionage in America,* pp. 53–55.

35. Ibid., p. 107.

36. Ibid., pp. 104–7.

37. See interview with retired CIA counterintelligence expert Sandy Grimes, *Spies,* episode 21, January 30, 1998.

38. Milt Bearden and James Risen, *The Main Enemy,* pp. 193–94.

39. Ibid., p. 127. Examples were Colonel Polishchuk, KGB counterintelligence officer, and Sergey Federenko, a nuclear arms expert in the Soviet delegation to the UN. He also compromised two KGB officers stationed at the KGB *rezidentura* (station) in Washington, D.C.; Valery Martynov, a Line X (technical and scientific intelligence) officer, and Sergei Motorin, a Line PR (political intelligence) officer. Both were arrested, sent back to Moscow, and subsequently executed.

40. David C. Martin, *Wilderness of Mirrors.* p. 54.

v. The New Dealer

1. Alger Hiss, *Recollections of a Life,* p. 82.
2. White, *Alger Hiss's Looking-Glass Wars,* p. 208, quoted in David Remnick's "Alger Hiss: Unforgiven and Unforgiving," *Washington Post Magazine,* October 12, 1986, pp. 27, 31–32, 34.
3. John Ehrman, Center for the Study of Intelligence, "The Alger Hiss Case," May 8, 2007.
4. Hiss Family Papers, TAM 134, Box 4, Folder 38, "Hiss's Handwritten Notes Praising the New Deal."
5. Alger Hiss, *Recollections of a Life,* p. 66.
6. Ibid., pp. 62–69.
7. Ibid., p. 66.
8. Ibid., pp. 16–17.
9. Ibid., p. 17.
10. Ibid., p. 62.
11. Rebecca West, *The New Meaning of Treason,* p. 141.
12. Alger Hiss, *Recollections of a Life,* p. 59.
13. Ibid., p. 57.
14. Ibid., p. 60.
15. Ibid., p. 67.
16. Ibid., p. 69.
17. Ibid., p. 70.
18. Smith, *Alger Hiss: The True Story,* p. 21.
19. Alger Hiss, *Recollections of a Life,* p. 63.
20. Weinstein, *Perjury,* p. 153.
21. Tony Hiss, *Laughing Last,* p. 83.
22. Chambers, *Witness,* p. 336.
23. Hiss Family Papers, TAM 134, Box 7, Folder 156, "Reminiscences of Alger Hiss."
24. Ibid., p. 24.
25. Ibid., pp. 131–32.
26. Ibid., pp. 132–34.

vi. The Ware Group

1. Chambers, *Witness,* pp. 332–33.
2. Weinstein, *Perjury,* p. 134.
3. Those individuals in the "underground" were Communist Party members who kept secret their party affiliation, as opposed to those who were openly Communists and publicly worked on behalf of and supported Communists.

4. Chambers, *Witness*, p. 32.
5. Weinstein, *Perjury*, p. 140.
6. Chambers, *Witness*, p. 560.
7. Ibid., p. 339.
8. Ibid., pp. 349–50.
9. Ibid., p. 359.
10. Ibid., pp. 340–41.
11. Ibid., p. 342.
12. Ibid., p. 343.
13. Ibid.
14. Isaac Don Levine, *Eyewitness to History*, pp. 182–83.
15. Weinstein, *Perjury*, p. 132.
16. Chambers, *Witness*, p. 335.
17. Ibid.
18. M. Stanton Evans, *Blacklisted by History*, p. 143.
19. For additional material on the Ware Group see Weinstein, *Perjury*, pp. 132–41, and Chambers, *Witness*, pp. 340–50.
20. Weinstein, *Perjury*, p. 124.
21. Ibid., pp. 43–44.
22. Ibid., pp. 144–45.
23. Dartmouth College Library, Rauner Special Collections: Library ML-66, Box 1, Folder 7, interview with *U.S. News & World Report*, January 9, 1953.
24. Ibid.
25. Ibid.
26. Ibid.
27. Ibid.
28. Ibid.
29. Ibid.
30. "LABOR: End of the Line?" *Time*, February 16, 1948.
31. Chambers, *Witness*, pp. 335, 436; Weinstein, *Perjury*, p. 135.
32. *New York Times* obituary, August 13, 1991.
33. Chambers, *Witness*, p. 344.
34. *New York Times* obituary, August 13, 1991.
35. Chambers, *Witness*, p. 335.
36. *New York Times* obituary, August 13, 1991.
37. Chambers, *Witness*, p. 344.
38. *New York Times* obituary, February 20, 1982.
39. FBI Files, Memorandum 65-14920 Vol. II, December 14, 1948.

40. Weinstein, *Perjury*, p. 24.

41. Chambers, *Witness*, p. 341.

42. Ibid., p. 345.

43. Weinstein, *Perjury*, p. 208.

44. John Earl Haynes, Harvey Klehr, and Alexander Vassiliev, *Spies: The Rise and the Fall of the KGB in America*, p. 279.

45. Allen Weinstein and Alexander Vassiliev, *The Haunted Wood: Soviet Espionage in America—The Stalin Era*, p. 232.

46. Haynes, Klehr, and Vassiliev, *Spies*, pp. 282–83.

47. Weinstein, *Perjury*, p.156. Weinstein wrote that the letter also went to the FBI. See note 43.

48. Chambers, *Witness*, p. 430.

49. T. Michael Ruddy, *The Alger Hiss Espionage Case*, p. 100.

50. *New York Times* obituary, December 10, 1999.

51. Chambers, *Witness*, p. 469; Vassiliev Black Notebook File 43173 v. 2c, p. 49.

52. Chambers, *Witness*, p. 569.

53. Ibid., p. 418.

54. Weinstein, *Perjury*, pp. 174–75.

55. David E. Murphy, *What Stalin Knew: The Enigma of Barbarossa*, p. 102.

56. Herbert Romerstein and Eric Breindel, *The Venona Secrets: Exposing Soviet Espionage and America's Traitors*, pp. 154–55, 301.

57. Chambers, *Witness*, p. 27.

58. Ibid., p. 383.

59. Christopher Andrew and Vasili Mitrokhin, *The Sword and the Shield*, p. 104.

60. Chambers, *Witness*, p. 386.

61. Romerstein and Breindel, *The Venona Secrets*, p. 30.

62. Ted Morgan, *Washington Post*, review of R. Bruce Craig, *Treasonable Doubt: The Harry Dexter White Spy Case*, 2004.

63. Weinstein, *Perjury*, p. 173.

64. Morgan, *Washington Post* review of *Treasonable Doubt*.

65. Romerstein and Breindel, *The Venona Secrets*, pp. 47–48.

66. Robert J. Lamphere and Tom Shactman, *The FBI-KGB War: A Special Agent's Story*, p. 284.

67. As quoted in Morgan, Washington Post review of *Treasonable Doubt*.

68. Venona Files, New York to Moscow, January 18, 1945, in Romerstein and Breindel, *The Venona Secrets*, p. 47.

69. See R. Bruce Craig's, *Treasonable Doubt: The Harry Dexter White Spy Case*.

70. Morgan, *Washington Post* review of *Treasonable Doubt*.

71. Hiss Family Papers, TAM 134, Box 11.

72. Chambers, *Witness*, p. 482.

73. Thomas Fleming, *The New Dealers' War: FDR and the War Within World War II*, pp. 319–20.

74. Weinstein, *Perjury*, p. 356.

75. Robert Conquest, *Reflections on a Ravaged Century*, p. 137.

76. "The Legacy of Alexander Orlov," Testimony of Orlov before the Senate Subcommittee on Internal Security, February 14–15, 1957, 93rd Congress, 1st Session, Committee Report (Washington, DC: U.S. Government Printing Office, 1973), p. 71.

77. Gordon Brook-Shepherd, *The Storm Petrels*, p. 218.

78. Ibid., p. 229.

79. Conquest, *Reflections on a Ravaged Century*, as quoted on p. 151.

80. George Kennan, *Memoirs*, vol. 2, chap. 9, from commentary by Wilson D. Miscamble, University of Notre Dame, published in H-DIPLO on February 9, 2003.

81. See Paul Monk, "Christopher Andrew and the Strange Case of Roger Hollis," *Quadrant Magazine* (Australia) online (Fall 2010). The article states that Chapman Pincher summarized the work of the Cambridge 5 spies: The KGB archives reveal that "the total take from these five spies alone—17,526 classified documents—is a measure of the number of their meetings with Russians and emphasizes the enormousness of their treachery, which was far worse than ever suspected, and more may yet be revealed."

82. Vladimir Lota, "Morris Makes Contact," *Krasnaya Zvezda (Red Star)*, May 5, 2006.

83. Chambers, *Witness*, pp. 32–33.

VII. WHITTAKER CHAMBERS
A. The Witness

1. Sam Tanenhaus, *Whittaker Chambers*, p. 3.

2. Ibid., p. 4.

3. Ibid., p. 5.

4. "Death of the Witness," *Time* magazine historical notes, July 21, 1961.

5. Tanenhaus, *Whittaker Chambers*, pp. 8–9.

6. Ibid., p. 7.

7. Chambers, *Witness*, p. 145.

8. Ibid.

9. Tanenhaus, *Whittaker Chambers*, p. 68.

10. Chambers, *Witness*, p. 150.

11. Ibid., p. 160.

12. Tanenhaus, *Whittaker Chambers*, p. 19.

13. Ibid., p. 22.

14. Ibid., pp. 22–23.

15. Kempton, *Part of Our Time*, p. 28.

16. Tanenhaus, *Whittaker Chambers*, p. 23.

17. Ibid., p. 24.

18. Ibid., p. 40.

19. Ibid., pp. 31–32.

20. Chambers, *Witness*, p. 166.

21. Ibid., p. 167.

22. Tanenhaus, *Whittaker Chambers*, p. 21.

23. Ibid., p. 41.

24. William F. Buckley, "Remembering Whittaker Chambers on the Centennial of His Birth," *National Review*, August 6, 2001.

25. "Death of the Witness," *Time*, July 21, 1961.

26. Chambers, *Witness*, p. 173.

27. Ibid., p. 185.

28. Tanenhaus, *Whittaker Chambers*, p. 502.

29. Ibid., pp. 64–65.

30. Ibid., pp. 79–82.

31. Chambers, *Witness*, p. 225.

32. Ibid., p. 288.

33. Tanenhaus, *Whittaker Chambers*, p. 96.

34. See Weinstein, *Perjury*, pp. 115–16; Chambers, *Witness*, p. 352; Swann, ed., *Alger Hiss, Whittaker Chambers, and the Schism in the American Soul*, p. 221; Hugh Kenner, "Chambers's Music and Alger Hiss," *American Spectator*, June 1979.

35. Tanenhaus, *Whittaker Chambers*, pp. 88–89.

36. Chambers, *Witness*, pp. 72, 350.

37. Ibid., p. 70.

38. Ibid.

39. Ibid., p. 363.

40. Ruddy, *The Alger Hiss Espionage Case*, p. 166.

41. Chambers, *Witness*, p. 422.

42. Ibid., p. 421.

43. Ibid., pp. 421–22.

44. Ibid., p. 380.

45. Christopher Andrew and Vasili Mitrokhin, *The Sword and the Shield: The Mitrokhin Archive and the Secret History of the KGB*, part 1, p. 105.

46. Chambers, *Witness*, pp. 381–82.

47. Chambers, *Witness*, p. 58; Tanenhaus, *Whittaker Chambers*, p. 136.

48. Chambers, *Witness*, p. 72.

49. Ibid.

50. Ibid., p. 73.

51. J. B. Matthews, *Odyssey of a Fellow Traveler*, p. 92.

52. See Dame Rebecca West's *The New Meaning of Treason*, which contains psychological insights and analyses of ideological treason and the rationalizations of traitors, and of the blindness of those who dismiss the whole subject as inconsequential. She mostly profiles British spies.

53. Nicolas Berdyaev, *The Origin of Russian Communism*, pp. 63–64.

54. Richard Pipes, ed., *The Unknown Lenin: From the Secret Archive*, p. 153.

55. Chambers, *Witness*, pp. 76–79.

56. Ibid., p. 41.

57. Alexander Foote, *Handbook for Spies*, p. 9. Foote, a radio operator, was a member of the Rota Capella (Red Orchestra), the famous Soviet espionage network operating inside Germany during the war. According to various sources, Foote actually was an MI6 (SIS) double agent.

58. Gary Kerns, *A Death in Washington: Walter G. Krivitsky and the Stalin Terror*, pp. 368–78.

59. Chambers, *Witness*, p. 486.

60. Carlo Tresca, "Where Is Juliet Stuart Poyntz?" *Modern Monthly* 10, no. 11 (March 1938), pp. 12–13.

61. Weinstein, *Perjury*, p. 312.

62. "Death of the Witness," *Time*, July 21, 1961.

63. Chambers, *Witness*, pp. 472–73.

64. Ibid.

65. Buckley, "Remembering Whittaker Chambers on the Centennial of His Birth."

66. Dwight Macdonald, book review, *Observer*, 1957.

67. Tanenhaus, *Whittaker Chambers*, p. 506.

68. Ibid., pp. 504–7.

69. Ibid., p. 484.

70. "Death of the Witness," *Time*, July 21, 1961.

71. "The Centennial of Chambers's Birth," *National Review*, August 6, 2001.

72. See Whittaker Chambers testimony, HUAC Hearings, August 3, 1948.

73. "Death of the Witness," *Time,* July 21, 1961.
74. *World Affairs,* Spring 2008.

B. The GRU

75. Andrew and Mitrokhin, *The Sword and the Shield,* p. 104.
76. Romerstein and Breindel, *The Venona Secrets,* p. 143.
77. Andrew and Mitrokhin, *The Sword and the Shield,* p. 104.
78. Ibid., p. 106.
79. Ibid., p. 109.
80. Weinstein and Vassiliev, *The Haunted Wood,* pp. 153–55.
81. Andrew and Mitrokhin, *The Sword and the Shield,* p. 105.
82. Andrew and Gordievsky, *KGB,* p. 286.
83. Andrew and Mitrokhin, *The Sword and the Shield,* p. 127.
84. Ibid., p. 597, fn. 31.
85. Jerrold Schecter and Leona Schecter, *Sacred Secrets,* p. 35.
86. Andrew and Mitrokhin, *The Sword and the Shield,* p. 109.
87. Michael Walsh, "Iowa-Born, Soviet-Trained," *Smithsonian,* May 2009, pp. 40–47.
88. Ibid.
89. Owen A. Lock, "Chiefs of the GRU: 1918–1947," Hayden B. Peake and Samuel Halpern, eds., *In the Name of Intelligence: Essays in Honor of Walter Pforzheimer,* pp. 353–78. Owen Lock was a senior editor at Ballantine Books (a subsidiary of Random House) and a former U.S. Air Force linguist in Russian and Chinese.
90. John Earl Haynes and Harvey Klehr, *In Denial: Historians, Communism, and Espionage,* p. 188.
91. Romerstein and Breindel, *The Venona Secrets,* p. 143.

VIII. THE STATE DEPARTMENT BUREAUCRAT

1. Louis Budenz, *Men Without Faces,* p. 1.
2. Stanislav Levchenko, *On the Wrong Side: My Life in the KGB,* p. 49.
3. Chambers, *Witness,* p. 332.
4. Andrew and Gordievsky, *KGB,* p. 230.
5. Weinstein, *Perjury,* p. 230. Julian Wadleigh, a State Department official who had passed classified material to Chambers, confirmed Chambers's assertion that Bykov wanted to increase the flow of information from within the U.S. government.
6. Weinstein, *Perjury,* pp. 350–51; Maria Schmidt, "Noel Field—The American Communist at the Center of Stalin's East European Purge: From the

Hungarian Archives," *American Communist History*, Vol. 3, no. 2 (2004), pp. 233–34.

7.   FBI Report: Whittaker Chambers Internal Security–C, Sep. 5, 1948 (FBI File Hiss-Chambers, Vol. 1).

8.   White, *Alger Hiss's Looking-Glass Wars*, p. 68.

9.   Lionel Trilling, in Swan, ed., *Alger Hiss, Whittaker Chambers, and the Schism in the American Soul*, p. 194.

10. Weinstein, *Perjury*, p. 448.

11. Alger Hiss, *Recollections of a Life*, p. 93.

12. Ibid., p. 94.

13. See General Albert C. Wedemeyer, *Wedemeyer Reports* (1958); Theodore Harold White, *Thunder Out of China* (1980); and Maochun Yu, *OSS in China* (1997).

14. Chinese-language source *Biography of Mao Tse-tung*, by Juang Chang (a former member of the Maoist Red Guards), as cited in Evans, *Blacklisted by History*, p. 108.

15. John Costello, *Mask of Treachery*, p. 482.

16. Evans, *Blacklisted by History*, pp. 100–1.

17. Ibid., pp. 102–4.

18. Ibid., p. 106.

19. Tanenhaus, *Whittaker Chambers*, p. 222.

20. Weinstein, *Perjury*, p. 570, and see p. 582 for discussion of the *Amerasia* case.

21. Alger Hiss, *Recollections of a Life*, pp. 128–29.

22. Andrew and Mitrokhin, *The Sword and the Shield*, p. 134.

23. Alger Hiss, *Recollections of a Life*, p. 146.

24. Bryton Barron, *Inside the State Department*, pp. 33, 127.

25. Thomas M. Campbell and George C. Herring, eds., *The Diaries of Edward R. Stettinius, Jr., 1943–1946*, pp. 302–3.

26. Weinstein, *Perjury*, pp. 362–63.

27. Alger Hiss, *Recollections of a Life*, pp. 140, 146.

28. Hiss Family Papers, TAM 134, Box 2, Folders 1 and 2.

29. Campbell and Herring, eds., *The Diaries of Edward R. Stettinius, Jr. 1943–1946*, p. 416.

30. Weinstein, *Perjury*, p. 361.

31. Alger Hiss, *Recollections of a Life*, p. 140.

32. Hiss Family Papers, TAM 134, Box 4, Folder 97.

33. Alger Hiss, *Recollections of a Life*, pp. 138–39.

34. Ibid., p. 143.

35. Ibid., p. 145.

36. FBI File: Report 65-14920, Vol. II, March 19, 1946.

37. Weinstein, *Perjury*, p. 356.

38. Ibid.

39. Ibid., pp. 357–58.

40. White, *Alger Hiss's Looking-Glass Wars*, p. 50; Weinstein, *Perjury*, p. 358; Alger Hiss, *Recollections of a Life*, p. 149.

41. FBI File: Report 65-14920, Vol. II, March 19, 1946.

42. FBI File: Ladd's Memorandum to Hoover, March 25, 1946.

43. Weinstein, *Perjury*, pp. 358–59.

44. Ibid., p. 365. For cites of various memos, see p. 630, fn. 75.

45. Tanenhaus, *Whittaker Chambers*, p. 519. For a list of memos, see p. 600, fn. 11.

46. Ibid.; Weinstein, *Perjury*, p. 361.

47. Weinstein, *Perjury*, p. 362.

48. Ibid., pp. 364–65.

49. Evans, *Blacklisted by History*, p. 158.

50. John Earl Haynes and Harvey Klehr, *Venona: Decoding Soviet Espionage in America*, pp. 52–55.

51. Weinstein, *Perjury*, p. 364. Weinstein cites "Notes Taken from Desk Calendar of A. Hiss on October 11, 1946," Document #23 State.

52. Romerstein and Breindel, *The Venona Secrets*, pp. 137–38.

53. Chambers, *Witness*, p. 510.

54. Levine, *Eyewitness to History*, pp. 193–94.

55. Chambers, *Witness*, p. 457.

56. Levine, *Eyewitness to History*, pp. 194–195; Tanenhaus, *Whittaker Chambers*, p.16; Chambers, *Witness*, pp. 463–70.

57. Thomas Fleming, *The New Dealers' War*, p. 320.

58. FBI File: NY 65-14920, Vol. II, December 14, 1948.

59. Tanenhaus, *Whittaker Chambers*, p. 162; Levine, *Eyewitness to History*, p. 198.

60. Weinstein, *Perjury*, p. 350; Levine, *Eyewitness to History*, p. 198.

61. Levine, *Eyewitness to History*, p. 198.

62. FBI Files on Priscilla Hiss, NY 65-15867.

63. Tanenhaus, *Whittaker Chambers*, p. 207 (Source: FBI memo, sec. 33, January 26, 1949).

64. Weinstein, *Perjury*, p. 366; Tanenhaus, *Whittaker Chambers*, p. 203.

65. William F. Buckley, Jr., ed., *Odyssey of a Friend: Whittaker Chambers' Letters to William F. Buckley, Jr., 1954–1961*, pp. 13–14.

66. Tanenhaus, *Whittaker Chambers,* p. 519.

67. White, *Alger Hiss's Looking-Glass Wars,* p. 68.

68. Alger Hiss, *Recollections of a Life,* p. 150.

69. Weinstein, *Perjury,* p. 367.

70. Ibid., p. 366.

71. Hiss Family Papers, TAM 134, Box 2, Folder 2.

72. Hiss Family Papers, TAM 134, Box 2, Folder 3.

73. Ruddy, *The Alger Hiss Espionage Case,* p. 25.

74. Ibid., p. 4.

75. "LABOR: End of the Line?" *Time,* February 16, 1948.

76. Tennent Bagley, *Spy Wars,* pp. 272–74.

77. Chambers, *Witness,* p. 427.

78. Ruddy, *The Alger Hiss Espionage Case,* p. 134, citing "Spy Papers Disclosed U.S. Code to Russians in 1937, Inquiry Finds; Jury Here Gets 'Real Evidence,'" *New York Herald Tribune,* December 8, 1948.

IX. YALTA

1. Anthony Eden, *The Reckoning,* pp. 335–45, as cited in J. K. Zawodny, *Nothing but Honor: The Story of the Warsaw Uprising,* pp. 79–80.

2. Winston Churchill, *The Second World War: The Hinge of Fate,* p. 327.

3. Zawodny, *Nothing but Honor,* pp. 80–81; Churchill, *The Hinge of Fate,* p. 327.

4. Zawodny, *Nothing but Honor,* p. 81.

5. Edward R. Stettinius, Jr., *Roosevelt and the Russians: The Yalta Conference,* p. 270.

6. Mikhail Heller and Aleksandr M. Nekrich, *Utopia in Power,* p. 414.

7. S. M. Plokhy, *Yalta: The Price of Peace,* p. 29.

8. Heller and Nekrich, *Utopia in Power,* p. 425.

9. François Furet, *The Passing of an Illusion: The Idea of Communism in the Twentieth Century,* p. 331.

10. Plokhy, *Yalta,* pp. 131–33.

11. Sumner Welles, *The Time for Decision,* p. 356.

12. Heller and Nekrich, *Utopia in Power,* p. 419.

13. Ibid., pp. 417, 419.

14. Ibid., p. 419.

15. Stettinius, *Roosevelt and the Russians,* p. 82.

16. Heller and Nekrich, *Utopia in Power,* p. 420.

17. Plokhy, *Yalta,* p. 78.

18. Ibid., p. 79; Haynes and Klehr, *Venona,* pp. 52–53.

19. Pavel Sudoplatov, Jerrold Schecter, and Leona Schecter, *Special Tasks*, p. 222.

20. Ibid.

21. Andrew and Gordievsky, *KGB*, p. 335.

22. Ilya Dzhirkvelov, *Secret Servant*, p. 32.

23. From conversations with John Dziak, fall 2010. Dziak is the author of *Chekisty: A History of the KGB*.

24. Gary Kern, *A Death in Washington: Walter G. Krivitsky and The Stalin Terror*, p. 230.

25. Schecter and Schecter, *Sacred Secrets*, pp. 129–32.

26. Tony Hiss, *Laughing Last*, pp. 106–10.

27. Alger Hiss, *Recollections of a Life*, pp. 98–100.

28. *Foreign Relations of the United States, Diplomatic Papers: The Conferences at Malta and Yalta*, p. 439.

29. Romerstein and Breindel, *The Venona Secrets*, p. 183.

30. Stettinius, *Roosevelt and the Russians*, p. 31.

31. Ibid., pp. 129–32.

32. Ibid., pp. 36–45, 49.

33. Edward Stettinius Jr., Private Papers, University of Virginia. Information provided by M. Stanton Evans.

34. *Foreign Relations of the United States, Diplomatic Papers: The Conferences at Malta and Yalta*, p. 441.

35. Ibid., p. 442.

36. Bryton Barron, "The Role of Alger Hiss and Others Like Him," in *Inside the State Department*, p. 28.

37. Ibid., p. 34.

38. Ibid., p. 25.

39. Campbell and Herring, eds., *The Diaries of Edward R. Stettinius, Jr. 1943–1946*, p. 229.

40. Stettinius, *Roosevelt and the Russians*, p. 84.

41. Ibid., p. 238.

42. Alger Hiss, *In the Court of Public Opinion*, p. 148.

43. Stettinius, *Roosevelt and the Russians*, pp. 103–4.

44. Ibid., pp. 83–84.

45. Major General Mikhail Milshtein, *Through the Years of Wars and Destitution: Memoirs of a Military Intelligence Officer*, p. 32. And see Milshtein obituary in *Krasnaya Zvezda*, August 25, 1992.

46. Milshtein, *Memoirs*, p. 49.

47. Schecter and Schecter, *Sacred Secrets*, p. 131.

48. Chervonnaya and Kai Bird presented a paper titled "Mystery of Ales" at the Hiss Conference at New York University in April 2007; "Essays on Espionage: Soviet Espionage in the 1930s and 1940s," March 26, 2008.

49. Alger Hiss, *Recollections of a Life*, p. 96.

50. Ibid., pp. 120–23.

51. Ibid., pp. 120–25.

52. Ibid., p. 120.

53. Ibid., p. 118.

54. Ibid., p. 119.

55. Ibid., p. 126.

56. Andrew and Gordievsky, *KGB*, p. 332.

57. Ibid., p. 287.

58. Ibid.

59. "There were two KGB chiefs in the United States during World War II. One was Vassiliy Zarubin, head of the 'legal' *rezidentura*. The other was Iskhak Akhmerov, head of the 'illegal' *rezidentura*. The difference was that Zarubin was employed at the Soviet Embassy as Third, later Second, Secretary and had diplomatic immunity. Akhmerov pretended to be an American and had an American birth certificate and passport, which had been illegally secured for him in 1934. He even registered for the draft under the pseudonym William Grienke, the name on his birth certificate. He had a fur and clothing business in Baltimore as a cover. . . . His Iowa-born wife was the niece of the CPUSA Earl Browder." Herbert Romerstein, "A Valuable New Book on the KGB," *Accuracy in Media*, May 13, 2009. Also see Andrew and Mitrokhin, *The Sword and the Shield*, pp. 107–9.

60. Andrew and Gordievsky, *KGB*, pp. 332–33.

61. Ibid., pp. 287–88.

62. Vojtech Mastny, *Russia's Road to the Cold War*, p. 242.

63. Plokhy, *Yalta*, pp. 110–12.

64. Mastny, *Russia's Road to the Cold War*, p. 243.

65. Ibid.

66. Winston Churchill, *The Second World War: Triumph and Tragedy*, p. 365.

67. *Foreign Relations of the United States, Diplomatic Papers: The Conferences at Malta and Yalta* (H. Freeman Matthews, director of European affairs, minutes of the Third Plenary Session February 6, 1945), p. 677.

68. Mastny, *Russia's Road to the Cold War*, p. 245.

69. *Foreign Relations of the United States, Diplomatic Papers: The Conferences at Cairo and Tehran* (1943), p. 604.

70. Churchill, *Triumph and Tragedy*, p. 373.

71. Ibid., p. 368.

72. Ibid., p. 422; Furet, *The Passing of an Illusion*, pp. 547–48, fn. 2.

73. Milovan Djilas, *The New Class*, p. 197.

74. Plokhy, *Yalta*, pp. 159–60.

75. Furet, *The Passing of an Illusion*, p. 330.

76. Stéphane Courtois et al., *The Black Book of Communism*, pp. 6, 211.

77. Furet, *The Passing of an Illusion*, p. 540, fn. 15.

78. Dmitry Zaks, "Russia Admits Stalin Ordered Katyn Massacre of Poles," Agence France-Presse, November 26, 2010.

79. Plokhy, *Yalta*, pp. 159–60.

80. Ibid., p. 162.

81. Zawodny, *Nothing But Honor*, p. 110; Churchill, *Triumph and Tragedy*, p. 145.

82. Churchill, *Triumph and Tragedy*, p. 144.

83. Alger Hiss, *Recollections of a Life*, pp. 119–20.

84. Ibid., p. 97.

85. Heller and Nekrich, *Utopia in Power*, p. 420.

86. Barron, *Inside the State Department*, pp. 124–26.

87. Plokhy, *Yalta*, pp. 189–90.

88. Campbell and Herring, eds., *The Diaries of Edward R. Stettinius, Jr. 1943–1946*, p. 252.

89. Stettinius, *Roosevelt and the Russians*, pp. 187–88.

90. Plokhy, *Yalta*, p. 218.

91. Stettinius, *Roosevelt and the Russians*, pp. 93–94.

92. Plokhy, *Yalta*, p. 220.

93. Mastny, *Russia's Road to the Cold War*, p. 252.

94. Alger Hiss, *Recollections of a Life*, p. 96.

95. Ibid., p. 120.

96. Andrew and Mitrokhin, *The Sword and the Shield*, p. 134.

97. Heller and Nekrich, *Utopia in Power*, pp. 425–26.

98. Robert Louis Benson and Michael Warner, eds., *Venona: Soviet Espionage and the American Response 1939–1957*, p. xviii.

99. Churchill, *Triumph and Tragedy*, p. 435.

100. Furet, *The Passing of an Illusion*, p. 547, fn. 2.

101. Heller and Nekrich, *Utopia in Power*, p. 504.

102. Furet, *The Passing of an Illusion*, p. 547, fn. 2.

103. Levine, *Eyewitness to History*, pp. 158–59.

104. R. R. Palmer, *A History of the Modern World*, p. 870.

105. Furet, *The Passing of an Illusion*, p. 548, fn. 7.

106. Tanenhaus, *Whittaker Chambers*, p. 192, as quoted from George Kennan's *Memoirs*, pp. 547–59.

107. Heller and Nekrich, *Utopia in Power*, p. 459.

108. Tanenhaus, *Whittaker Chambers*, pp. 192–93.

109. Weinstein, *Perjury*, p. 470.

110. Tanenhaus, *Whittaker Chambers*, p. 192.

111. Beatrice Bishop Berle and Travis Beal Jacobs Berle, eds., *Navigating the Rapids: 1918–1971: From the Papers of Adolf Berle*, in Fleming, *The New Dealers' War*, p. 498.

112. Stettinius, *Roosevelt and the Russians*, p. 324.

113. William C. Bullitt, "How We Won the War & Lost the Peace," Part I, *Life*, September 6, 1948.

114. Aleksandr Solzhenitsyn provided his take on Yalta in his *GULAG* series on the conference: The Vlasov army consisted of Russian units that fought on the German side. At the end of the war, after hoping to be turned over to the U.S. side, "the Americans forced them to surrender to Soviet hands, as stipulated by the Yalta Conference." And Churchill performed the same 'act of a loyal ally'; . . . he turned over to the Soviet Command the Cossack corps of 90,000 men," along with many elderly people, women, and children who did not want to return to their native land. Knowing they would never surrender, the British tricked the Cossack military into a situation where they had their weapons removed and went to an area where they were surrounded by Soviet tanks. Many jumped from a viaduct rather than surrender. In effect, they were all being surrendered to their death. Solzhenitsyn and his fellow prisoners in the camps saw this U.S.-English treachery and Allied postwar diplomacy as stupid and shortsighted. "How could they [i.e., Roosevelt and Churchill] . . . fail to secure any guarantees whatsoever of the independence of Eastern Europe? How could they give away broad regions of Saxony and Thuringia in return for the preposterous toy of a four-zone Berlin, their own future Achilles' heel? And what was the military or political sense in their surrendering to destruction at Stalin's hands hundreds of thousands of armed Soviet citizens determined not to surrender? They say it was the price they paid for Stalin's agreeing to enter the war against Japan. With the atom bomb already in their hands, they paid Stalin for not refusing to occupy Manchuria, for strengthening Mao Tse-tung in China, and for giving Kim Il Sung control of half Korea!" Aleksandr Solzhenitsyn, *The GULAG Archipelago 1918–1956*, pp. 259–60.

x. Fascism and Communism

1. John Earl Haynes and Harvey Klehr interview, December 1, 2003. The interview was conducted by historian Jamie Glazov, the managing editor of frontpagemag.com, where the interview was first published.
2. John Ehrman, "The Alger Hiss Case: A Half-Century of Controversy," Center for the Study of Intelligence, Central Intelligence Agency, May 8, 2007.
3. Ibid.
4. A. James Gregor, *The Faces of Janus: Marxism and Fascism in the Twentieth Century*, p. 20.
5. Gene Edward Veith Jr., *Modern Fascism*, p. 26.
6. Marxism defines the bourgeoisie as the social class that owns the means of production in a capitalist society. Marxism views this group as emerging from the wealthy urban classes in pre- and early capitalist societies. It also can refer to the middle or merchant class.
7. Timothy Snyder, *Bloodlands: Europe Between Hitler and Stalin*, p. 388.
8. Veith, *Modern Fascism*, p. 26.
9. Gregor, *The Faces of Janus*, p. 181.
10. See Vadim Borisov in *From Under the Rubble*, pp. 198–203.
11. Conquest, *Reflections on a Ravaged Century*, pp. 136–37.
12. Ibid., p. 62.
13. Ibid., pp. 63–64.
14. Ibid., p. 64.
15. J. B. Matthews, *Odyssey of a Fellow Traveler*, p. 148.
16. Furet, *The Passing of an Illusion*, p. 159.
17. Ibid., p. 160.
18. Ibid., p. 166.
19. Ibid., p. 169.
20. Furet may think it is accepted in Europe. And it is even in Russia. But this is not the case in the United States.
21. Furet, *The Passing of an Illusion*, p. 180.
22. Ibid., p. 181.
23. Ibid., pp. 191–92.
24. Ibid., pp. 205–6.
25. F. A. Hayek, *The Road to Serfdom*, pp. 31–35.
26. Courtois, Werth, Panne, Paczkowski, Bartosek, Margolin, *The Black Book of Communism: Crimes, Terror, Repression*, pp. x, xii.
27. Ibid., p. xiii.
28. Ibid., p. xv.

29. Ibid., p. xvi.
30. Ibid., p. xvii.
31. Ibid., p. xx.
32. Milovar Djilas, *Conversations with Stalin*, p. 187.
33. Dmitry Medvedev, interview in *Izvestiya*, May 7, 2010.
34. Ibid.
35. Ibid.
36. Haynes and Klehr interview, December 1, 2003.
37. Nicolas Berdyaev, *The Origins of Russian Communism*, pp. 117, 125.
38. Pipes, ed., *The Unknown Lenin*, pp. 8, 150, 153.
39. Granville Hicks quoted Krivitsky in Swan, ed., *Alger Hiss, Whittaker Chambers, and the Schism in the American Soul*, p. 63. The 1921 Kronstadt Rebellion was an uprising among Soviet sailors in Kronstadt. The sailors, who had supported the Bolsheviks during the revolution, demanded economic reforms and an end to Bolshevik political domination. Red Army forces, led by Tukhachevsky, under Lenin's orders, crushed the rebellion. See Richard Pipes, *Russia Under the Bolshevik Regime*, pp. 382–86, for full discussion of the rebellion.
40. Haynes and Klehr interview, December 1, 2003.

xi. The Case

1. Geoffrey Wheatcroft, "A Tale of Treachery," *Spectator*, February 22, 2007.
2. "Death of the Witness," *Time*, July 21, 1961.
3. White, *Alger Hiss's Looking-Glass Wars*, p. 68.
4. Tanenhaus, *Whittaker Chambers*, p. 383.
5. "Death of the Witness," *Time*, July 21, 1961.
6. Congress, House, Committee on Un-American Activities, Hearings Regarding Communist Espionage in the United States government, 80th Congress, 2nd Session, July–September 1948, pp. 564–66, 572, 580–82. "Hearings held Tuesday, August 3, 1948."
7. Ibid.
8. Isaac Don Levine, who was at the Berle meeting with Chambers, confirmed in his book that Chambers named six individuals in the State Department, and stated that they knowingly furnished classified data to Soviet underground agents. See Levine, *Eyewitness to History*, pp. 194–95.
9. FBI Memo 1-26-49, in Tanenhaus, *Whittaker Chambers*, p. 207, fn. 12.
10. Chambers, *Witness*, p. 509.
11. Ibid., p. 511.

12. Tanenhaus, *Whittaker Chambers*, p. 221.

13. Ibid., pp. 216–17.

14. FBI Memo 1-26-49, in Tanenhaus, *Whittaker Chambers*, p. 207, fn. 12.

15. Chambers, *Witness*, p. 511.

16. Weinstein, *Perjury*, p. 351. Weinstein cites "A Memorandum on Alger Hiss," n.d. (ca. 1951), Stanley K. Hornbeck MSS, Hoover Institution.

17. Congress, House, Committee on Un-American Activities, Hearings Regarding Communist Espionage in the United States government, 80th Cong., 2nd Sess., July–September 1948. "Hearings held Thursday, August 5, 1948."

18. Chambers, *Witness*, pp. 415–17.

19. FBI File: Hiss, NY 65-14920, Vol. II December 15, 1948.

20. Hiss Testimony to the HUAC Executive Session, August 16, 1948, in Ruddy, *The Alger Hiss Espionage Case*, pp. 49–67.

21. Kempton, *Part of Our Time*, p. 25.

22. Ruddy, *The Alger Hiss Espionage Case*, p. 90.

23. Ibid., p. 92.

24. Chambers, *Witness*, p. 572.

25. Ibid., p. 685.

26. Tanenhaus, *Whittaker Chambers*, pp. 223–24.

27. Chambers, *Witness*, p. 335.

28. Ruddy, *The Alger Hiss Espionage Case*, pp. 161–62.

29. Tanenhaus, *Whittaker Chambers*, p. 387.

30. *New York Times*, December 12, 1948.

31. Weinstein, *Perjury*, p. 58.

32. Ruddy, *The Alger Hiss Espionage Case*, p. 106.

33. Tony Hiss, *The View from Alger's Window*, p. 66.

34. Weinstein, *Perjury*, pp. 172–73.

35. Tanenhaus, *Whittaker Chambers*, p. 217.

36. Weinstein, *Perjury*, p. 64.

37. Ibid., pp. 65–66.

38. Ibid., p. 168.

39. FBI summary report #3220, May 11, 1949, pp. 135–36.

40. Weinstein, *Perjury*, p. 188.

41. Ruddy, *The Alger Hiss Espionage Case*, p. 121.

42. Ibid., p. 106.

43. Hiss Family Papers, TAM 134, Box 2, Folder 9, letter dated May 12, 1949.

44. Weinstein, *Perjury*, p. 278.

45. Ruddy, *The Alger Hiss Espionage Case*, p. 144.
46. Weinstein, *Perjury*, p. 281.
47. Ibid., p. 176.
48. Ibid., p. 177; fn. 39, p. 609. The testimony was quoted at Hiss's second trial for perjury (pp. 350–51).
49. FBI File: Hiss, NY 65-14920, Vol. II, December 15, 1948.
50. Weinstein, *Perjury*, p. 300.
51. FBI file: Hiss, NY 65-14920, Vol. II, December 15, 1948.
52. Chambers, *Witness*, pp. 673–75.
53. Weinstein, *Perjury*, p. 433.
54. Weinstein, *Perjury*, updated ed. (1997), pp. 147–48.
55. Alger Hiss, *Recollections of a Life*, pp. 151–53.
56. Hiss Family Papers, TAM 134, Box 2, Folder 10.
57. Hiss Family Papers, TAM 134, Box 2, Folder 7 (May–August 1948).
58. Weinstein, *Perjury*, pp. 467–69.
59. Ruddy, *The Alger Hiss Espionage Case*, p. 186.
60. Tony Hiss, *The View from Alger's Window*, p. 87.
61. Ruddy, *The Alger Hiss Espionage Case*, pp. 193–94.
62. Ibid., p. 198.
63. Ibid., p. 203.
64. Weinstein, *Perjury*, p. 477.
65. Swan, ed., *Alger Hiss, Whittaker Chambers, and the Schism in the American Soul*, pp. 202–3.
66. Ruddy, *The Alger Hiss Espionage Case*, p. 204.
67. Alger Hiss, *Recollections of a Life*, pp. 153–57.
68. Ibid., pp. 150–53.
69. Leslie A. Fiedler, as quoted in Swan, ed., *Alger Hiss, Whittaker Chambers, and the Schism in the American Soul*, p. 3.
70. Weinstein, *Perjury*, p. 347.
71. As quoted in Tanenhaus, *Whittaker Chambers*, p. 434.
72. *World Affairs* (Spring 2008).
73. "Death of the Witness," *Time*, July 21, 1961.
74. Chambers, *Witness*, p. 789.

XII. LEWISBURG PRISON

1. Alger Hiss, *Recollections of a Life*, pp. 162–63.
2. Weinstein, *Perjury*, p. 524.
3. White, *Alger Hiss's Looking-Glass Wars*, pp. 104–5.
4. Ibid., p. 86.

5. Smith, *The True Story*, p. 433, as quoted in White, *Alger Hiss's Looking-Glass Wars*, p. 93.

6. Tony Hiss, *Laughing Last*, pp. 119, 151–54, 229; White, *Alger Hiss's Looking-Glass Wars*, pp. 109–12.

7. White, *Alger Hiss's Looking-Glass Wars*, p. 97, as quoted from Murray Kempton "Alger Hiss—an Argument for a Good Con," *New York Post*, April 22, 1978, p. 11.

8. Weinstein, *Perjury*, pp. 526–27.

9. Tony Hiss, *Laughing Last*, p. 74.

10. Tony Hiss, *The View from Alger's Window*, p. 65.

11. Alger Hiss, *Recollections of a Life*, p. 163.

12. White, *Alger Hiss's Looking-Glass Wars*, p. 90.

13. Ibid., p. 88. See also Alger Hiss, *Recollections of a Life*, for his memories of prison life (pp. 168–75).

14. Tony Hiss, *Laughing Last*, p. 151.

15. Ibid., pp. 153–55.

16. Ibid., p. 152.

17. White, *Alger Hiss's Looking-Glass Wars*, p. 106; Tony Hiss, *The View from Alger's Window*, p. 182.

18. White, *Alger Hiss's Looking-Glass Wars*, p. 105.

19. Ibid., p. 109.

20. Tony Hiss, *The View from Alger's Window*, p. 33.

21. Ibid., p. 30.

22. White, *Alger Hiss's Looking-Glass Wars*, p. 109.

23. Tony Hiss, *The View from Alger's Window*, p. 42.

24. Ibid.

25. Ibid., pp. 213–15; White, *Alger Hiss's Looking-Glass Wars*, p. 106.

26. Aaron Finestone, "Prison Visitor," http://www.microbrewjournalism.com/page8/page30/page30.html. The Bryn Mawr archives contain an article from *This Week*, a Sunday newspaper supplement dated February 24, 1954: Rowland T. Moriarty, "Alger Hiss in Prison."

27. Alger Hiss, *Recollections of a Life*, p. 185.

28. *Time*, December 6, 1954.

XIII. CRUSADE FOR VINDICATION, 1954–96

1. *Time*, December 6, 1954.

2. Smith, *Alger Hiss: The True Story*, p. 433.

3. Tony Hiss, *Laughing Last*, p. 171.

4. Alger Hiss, *Recollections of a Life,* pp. 187–88.

5. Ibid., pp. 189–91.

6. Hiss Family Papers, TAM 134, Box 4, Folder 97.

7. Alger Hiss, *Recollections of a Life,* p. 186.

8. Tony Hiss, *The View from Alger's Window,* p. 77.

9. Tony Hiss, *Laughing Last,* p. 142.

10. Alger Hiss, *Recollections of a Life,* p. 187.

11. Ibid.

12. Ibid.

13. Ibid., p. 190.

14. Arthur and Elizabeth Schlesinger Library on the History of Women in America, Radcliffe Institute for Advanced Study, Harvard University, Isabel Hiss Papers 1907–2000; *New York Times* obituary, May 7, 2000.

15. FBI File: P. Hiss, July 18, 1955; 5-Bureau (100-376016) RM; 3—New York 65-15867.

16. Tony Hiss, *Laughing Last,* p. 172.

17. Tony Hiss, *The View from Alger's Window,* p. 37.

18. Alger Hiss, *Recollections of a Life,* p. 192.

19. Tony Hiss, *Laughing Last,* p. 173.

20. Ibid., pp. 174–76.

21. Ibid., p. 176.

22. Ibid.

23. Ibid., p. 178.

24. Tony Hiss, *The View from Alger's Window,* p. 220.

25. *New York Times,* October 16, 1984.

26. James L. Kilgallen, International News Service; sixth article in series on life of Alger Hiss.

27. Alger Hiss, *Recollections of a Life,* p. 186.

28. Ibid., pp. 190–91.

29. Ibid., pp. 186–87.

30. Ibid., p. 194.

31. Ibid., pp. 198–99.

32. Ibid., pp. 197–98.

33. See Weinstein, *Perjury,* book jacket.

34. Hiss, *Recollections of a Life,* p. 217.

35. Ibid., p. 225.

36. Ibid., p. 153.

37. White, *Alger Hiss's Looking-Glass Wars,* p. 213.

38. Ibid., pp. 213–16.

39. Ibid., pp. 216–19.

40. George McGovern, "George McGovern Reflects on Nixon," in "Nixon and Historical Memory: Two Reviews," *Perspectives* 34, nos. 1, 4 (March 1996), as quoted in White, *Alger Hiss's Looking-Glass Wars*, p. xvii.

41. Hiss Family Papers, TAM 134, Box 3, Folder 22.

42. John Ehrman, "The Mystery of 'ALES': Once Again, the Alger Hiss Case," Center for the Study of Intelligence, December 11, 2007, and "The Alger Hiss Case," Center for the Study of Intelligence, May 8, 2007.

43. Ehrman, "The Mystery of 'ALES.'"

44. Janny Scott, "Alger Hiss, 92, Central Figure in Long-Running Cold War Controversy," obituary, *New York Times*, November 16, 1996.

45. Hiss Family Papers, TAM 134, Box 7, Folder 15. See also *New York Times*, December 6, 1996.

46. Budenz, *Men Without Faces*, pp. 30–31.

XIV. Testimonies

1. Weinstein, *Perjury*, p. 351; FBI File: Hiss & Chambers, FOIA 1117764, Vol. II, NY65-14920, December 14, 1948.

2. Alexander Barmine, *One Who Survived*, pp. 59, 60, 64, 68, 81, 85, and 87.

3. Lock, "Chiefs of the GRU: 1918–1947," pp. 353–78.

4. Brook-Shepherd, *The Storm Petrels*, p. 144.

5. Bagley, *Spy Wars*, p. 272.

6. Will Brownell and Richard N. Billings, *So Close to Greatness: A Biography of William C. Bullitt*, p. 318.

7. Weinstein, *Perjury*, p. 350.

8. Ibid., p. 351. Weinstein cites "A Memorandum on Alger Hiss," n.d. (ca. 1951), Stanley K. Hornbeck MSS, Hoover Institution.

9. Ibid., p. 350.

10. William Hood, preface in Walter Krivitsky's *In Stalin's Secret Service*, p. xxi.

11. J. L. Black and Andrew Donskov, *The Gouzenko Affair: Canada and the Beginnings of Cold War Counterespionage*, Center for Research on Canadian-Russian Relations. Canada/Russia Series, vol. 8; Schecter and Schecter, *Sacred Secrets*, p. 114.

12. FBI, J. E. Hoover Memorandum, September 24, 1945.

13. Weinstein, *Perjury*, pp. 356–57.

14. Ibid., pp. 22–23, 357; Schecter and Schecter, *Sacred Secrets*, p. 115. For a summary of Elizabeth Bentley's 1945 comments to the FBI, see D. M. Ladd Memo to Director, FBI, January 28, 1949 #2058, pp. 4–5.

15. FBI Report: "Soviet Espionage Activities in the United States Between World War I and World War II," November 27, 1945, p. 13.

16. See Chambers's HUAC testimony, August 25, 1948.

17. See HUAC testimony of Alger Hiss, August 16, 1948, in Ruddy, *The Alger Hiss Espionage Case.*

18. See the HUAC testimony of Whittaker Chambers, August 3 and August 25, 1948.

19. Haynes and Klehr, *Venona,* p. 169.

20. Chambers, *Witness,* p. 417.

21. Ibid., p. 39; White, *Alger Hiss's Looking-Glass Wars,* p. 73.

22. Weinstein, *Perjury,* p. 455.

23. Tanenhaus, *Whittaker Chambers,* p. 323.

24. Ibid., p. 517.

25. Ruddy, *The Alger Hiss Espionage Case,* p. 203.

26. FBI Files: FBI Memo, Field Office, NY 65-14920-2475, March 2, 1949.

27. Weinstein, *Perjury,* pp. 230–31.

28. Chambers, *Witness,* pp. 465–66.

29. Weinstein, *Perjury,* p. 173.

30. Ruddy, *The Alger Hiss Espionage Case,* p. 117.

31. Ibid., pp. xi, xii.

32. John Earl Haynes and Harvey Klehr, *In Denial: Historians, Communism, and Espionage,* pp. 182–83.

33. Hede Massing, *This Deception: KGB Target: America,* pp. 271–79.

34. Weinstein, *Perjury,* p. 477.

35. Massing, *This Deception,* pp. 146–52; also see Vassiliev Yellow Notebook #2, p. 23; and #2, pp. 22, 24.

36. See also White, *Alger Hiss's Looking-Glass Wars,* pp. 228–29; Haynes, Klehr, and Vassiliev, *Spies,* p. 11.

37. Andrew and Gordievsky, *KGB,* p. 286.

38. Ibid.; FBI File on Akhmerov, 65-57905, Letter to New York, Sect. 22 044231-03.

39. Andrew and Gordievsky, *KGB,* p. 287.

40. Dartmouth College Library, Rauner Special Collections: Library ML-66, Box 1, Folder 7, interview with *U.S. News & World Report,* January 9, 1953.

41. Ruddy, *The Alger Hiss Espionage Case,* p. 161, 194–95.

42. Weinstein, *Perjury,* p. 280.

43. Haynes and Klehr, *In Denial,* p. 166.

44. Haynes, Klehr, and Vassiliev, *Spies,* p. 30.

45. Weinstein, *Perjury,* p. 156.

46. Ibid., p. 24.

47. FBI Memorandum, Ladd to Hoover, January 28, 1949 (FBI File: Hiss-Chambers, Vol. 44, p. 30).

48. Budenz, *This Is My Story*, p. 192.

49. Weinstein, *Perjury*, p. 360.

50. Schecter and Schecter, *Sacred Secrets*, p. 114.

XV. VENONA PROGRAM

1. Benson and Warner, eds., foreword, *Venona*, pp. viii, xiii.

2. Ibid., p. xxii.

3. Ibid., pp. vii–xxxiii.

4. Haynes and Klehr, *Venona*, p. 11.

5. Benson and Warner, eds., *Venona*, p. 191.

6. Haynes and Klehr, *Venona*, p. 12.

7. Ibid., pp. 14–15.

8. Ehrman, "The Alger Hiss Case."

9. Haynes and Klehr, *Venona*, p. 51.

10. Ehrman, "The Alger Hiss Case."

11. Haynes and Klehr, *Venona*, p. 5.

12. Haynes, Klehr, and Vassiliev, *Spies*, p. 16. The authors state that Glasser described "Pol" (Maxim Lieber) as "Karl's" successor.

13. Benson and Warner, eds., *Venona*, p. 423.

14. Haynes and Klehr, *Venona*, p. 22; Eduard Mark, "*In Re* Alger Hiss: A Final Verdict from the Archives of the KGB," *Journal of Cold War Studies* Vol. 11, no. 3 (Summer 2009), pp. 56–59.

15. Vladimir Lota, "Morris Makes Contact," *Krasnaya Zvezda* (*Red Star*), May 5, 2006.

16. The American delegation to Yalta included—as listed in "The Crimea Conference" Report to the Conference, U.S. National Archives, College Park, Maryland, RG 43 WW II, Box 5, Conference Arc ID 1137445/ MLR #A1303—President Roosevelt; Edward R. Stettinius, Secretary of State; Harry L. Hopkins, Special Assistant to the President; Justice James F. Byrnes Director, Office of War Mobilization and Reconversion; W. Averell Harriman, Ambassador to the USSR; H. Freeman Matthews, Director, Office of European Affairs, State Department; Alger Hiss, Deputy Director, Office of Special Political Affairs, Department of State; Charles E. Bohlen, Assistant to the Secretary of State, together with political, military, and technical advisors; and six senior military officers: Fleet Admiral William D. Leahy, USN, Chief of Staff to the President;

General of the Army George C. Marshall, USA, Chief of Staff, U.S. Army; Fleet Admiral Ernest J. King, USN, Chief of Naval Operations, and Commander in Chief, U.S. Fleet; Lieutenant General Brehon B. Somervell, Commanding General, Army Service Forces; Vice Admiral Emory S. Land, War Shipping Administrator; Major General L. S. Kuter, USA, Staff of Commanding General, U.S. Army Air Forces. Wilder Foote is not listed by name; presumably he is one of Bohlen's group of advisors.

17. Eduard Mark, "Who was Venona's 'Ales'?" *Intelligence and National Security* Vol. 18, no. 3 (Autumn 2003), pp. 45–72; Mark, "*In Re* Alger Hiss"; pp. 26–67; Kai Bird and Svetlana Chervonnaya, "The Mystery of Ales," *American Scholar,* Summer 2007.

18. Haynes and Klehr, *Spies,* p. 25; Haynes and Klehr, "Hiss Was Guilty," History News Network, April 16, 2007; Mark, "*In Re* Alger Hiss," pp. 54–55, 59.

19. Haynes and Klehr, *Venona,* p. 170.

20. Mark, "*In Re* Alger Hiss," pp. 47, 49.

21. Venona Document, September 28, 1943, No. 1579, from New York to Moscow, printed in Ruddy, *The Alger Hiss Espionage Case,* p. 233.

22. Moynihan Commission, Appendix A A-36 (PDF 36).

23. Mark, "*In Re* Alger Hiss," p. 50. Wilder Foote lived in Vermont from 1931 to 1941 as a newspaper publisher; there is no evidence that connected him with the GRU or Karl's Group during that period.

24. "Hiss in Venona: The Continuing Controversy," symposium at the John R. Schindler Center for Cryptologic History, October 27, 2005.

25. Ehrman, "The Mystery of 'ALES,'" Volume 51, Number 4, 2007.

26. Mark Kramer, "Alger Hiss and Venona," H-HOAC online, 3 November 3, 2005.

XVI. Archival Material
A. Hungarian Archives

1. See Maria Schmidt, *Battle of Wits* (by Maria S. 2007 XX Szazad Intezet); Schmidt, "Noel Field," *American Communist History* Vol. 3, No. 2, 2004; and Schmidt, "The Hiss Dossier," *New Republic,* November 8, 1993.

2. Schmidt, "Noel Field," p. 228.

3. Flora Lewis, *Red Pawn: The Story of Noel Field,* p. 79.

4. Schmidt, "Noel Field," p. 230.

5. Hede Massing, *This Deception,* pp. 240–43.

6. Lewis, *Red Pawn,* p. 121; Schmidt, "Noel Field," p. 234.

7. Schmidt, "Noel Field," pp. 234–35.

8. Ibid., pp. 234–37.

9. Ibid., pp. 217–20.

10. Ibid., p. 221.

11. FBI File: Akhmerov, NY 65-14737, Section 4; Lewis, *Red Pawn*, p. 58.

12. Lewis, *Red Pawn*, p. 194.

13. HIA (Hungarian Intelligence Security Service), Noel Field Interrogation Material, September 23 and 29, 1954.

14. KGB File 36857, vol. 1, p. 23. See also Vassiliev, Yellow Notebook #2, pp. 23, 24, 25.

15. Massing, *The Deception*, p. 148; Lewis, *Red Pawn*, p. 73.

16. HIA Noel Field Interrogation Material.

17. Schmidt "Noel Field," p. 233.

18. Ibid.

19. Schmidt, "The Hiss Dossier."

20. Ibid.

21. Ibid.

22. Schmidt, "Noel Field," p. 224.

23. Ibid., p. 225.

24. Ibid., p. 228.

25. Schmidt, *Battle of Wits*, pp. 122–23.

26. Schmidt, "Noel Field," p. 240.

27. Ibid., p. 242.

28. Ibid., p. 243.

29. Schmidt, *Battle of Wits*, p. 209.

30. Schmidt, "Noel Field," p. 229.

31. Ibid., p. 230.

32. Haynes and Klehr, *In Denial*, pp. 147–48.

B. KGB Archives

33. Weinstein and Vassiliev, *The Haunted Wood*, p. xv.

34. Vassiliev did not have unrestricted access to KGB files. He was limited by two years' work in the archives and by the unwillingness of the KGB to provide certain types of files. The handwritten notebooks include KGB archival file numbers and contain details that could come only from internal KGB documents. See Haynes, Klehr, and Vassiliev, *Spies*, pp. xvi, xix.

35. The notebooks are available online through the Cold War International History Project, Woodrow Wilson International Center for Scholars.

36. Haynes, Klehr, and Vassiliev, *Spies,* p. i.

37. H-DIPLO is an online site where scholarly discussions on diplomatic and international history take place.

38. Haynes, Klehr, and Vassiliev, *Spies,* p. liii.

39. Ibid., p. 29.

40. Ibid.

41. Haynes and Klehr, "Professors of Denial: Ignoring the Truth about American Communists," *Weekly Standard,* March 21, 2005.

42. Vassiliev, Black Notebook File 43173 v. 2c, pp. 46–49.

43. Weinstein and Vassiliev, *The Haunted Wood,* p. 266; Mark, "*In Re* Alger Hiss," p. 42.

44. Chambers, *Witness,* p.414. When Bykov found out that Hiss was a lawyer, he told Chambers that from now they would call him "Der Advokat" ("The Lawyer").

45. Haynes and Klehr, "Professors of Denial."

46. Haynes, Klehr, and Vassiliev, *Spies,* p. 7.

47. Vassiliev, Yellow Notebook #2, pp. 23–24.

48. Vassiliev, White Notebook #3, pp. 73–118.

49. Haynes, Klehr, and Vassiliev, *Spies,* p. 12.

50. Vassiliev, White Notebook #3, p. 78.

51. Weinstein and Vassiliev, *The Haunted Wood,* pp. 267–68; Vadim to Moscow Center, April 2, 1945, KGB file 43072, v.1, p. 82; Vassiliev, White Notebook #3, p. 57; Haynes, Klehr, and Vassiliev, *Spies,* pp. 25–26.

52. Vassiliev, White Notebook #3, p. 82; Haynes, Klehr, and Vassiliev, *Spies,* p. 26.

53. Mark, "*In Re* Alger Hiss," pp. 47, 49.

54. Haynes, Klehr, and Vassiliev, *Spies,* p. 24.

55. Ibid., p. 25.

56. Ibid., pp. 24–25.

57. Ibid., pp. 22–23.

58. Ibid., p. 27.

59. Vassiliev, Black Notebook 72, p. 479.

60. Vassiliev, Black Notebook, p. 203. By December 1948, when this message was written, Hiss was a "former agent." He had been indicted for perjury by a grand jury that month.

61. Haynes, Klehr, and Vassiliev, *Spies,* p. 27.

62. Vassiliev, Black Notebook, p. 82; Haynes, Klehr, and Vassiliev, *Spies,* p. 30.

EPILOGUE

1. Tony Hiss, *The View from Alger's Window,* p. 51.
2. Ibid., p. 57.
3. Ibid., p. 56.
4. Vladimir Bukovsky, "Analysis of European Union (EU) in comparison to Soviet Union," http://www.youtube.com/watch?v=rg58wRRmWL0.

BIBLIOGRAPHY

The Alger Hiss Story: The Search for the Truth. https://files.nyu.edu/th15/public/home.html.

Andrew, Christopher, and Oleg Gordievsky. *KGB: The Inside Story.* New York: HarperCollins, 1990.

Andrew, Christopher, and Vasili Mitrokhin. *The Mitrokhin Archive and the Secret History of the KGB.* New York: Basic Books, 1999.

———. *The Sword and the Shield: The Mitrokhin Archive and the Secret History of the KGB.* Part 1, unabridged. New York: Basic Books, 2000.

Arendt, Hannah. *The Origins of Totalitarianism.* New York: Harcourt Brace Jovanovich, 1973.

Bagley, Tennent H. *Spy Wars: Moles, Mysteries, and Deadly Games.* New Haven, CT: Yale University Press, 2007.

Barmine, Alexander. *One Who Survived.* New York: G. P. Putnam's Sons, 1945.

Barron, Bryton. *Inside the State Department.* 1956; reprint, New York: Book Mailer, 1961.

Barron, John. *KGB: The Secret Work of Soviet Secret Agents.* New York: Reader's Digest Press, 1974.

Bearden, Milt, and James Risen. *The Main Enemy: The Inside Story of the CIA's Final Showdown with the KGB.* New York: Random House, 2003.

Benson, Robert Louis, and Michael Warner, eds. *Venona: Soviet Espionage and the American Response 1939–1957.* Washington, DC: National Security Agency and Central Intelligence Agency, 1996.

Bentley, Elizabeth. *Out of Bondage.* With afterword by Hayden B. Peake. New York: Ballantine Books, 1988.

Berdyaev, Nikolai. *The Origin of Russian Communism.* Ann Arbor: University of Michigan Press, 1969.

———. *The Russian Idea.* Rev. ed. New York: Lindisfarne Press, 1992.

Black, J. L., and Andrew Donskov, eds. *The Gouzenko Affair: Canada and the Beginnings of the Cold War Counterespionage.* Canada/Russia Series, vol. 8.

Center for Research on Canadian-Russian Relations at Carleton University, Slavic Research Group at University of Ottawa, 2006.

Brook-Shepherd, Gordon. *The Storm Petrels: The Flight of the First Soviet Defectors.* New York: Harcourt Brace Jovanovich, 1977.

Brownell, Will, and Richard N. Billings. *So Close to Greatness: A Biography of William C. Bullitt.* New York: Macmillan, 1987.

Buckley, William F., Jr. *Odyssey of a Friend: Whittaker Chambers' Letters to William F. Buckley, Jr. 1954–1961.* New York: G. P. Putnam's Sons, 1961.

Budenz, Louis Francis. *Men Without Faces: The Communist Conspiracy in the USA.* New York: Harper & Brothers, 1948.

———. *This Is My Story.* New York: McGraw-Hill, 1947.

Chen, Ivan. "Alger Hiss 1926–1929." Manuscript, Harvard Law School, online, 2006.

Chernow, Ron. *Alexander Hamilton.* New York: The Penguin Press, 2004.

Churchill, Winston. *The Second World War: The Grand Alliance.* Boston: Houghton Mifflin, 1950.

———. *The Second World War: The Hinge of Fate.* Boston: Houghton Mifflin, 1950.

———. *The Second World War: Triumph and Tragedy.* Boston: Houghton Mifflin, 1953.

Clarridge, Duane R., with Digby Diehl. *A Spy for All Seasons.* New York: Scribner, 1997.

Congressional Record. The Legacy of Alexander Orlov: Testimony of Orlov before the Senate Subcommittee on Internal Security, February 14–15, 1957. 93rd Congress, 1st Session. Committee Report. Washington, DC: U.S. Government Printing Office, August 1973.

Conquest, Robert. *Reflections on a Ravaged Century.* New York: Norton, 2000.

———. *The Great Terror: A Reassessment.* Oxford: Oxford University Press, 1990.

Costello, John. *Mask of Treachery.* New York: William Morrow, 1988.

Courtois, Stéphane, et al. *The Black Book of Communism: Crimes, Terror, Repression.* Cambridge, MA: Harvard University Press, 1999.

Deakin, F. W., and G. R. Storry. *The Case of Richard Sorge.* New York: Harper & Row, 1966.

Djilas, Milovan. *Conversations with Stalin.* New York: Harcourt, Brace & World, 1962.

———. *The New Class.* New York: Praeger, 1957.

Duff, William E. *A Time for Spies: Theodore Stephanovich Mally and the Era of the Great Illegals.* Nashville, TN: Vanderbilt University Press, 1999.

Dzhirkvelov, Ilya. *Secret Servant: My Life with the KGB and the Soviet Elite.* London: William Collins Sons, 1987.

Dziak, John J. *Chekisty: A History of the KGB*. Lexington, MA: Lexington Books, 1988.

Evans, M. Stanton. *Blacklisted by History: The Untold Story of Senator Joe McCarthy*. New York: Crown Forum, 2007.

FBI Files, Alger Hiss and Whittaker Chambers. FOIA: 1117764 Vols. 1–52, Exhibits 1–7; 1117764, Sections 1–27; and 1117764; Alger Hiss, FOIA #1117764 1–15.

FBI Files, FOIA: Iskhak Akhmerov.

FBI Files, FOIA: Priscilla Hiss: NY, 65-15867.

Fleming, Thomas. *The New Dealers' War: FDR and the War Within World War II*. New York: Basic Books, 2001.

Foote, Alexander. *Handbook for Spies*. London: Museum Press, 1949.

Foreign Relations of the United States. Diplomatic Papers: The Conferences at Malta and Yalta. Westport, CT: Greenwood Press, 1945.

Furet, Francois. *The Passing of an Illusion: The Idea of Communism in the Twentieth Century*. Chicago: University of Chicago Press, 1999.

Gregor, A. James. *The Faces of Janus: Marxism and Fascism in the Twentieth Century*. New Haven, CT: Yale University Press, 2000.

Grogin, Robert C. *Natural Enemies: The United States and the Soviet Union in the Cold War, 1917–1991*. Lanham, MD: Lexington Books, 2001.

Hayek, F. A. *The Road to Serfdom*. 50th anniv. ed. Chicago: University of Chicago Press, 1994.

Haynes, John Earl, and Harvey Klehr. *In Denial: Historians, Communism, and Espionage*. San Francisco: Encounter Books, 2003.

———. *Venona: Decoding Soviet Espionage in America*. New Haven, CT: Yale University Press, 2000.

Haynes, John Earl, Harvey Klehr, and Alexander Vassiliev. *Spies: The Rise and Fall of the KGB in America*. New Haven, CT: Yale University Press, 2009.

Heller, Mikhail, and Aleksandr M. Nekrich. *Utopia in Power: The History of the Soviet Union from 1917 to the Present*. New York: Summit Books, 1982.

Hiss, Alger. *In the Court of Public Opinion*. London: John Calder, 1957.

———. *Recollections of a Life*. New York: Seaver Books, 1988.

Hiss, Tony. *Laughing Last*. Boston: Houghton Mifflin, 1977.

———. *The View from Alger's Window*. New York: Knopf, 1999.

Hood, William. *Mole*. New York: Norton, 1982.

Jacoby, Susan. *Alger Hiss and the Battle for History*. New Haven, CT: Yale University Press, 2009.

Kempton, Murray. *Part of Our Time: Some Ruins and Monuments of the Thirties*. New York: Simon and Schuster, 1955.

Kern, Gary. *A Death in Washington: Walter G. Krivitsky and the Stalin Terror.* New York: Enigma Books, 2003.

Kessler, Lauren. *Clever Girl: Elizabeth Bentley, The Spy Who Ushered in the McCarthy Era.* New York: HarperCollins, 2003.

Knightley, Phillip. *Philby: KGB Masterspy.* London: Andre Deutsch, 1988.

Koestler, Arthur. *Darkness at Noon.* New York: Macmillan, 1941.

Krivitsky, Walter. *In Stalin's Secret Service.* New York: Harper & Brothers, 1939.

———. *MI5 Debriefing and Other Documents on Soviet Intelligence.* Edited by Gary Kern. Riverside, CA: Xenos Books, 2004.

Lamphere, Robert J., and Tom Shachtman. *The FBI-KGB War: A Special Agent's Story.* New York: Random House, 1986.

Levchenko, Stanislav. *On the Wrong Side: My Life in the KGB.* McLean, VA: Pergamon-Brassey's, 1988.

Levine, Isaac Don. *Eyewitness to History.* New York: Hawthorne Books, 1973.

Lewis, Flora. *Red Pawn: The Story of Noel Field.* Garden City, NY: Doubleday, 1965.

Linden, Carl A. *The Soviet-Party-State: The Politics of Ideocratic Despotism.* New York: Praeger, 1983.

Lock, Owen A. "Chiefs of the GRU: 1918–1947." *In the Name of Intelligence: Essays in Honor of Walter Pforzheimer.* Edited by Hayden B. Peake and Samuel Halpern. Washington, DC: NIBC Press, 1994.

Martin, David C. *Wilderness of Mirrors.* New York: Harper & Row, 1980.

Massing, Hede. *This Deception.* New York: Ballantine Books, 1951.

Mastny, Vojtech. *Russia's Road to the Cold War.* New York: Columbia University Press, 1979.

Matthews, J. B. *Odyssey of a Fellow Traveler.* New York: Mount Vernon, 1938.

Milshtein, Mikhail. *Through the Years of Wars and Destitution: Memoirs of a Military Intelligence Officer.* Moscow: ITAR-TASS, 2000.

Murphy, David E. *What Stalin Knew: The Enigma of Barbarossa.* New Haven, CT: Yale University Press, 2005.

National Archives. College Park, MD. Papers on Alger Hiss and Yalta.

New York University, Tamiment Library. Robert F. Wagner Labor Archives. Alger Hiss Family Papers (1892–2007). TAM 134.

Orlov, Alexander. *The Secret History of Stalin's Crimes.* New York: Random House, 1953.

Palmer, R. R. *A History of the Modern World.* 2nd ed. New York: Knopf, 1960.

Pipes, Richard. *Russia Under the Bolshevik Regime.* New York: Knopf, 1994.

————, ed. *The Unknown Lenin: From the Secret Archive.* New Haven, CT: Yale University Press, 1996.

Plokhy, S. M. *Yalta: The Price of Peace.* New York: Viking, 2010.

Poretsky, Elizabeth K. *Our Own People: A Memoir of Ignace Reiss and His Friends.* London: Oxford University Press, 1969.

Rocca, Raymond G., and John J. Dziak. *Bibliography on Soviet Intelligence and Security Services.* Boulder, CO: Westview, 1985.

Romerstein, Herbert, and Eric Breindel. *The Venona Secrets: Exposing Soviet Espionage and America's Traitors.* Washington, DC: Regnery, 2000.

Romerstein, Herbert, and Stanislav Levchenko. *The KGB Against the "Main Enemy."* Lexington, MA: Lexington Books, 1989.

Ruddy, T. Michael. *The Alger Hiss Espionage Case.* Belmont, CA: Thomson & Wadsworth, 2005.

Schecter, Jerrold, and Leona Schecter. *Sacred Secrets: How Soviet Intelligence Operations Changed American History.* Washington, DC: Brassey's, 2002.

Schmidt, Maria. *Battle of Wits: Beliefs, Ideologies, and Secret Agents in the 20th Century.* Budapest: XX Század Intezet, 2007.

————. "The Hiss Dossier." *New Republic,* November 8, 1993.

————. "Noel Field—The American Communist at the Center of Stalin's East European Purge: From the Hungarian Archives." *American Communist History,* Vol. 3, no. 2 2004.

Shatz, Marshall S., and Judith E. Zimmerman, trans. and eds., *VEKHI: Landmarks.* Armonk, NY: M. E. Sharpe, Inc. 1994.

Smith, John Chabot. *Alger Hiss: The True Story.* New York: Holt, Rinehart & Winston, 1976.

Snyder, Timothy. *Bloodlands: Europe Between Hitler and Stalin.* New York: Basic Books, 2010.

Solzhenitsyn, Aleksandr. *The GULAG Archipelago, 1918–1956.* New York: Harper & Row, 1973.

Solzhenitsyn, Aleksandr, et al. *From Under the Rubble.* Chicago: Regnery Gateway, 1974.

Stettinius, Edward R., Jr. *The Diaries of Edward R. Stettinius Jr., 1943–1946.* Edited by Thomas M. Campbell and George C. Herring. New York: New Viewpoints, 1975.

————. *Roosevelt and the Russians: The Yalta Conference.* Edited by Walter Johnson. New York: Doubleday, 1949.

Sudoplatov, Pavel, and Anatoli Sudoplatov, with Jerrold Schecter and Leona Schecter. *Special Tasks.* Boston: Little, Brown, 1994.

Swan, Patrick A., ed. *Alger Hiss, Whittaker Chambers, and the Schism in the American Soul.* Wilmington, DE: ISI Books, 2003.

Tanenhaus, Sam. *Whittaker Chambers: A Biography.* New York: Random House, 1997.

Tice, Louis E. *Personal Coaching for Results.* Nashville, TN: Thomas Nelson, 1997.

———. *Smart Talk for Achieving Your Potential.* Seattle: Pacific Institute, 1995.

Ulam, Adam B. *Stalin: The Man and His Era.* New York: Viking Press, 1973.

Vassiliev, Alexander. *Notebooks.* Material from KGB archives. Woodrow Wilson International Center for Scholars, Cold War International History Project. http://legacy.wilsoncenter.org/va2/index.cfm?topic_id=1409&fuseaction =home.browse&sort=collection&item=Vassiliev%20Notebooks.

Veith, Gene Edward, Jr. "Modern Fascism: Liquidating the Judeo-Christian Worldview." *Concordia Scholarship Today* (1973).

Volkogonov, Dmitri. *Lenin: A New Biography.* New York: Free Press, 1994.

Weinstein, Allen. *Perjury: The Hiss-Chambers Case.* New York: Knopf, 1978.

Weinstein, Allen, and Alexander Vassiliev. *The Haunted Wood: Soviet Espionage in America—The Stalin Era.* New York: Random House, 1999.

Weiser, Benjamin. *A Secret Life: The Polish Officer, His Covert Mission, and the Price He Paid to Save His Country.* New York: Public Affairs, 2004.

Welles, Sumner. *The Time for Decision.* New York: Harper & Brothers, 1944.

West, Nigel. *MI6: British Secret Intelligence Service Operations, 1909–1945.* New York: Random House, 1983.

West, Rebecca. *The New Meaning of Treason.* New York: Viking Press, 1964.

White, G. Edward. *Alger Hiss's Looking-Glass Wars.* New York: Oxford University Press, 2004.

Winks, Robin W., ed. *The Historian as Detective: Essays on Evidence.* New York: Harper & Row, 1968.

Wright, Peter. *Spy Catcher: The Candid Autobiography of a Senior Intelligence Officer.* New York: Viking Press, 1987.

Zawodny, J. K. *Nothing But Honor: The Story of the Warsaw Uprising, 1944.* Stanford, CA: Hoover Institution Press, 1978.

INDEX